WITHDRAWN

MAKEOVER NATION

MAKEOVER NATION

THE UNITED STATES OF REINVENTION

Toby Miller

 THE OHIO STATE UNIVERSITY PRESS / COLUMBUS

Library of Congress Cataloging-in-Publication Data
Miller, Toby.
Makeover nation : the United States of reinvention / Toby Miller.
   p. cm.
Includes bibliographical references and index.
ISBN 978-0-8142-5169-0 (pbk. : alk. paper)—ISBN 978-0-8142-1093-2 (cloth : alk. paper)
1. Social problems—United States. 2. Social change—United States. 3. United States—
Social conditions. I. Title.
HN59.2.M545 2008
306.4'20973—dc22
                    2008018820

This book is available in the following editions:
Paperback (ISBN 978-0-8142-5169-0)
Cloth (ISBN 978-0-8142-1093-2)
CD-ROM (ISBN 978-0-8142-9173-3)

Cover design by Jason Moore.
Text design by Jennifer Shoffey Forsythe.
Type set in Adobe Minion Pro.
Printed by Thomson Shore, Inc.

♾ The paper used in this publication meets the minimum requirements of the American
National Standard for Information Sciences—Permanence of Paper for Printed Library Materials.
ANSI Z39.48–1992.

9 8 7 6 5 4 3 2 1

CONTENTS

ACKNOWLEDGMENTS

MANY THANKS to everyone involved in publishing the book, plus Ece Algan, Peter Bliss, Jenny Burton, Sandy Crooms, Paula Gardner, Dana Heller, Virginia Keeny, Marie Leger, Ann McClintock, Richard Maxwell, Stephen Muecke, Chris Straayer, and Steve Sussman. *Recuerdo la pareja dentro mi cuerpo.*

INTRODUCTION

[We live in] a State where there is no fever of speculation, no inflamed desire for sudden wealth, where the poor are all simple-minded and contented, and the rich are all honest and generous, where society is in a condition of primitive purity and politics is the occupation of only the capable and the patriotic.
  —Mark Twain and Charles Dudley Warner (1874)

Ready for a free, fun, no-hassle virtual makeover? The Makeover-o-Matic virtual makeover game lets you try on virtual hairstyles, makeup and accessories with your own photo or a model photo. Find your best online virtual makeover look and style using the latest beauty products, without the risk! Select from hundreds of hairstyles, cosmetic colors and accessories in the privacy of your own home. Blend, highlight, mix and match to create your new online look. What are you waiting for? Go ahead and get beautiful!
  —http://beauty.ivillage.com/0,,9jlxfdd5,00.html

THE NEW YORK satirical magazine *Vanity Fair* (unrelated to its latter-day lounge-lizard/coffee-table/hairdressing salon namesake) ran from 1859 to 1863. Page 215 of the October 27, 1860, edition earned the periodical enduring fame, because the first known use of the word "makeover" appeared there, in a notice headed "Adornment." It referred to a fictional figure: "Miss Angelica Makeover. The men like her and the women wonder why." Angelica's gift was the ability to transform her "coarse" hair "into waves of beauty" through "miracles of art and patience." Her "eyes were by no means handsome, but she . . . learned how to use them," utilizing "art and culture" to pass "for a fine woman" ("Adornment" 1860).[1]

The word "makeover" reappeared in women's magazines of the 1920s and 1960s. In 1936, *Mademoiselle* magazine offered what has been described as the first formal makeover of an "average" reader, who had asked for tips on how to "make the most" of a self that she deemed "homely as a hedgehog"

1

and "too skinny" (quoted in Fraser 2007: 177). The article turned into a regular feature, and the term "makeover" entered routine parlance in the 1970s. I argue in this book that it describes a long-term tendency in US culture that has intensified in the contemporary moment.

The grand promise of the United States is that what its people were born as need not define them ever more. The Latin@ writer James Truslow Adams coined the signal term "the American Dream" in 1931 as the core of his wide-ranging overview of national history, *The Epic of America*.[2] Adams argued that since the 17th century, voluntary immigrants had been attracted here not only by "the economic motive" but also by "the hope of a better and freer life, a life in which a man might think as he would and develop as he willed" (1941: 31). The "*American Dream*" was "of a land in which life should be better and richer and fuller . . . , with opportunity for each according to his ability or achievement." Measured by something beyond commodities ("merely material plenty"), it was "a dream of being able to grow to fullest development as man and woman," defying class barriers (405, 411).[3]

That grand meritocratic promise still has the power to fascinate. It is expressed and achieved through the ultimate Yanqui desire: self-invention via commodities. This is an irony, for, as Marx noted, commodities originate "outside us" (1987: 43). But commodities are quickly internalized, wooing consumers by appearing attractive in ways that borrow from romantic love but reverse that relationship: People learn about romance from commodities, which proceed to become part of them through the double-sided nature of advertising and "the good life" of luxury: the culture industries encourage competition between consumers at the same time as they standardize processes to manufacture unity in the face of diversity. Transcendence is articulated to objects, and commodities dominate the human and natural landscape. The corollary is the simultaneous triumph and emptiness of the sign as a source and measure of value. Commodities hide not only the work of their creation but their postpurchase existence as well. Designated with human characteristics (beauty, taste, serenity, and so on), they compensate for the absence of these qualities in everyday capitalism via a "permanent opium war" (Debord 1995: 26–27, 29–30). Wolfgang Haug's term "commodity aesthetics" captures this paradox (1986: 17, 19, 35), what Seyla Benhabib calls "the *promesse du bonheur* that advanced capitalism always holds before [consumers], but never quite delivers" (2002: 3). It is embodied in the difference between those with and those without the class position and capital to define luxury and encourage emulation through identity goods such as fashion items (Sarah Berry 2000).

Commodities appeal because they provide a way to dodge that old Hegelian dilemma: what to do about ethical substance? In the United States, a sense of ethical incompleteness comes courtesy of origins in the underclass of Europe and Asia, the enslaved of Africa, and the dispossessed of the Americas. It encourages an ongoing self-criticism that falls back on faith and consumerism as means of surviving and thriving. *One* alternately loving and severe world of superstition (AKA religion) is matched by a *second* alternately loving and severe world of superstition (AKA consumption). In times of economic dynamism and uncertainty, these worlds merge with old myths about meritocracy and religion to inform the way we think about the nation. D. H. Lawrence identified *"the true myth of America"* as: *"She starts old, old, wrinkled and writhing in an old skin. And there is a gradual sloughing of the old skin, towards a new youth"* (1953: 64). The detritus of other lands needs remaking, as do successive newcomers and newborns.

Life is very much a project in the United States—but not a straightforwardly individual one. A duality of free choice and disciplinary governance is the grand national paradox. For example, many migrants arrive here cognizant of the country's extravagant claims to being *laissez-faire*—but they encounter the most administered society they have lived in! From dawn to dusk, life is laid out across a bewildering array of public and private institutions. Various forms of government are present every day and in every way, from municipal to state to federal agencies, along with less accountable intruders such as church and business bureaucrats—not to mention the venerable third sector of venture philanthropists, nosy foundations, and do-gooder associations. Even the summer break from school for young people is orchestrated via the bizarre ritual of camp, while those preparing for college entry must ritualistically embark on volunteerism to boost their application packets. Simply being—leading life without a bumper sticker avowing one's elective institutional affinities—seems implausible. The corollary is an earnest search for a self that can operate within this disciplinary complex. Wander through virtually any bookstore across the country, for example, and you will be swamped by the self-help section, edging its way closer and closer to the heart of the shop, as the ancestral roots of an unsure immigrant culture are stimulated anew by today's risky neoliberal one. In the three decades to 2000, the number of self-help books in the United States more than doubled. Between a third and a half of Yanquis buy them, lending their credit to a $2.48 billion-a-year industry of tapes, DVDs, videos, books, and "seminars" on making oneself anew, frequently with "spiritual" alibis—a whole array of consumables in place of adequate social security. Each item promises fulfillment but delivers a never-ending project of work on the self (McGee 2005: 11–12). Consider another powerful instance: Hollywood's promise of the makeover, of turning an off-screen farm girl into a film star, or an on-screen librarian into a siren. It stands at the heart of such projects and has been advertised as such ever since 1930s fan magazines promoted the emulation of actresses through cosmetics, with stars like Joan Blondell instructing readers that "the whole secret of beauty is change" (quoted in Sarah Berry 2000: 106; also see 107, 27).

Many cultural critics demonize such tendencies. For example, Christopher Lasch's influential 1970s tract, *The Culture of Narcissism,* a requiem for the national "character," was rejected by most scholars but embraced by pop intellectuals and then-President Jimmy Carter. Lasch identified a turn for the worse caused by "bureaucracy, the proliferation of images, therapeutic ideologies, the rationalization of the inner life, the cult of consumption, and in the last analysis . . . changes in family life and . . . changing patterns of socialization." He discerned a "pathological narcissism" of the "performing self." People had become "connoisseurs of their own performance and that of others," with the "whole man" fragmented. This critique bought into a longstanding obsession, exhibited since the 19th century in literature and philosophy, that associated the nation with Adam prior to the Fall, as a site where new forms of life could be invented that reprised a life before desire (Lasch 1978: 32, 67–68, 93; Stearns 2006: 203; Crawley 2006).

This perverse US fixation on "character" is invoked with inquisitorial reverence in election campaign after election campaign to question presidential candidates. Distinctions are avidly drawn between "personality"—the psychological cards one is dealt—and "character"—how one plays them. A failing that derives from "personality" (which seems to be about fun and the id) can be overcome by "character" (which seems to be about repression and the ego/superego). In the 2000 elections, George Bush Minor's character was routinely valorized by the bourgeois media as distinct from the Republican norm, because of his putative compassion and bipartisan tendencies. He was not evaluated on the measurable materiality of his public service—spectacular public-educational underachievement and record high rates of execution while governor of somewhere named Texas—or his recreational drug record, nepotistic affirmative-action entry to the Ivy League, and sordid business history. It took years for *Newsweek's* alarming 2003 cover story "Bush and God" to uncover the policy implications of Minor's alcohol-addiction- and business-failure-fueled conversion to evangelical Protestantism and its electoral appeal (Republicans were overwhelmingly supported across class lines by white Protestants during the 2003 Iraq crisis and the 2004 presidential election). Conversely, Al Gore Minor's character was routinely problematized in 2000 because of his fundraising activities on behalf of Democrats and putative tall tales about inventing the Internet, inspiring *Love Story,* and investigating Love Canal. He was not evaluated on the measurable materiality of his public service— spectacular economic growth and record high rates of educational attainment under his vice-presidency (Newport and Carroll 2003; Pew Research Center for the People & the Press 2004).

This obsession with personality versus character has a long history. In Ancient Greece and Rome, the body was the locus for an ethics of the self, a combat with pleasure and pain that enabled people to find the truth by mastering themselves. Austerity and hedonism could be combined. Xenophon, Socrates, and Diogenes believed that decadence led to professional failure unless accompanied by regular examination of the conscience and by physical training. Carefully modulated desire could be a sign of fitness to govern others: Aristotle and Plato went so far as to favor regular flirtations with excess (Foucault 1986: 66–69, 72–73, 104, 120, 197–98). For Solon, the key task of any ruler was "to check the desires that are excessive" in order to "make crooked judgments straight" (1994: 39). This did not mean wishing pleasure away but modifying oneself to account for it. Five hundred years later, the sexual ethics of Ancient Rome saw spirituality emerge to complicate exercises of the self as training for governance:

> within an ethics that posits that death, disease, or even physical suffering do not constitute true ills and that it is better to take pains over one's soul than to devote one's care to the maintenance of the body. But in fact the focus of attention in these practices of the self is the point where the ills of the body and those of the soul can communicate with one another and exchange their distresses; where the bad habits of the soul can entail physical miseries, while the excesses of the body manifest and maintain the failings of the soul. (Foucault 1988: 56–57)

In place of the excesses that had preoccupied 4th-century B.C. Athens, 1st-century A.D. Rome was principally concerned with frailty: the finitude of life and fitness. Moral arguments were imbued with "nature and reason," so exercises of the self were joined to a more elevated search for truth (Foucault 1988: 238–39). For his part, Saint Augustine explained Adam and Eve's postapple physical shame as a problem of control: what had been easily managed organs prior to the Fall suddenly became liable to "a novel disturbance in their disobedient flesh," as per Adam's disobedience of God. The result: the rest of us are left with original sin. The *pudenda,* or "parts of shame," were named as such because lust could "arouse those members independently of decision." The "movements of their body" manifest "indecent novelty" and hence shame, because the "genital organs have become as it were the private property of lust" (Augustine 1976: 522–23, 578, 581). Such feelings derived from the capacity of desire to get out of whack. As Foucault puts it, what were once "like the fingers" in obeying the will of their owner came to elude the owner's control, a punishment for Adam's own attempt to evade God's will. Man exemplifies the Fall in the mutability of his penis. So Renaissance paintings of Jesus routinely depict him pointing to or touching his genitals as a sign of his human side: a begotten rather than a created Son (Foucault and Sennett 1982; Porter 1991: 206). For Kant, while the distinctively human capacity for intellection is laden with a moral purpose, it is indissoluble from a craven desire that comes from being alive and mediates access to knowledge. The two modulate each other, with principle and pleasure in a constant combat that is an entirely normal occurrence. Virtue derives not from resolving the conflict, which is impossible, but from governing it (McHoul and Rapley 2001: 439–40).

In the United States, I sense that all this palaver about personality, character, and the control and expression of drives works as a grand metaphor for managing the differences and difficulties of language, history, race, gender, class, and faith that color the nation's history. It references the risk and opportunity embodied in the longest-standing makeover aspect of US society: immigration. A triad of personality-character-immigrant indexes the coterminous pleasure and pain of a "touch-and-go" existence, a suddenly anonymous personal history of "individual independence and differentiation" and the "right to distrust," alongside a need to map new selves and spaces (Simmel 1976: 88–89; Jameson 1991; Gabaccia 2006).

Ironically, today's encounter with difference is finally making the United States look truly American—it is coming to resemble the Americas. The first great wave of immigrants at the turn of the 20th century left the country 87% white/Euro-American, a proportion that remained static through the 1950s. The 20th century saw the US population increase by 250% (the equivalent figures are below 60% for both France and Britain). In the past decade, its Asian and Pacific Islander population increased by 43%, and its Latin@ population by 38.8%. Latin@s and Asians are increasing at ten times the rate of Euros. The minority population topped 100 million in 2007—

44 million Latin@s, 40 million African Americans, 15 million Asians, 4.5 million Native Americans, and a million Pacific Islanders. Most people who live in California, Texas, New Mexico, and Hawaii are minorities. If today's trends continue, 82% of the increase in US population between now and 2050 will come from immigrants and their offspring. Whites will be a minority. The foreign-born segment of the country is 36 million—double the proportion from 1970, half as many again as in 1995, and back to Depression-era levels—and across the 1990s immigration was up 37.7% from the previous decade. Almost half the people living in Los Angeles and Miami were born beyond the border, and Latin@s accounted for half the growth in the nation's population between 2003 and 2004. Of course, these official figures do not disclose the full picture. It has been suggested that 9 million new residents lack immigration documents, and they are joined by 300,000 new arrivals annually. There was a net increase of 2.5 million people without papers between 2002 and 2006. A reaction of fear is clear in events such as the 2007 scuttling of immigration reform. And hybridity is increasingly the norm. In 1990, one in twenty-three US marriages crossed race and ethnicity. In 2005, the figure was one in fifteen, an increase of 65%. As for the labor force, in 1960, one in seventeen workers was born outside the United States, the majority in Europe. Today, the proportion is one in six, mostly from Latin America and Asia. And the trend is accelerating: between 1996 and 2000, people born overseas comprised close to half the net increase in labor ("Hispanic" 2000; *Hispanic* 2005: 46; "Centrifugal" 2005; El Nasser and Grant 2005b; United Nations Development Programme 2004: 99; Pew Hispanic Center 2006; "The Americano" 2005; US Census Bureau News 2007; Pew Research Center 2008; "Open Up" 2008; Massey 2003: 143; Bloemraad 2006: 27; *Hispanic* 2005; El Nasser and Grant 2005b; Mosisa 2002: 3, 9; Tienda 2002; Castles and Miller 2003: 5; Schweder et al. 2002: 27).

Coinciding with these cultural changes, economic life for many US residents, both long-term and recent, is getting worse and worse. Successive population waves—no longer just white ones—have fled the inner city, in vain search of a turn to Arcady. The United States recently became the first nation in the world to have more than half its people living in suburbia—a quarter of whom are minorities—and 75% of new office space is constructed there. But as this historic demographic shift continues the trend from a rural to an urban to a suburban country, middle-class people are increasingly disarticulated from subsistence, from the state, and from the experience of country and city life. By contrast with European welfare systems, the capacity to exit poverty in the United States has diminished over the last three decades of neoliberalism and suburbanization, thanks to a gigantic clumping of wealth at the apex of the nation, atop a poor, unskilled, and unhealthy base. For twenty years, the state has pursued monetary policies that favor financial over productive capital, with obvious results—40% of corporate profit is in finance sectors, which employ just 5% of private-sector workers ("The Gentleman's Bailout" 2008; "Wall Street's Crisis" 2008: 11). Forty-six million US residents are indigent (even the Bush Minor administration admits that 13.3% of the population lives in poverty, the greatest proportion in the Global North); 52 million are functionally analphabetic; and 46 million lack health insurance, with an additional 36 million going without it at some point in the two years to 2003. One in six adults who *has* medical insurance experiences severe difficulties meeting his or her medical expenses. And access to money and net worth are massively stratified by class, race, and gender. In 2003, black men earned 73% of the hourly wage rate of white people, for instance, and the gaps are widening. Migrants are disproportionately represented amongst the poor, with wages averaging 75 cents for every dollar paid to Yanquis. In the first six years of his rule, George Bush Minor presided over a 9% increase in the poverty rate, a 12% increase in people without heath insurance, and immobile family income. Minor himself has been forced to proclaim that "income inequality is real—it's been rising for more than 25 years" (Younge 2007; Minor quoted in Sawhill and Morton 2008: 3).

Twenty years ago, neoclassical economists hailed the impact of market precepts over social democracy, because just 20% of the public's future income was predictable based on paternal income. By the 1990s, and two more decades of deregulation, that figure had doubled. Some figures suggest it now stands at 60%. In the two decades from 1979, the highest-paid 1% of the population doubled its share of national pretax income, to 18%. Incomes of the top 1% increased by 194%; the top 20%, by 70%—and the bottom 20%, by just 6.4%. In 1967, chief executive officers (CEOs) of corporations were paid 24 times the average wage of employees. Thirty years later, they received 300 times that amount. The average Yanqui CEO "makes" more in an hour than an employee does in a month. The Congressional Budget Office reports that during the late 1990s, the wealthiest 1% of US households had a greater combined income than the poorest 40%. In California, where I live, the economy is larger than all but a few sovereign states around the world. So what? Working-class family income in California has increased by 4% since 1969, while its ruling-class equivalent has grown by 41%. Nationally, corporate profits are at their highest level in five decades, while wages and salaries have the lowest share of the national pie on record. Over Bush Minor's first term, corporate profits rose by 60%, but wages by just 10%. In 2004, after-tax profits for corporations grew to their highest proportion of Gross Domestic Product (GDP) since the Depression. In the eyes of *Fortune* magazine, corporations "deserve credit for their restraint," because "[i]nstead of hiring recklessly, they found ways to produce a trim workforce." The *Fortune 500* group of companies received $785 billion of income in 2006, up 29% from 2005, adding up to the biggest profits in the half-century life of the index. Half the money made goes to a tenth of the population, even as the tax burden has shifted dramatically away from companies and onto workers. In the three years 2003–6, hourly wages (adjusted for inflation) declined, despite the increase in productivity. Between 1999 and 2004, the bottom 90% of US households saw their income rise by 2%; for those "earning" over $1 million annually, income grew by more than 87%. In 2005, real wages fell for all but the top 5%, while productivity rose by 3% and GDP by 3.2%. The Gini index saw inequality attain the same level as during the Great Depression. The Organization for Economic Cooperation and Development categorizes the US halfway down its thirty member-nations in terms of the average worker's net income. Only Hungary has greater income inequality. Whereas there were 290,000 individual bankruptcies in 1980, 2005 saw more than 2 million. Over a similar period, mortgage foreclosures increased five times over, and the personal savings rate became negative for the first time since the pit of the Depression (Lexington 2005; Skocpol 2004; Webster and Bishaw 2006; Thelen 2000: 552; Freeman 2004; "Centrifugal" 2005; Sered and Fernandopulle 2007: 213, 222; Patrick Harris 2006; "Ever Higher" 2005; Madrick 2007: 20; "Breaking" 2005; Yates 2005; Hutton 2003b: 133, 148; Taibo 2003: 24; Bernstein 2006: 6, 34, 120; Henwood 2006; Kotkin and Friedman 2006; Hacker 2006: 13, 94, 138, ix, 2; Tully 2007; Wallechinsky 2006; "Time to Act" 2007; Francis 2005; Francis 2007; Sawhill and Morton 2008: 3).

Put another way, the gap between what labor produces and what it reaps is greater than at any point in recorded history. This bizarre reconcentration of wealth in the hands of the bourgeoisie is unprecedented in world history since the advent of working-class electoral franchises. No wonder *The Economist* captioned a photo of the Queen of England greeting Bush Minor and his wife, Laura, as "Liz, meet the royals." We are back in what Mark Twain and Charles Dudley Warner (1874) bitingly satirized as *The Gilded Age*, the 19th-century heyday of capital when Andrew Carnegie coined the term "The Gospel of Wealth" to legitimize his race, class, and gender privilege. No wonder Warren Buffet avowed in a 2003 letter to Berkshire investors that "if class warfare is being waged in America, my class is clearly winning" ("Ever Higher" 2005; Garfinkle 2006: 15). Even some unrepentant fans of capitalism complain that "many Americans are one lost job and one medical emergency away from bankruptcy," while James Glassman, one of the reactionary American Enterprise Institute's pop thinkers, acknowledges that "we've redistributed income about as much as we can." Almost half the population does not see hard work as the means to a better life. Employment is less secure and fluctuations in household income are more intense than people were brought up to remember. Risk is "offloaded by governments and corporations onto the increasingly fragile balance sheets of workers and their families." In sum, if we juxtapose aggregate prosperity against personal insecurity, the economy is doing well by ruling-class indices; but it is doing poorly by working-class indices, in terms of both inequality and instability. Non-supervisory employees remain driven by the "Dream"—and it's not about wealth but simply economic comfort. Despite this modest objective, their pursuit of it has failed in their own eyes, wrecked on the shoals of stagnating wages, accelerating costs of basic needs, agglomerating debt, and perishing retirement income. Workers are far from sanguine about their own future and their children's—and this anxiety is felt by college graduates, for the first time (Lake Research Partners 2006; Tully 2007; Cohen and DeLong 2005: 113; Glassman quoted in Hall 2006). Even the intellectual bloc of the plutocracy, represented by the American Enterprise Institute, the Brookings Institution, the Heritage Foundation, and the Urban Institute, concurs that the Dream has been disrupted by our national decline in economic mobility. They are posing the ultimate political quandary for capital: "What happens if the public begins to question its prospects for upward mobility?" (Sawhill and Morton 2008: 2).

And the reaction to these shocks and shifts in culture and economy? As immigration has become more diverse and complex, and wealth has been systematically redistributed upwards, vast numbers of people have pledged themselves to two potent forms of makeover: religion and psycho-pharmacology. These developments are reshaping a tendency toward reinvention that is central to the mythology and lived experience of the entire nation. Each trend comes complete with transformative claims, as if they were rescue columns promising deliverance from peril. I address them in turn.

God-Botherers

True conservatism flows from a singular unifying belief: God. In private life and in the public square good liberals can take Him or leave Him, but true conservatives must always seek Him and strive to heed Him. In the conservative creed human beings are moral and spiritual beings. Each of us has God-given personal rights and God-given social duties, God-given individual liberties and God-given moral responsibilities.
—John J. Dilulio, Jr., Bush Minor's first Director of the White House Office of Faith-Based and Community Initiatives (2003: 218)

At the time of its formation, the United States was not very religious (perhaps 15% to 20% of the population were God-botherers). In 1683, 83% of Salem (Salem!) taxpayers were not aligned with any church ("O Come" 2007: 8, 10). Three hundred years later, the same proportion of the US population regarded the Bible as the word. Its annual sales veered between $425 and $650 million ("The Battle" 2007: 80). Puritanism had long been the object of obloquy and mockery as much as adherence. The Constitution did not mention God, and 1797's Treaty of Tripoli specified that the country "is not in any sense founded on the Christian religion" (Kevin Phillips 2006: 108; Elliott 2001: ix; Treaty quoted in Allen 2005). But a clear relationship developed between immigration, economic change, and religious uptake in the United States. Religion offered comfort to new arrivals and reaction for nativists, very much as for today's right-wing religious rapture; and it became a national player because churches provided services in competition with one another to recruit migrants, who were not aided by the state. For free settlers and enslaved ones alike, faith provided reasons to flee, forms of succor, and means of collective identification. It helped maintain ethnic solidarity in a new environment, leavened a lack of class bearings, gave solace throughout the horrors of slavery, and delivered social services denied by the brutality of capital and the plutocracy of the state. With the emergence of industrial capitalism and its collective pressures, the selfish aspects of Protestant religion also offered a form of possessive individualism to counter the dictates of obedience at work. Immigration and economic change coincided between 1890 and 1920, as the mass arrival of Eastern and Central Europeans changed the ethnic equilibrium and factory life developed.

Now the two trends are cycling again via new racial formations and postindustrialization. Each period has been providential for the particular superstitions of Evangelicals, characterized by a demonization of secular positivism—most obviously evolutionary theory—and by imperialistic desire and militarism. These bigotries tie into a longstanding obsession with fertility and conversion as means of defending and expanding terrain. The nation's repeated bursts of God-bothering are called Great Awakenings. As measured by leaps in the percentage of the population attending and affiliating with churches, these bursts occurred in 1850 (34%), 1890 (45%), 1926 (56%), and 1980 (62%). Those dates correlate with devastating forms of economic faith: nutty Malthusian racism, embodied in the 1885 Chinese Exclusion Act; contractionary class inequality and the 1924 Immigration Act under Depression-era Republicans; and the neoliberal warlock craft of the contemporary moment, as per welfare reform and regressive taxation (Peck 1993: 11–14, 36, 81; Kaufmann 2006; Phillips 2006: 116; Greene 1999: 39, 44; Portes and Rumbaut 2006: 316).

Time magazine ran a cover story in 1966 entitled "Is God Dead?" and *The Economist* published his obituary in its millennial issue ("In God's Name" 2007: 5). Such secularism is inconceivable today. We can discern a homology between what Marx called "the mist-enveloped regions of the religious world," which conceal the secular reality of human action forging faith, and the way that the value of commodities is disarticulated from the labor that makes them (1987: 77, 84). Based on his extensive interviews with true believers across the country, Pulitzer Prize–winning former *New York Times* journalist and Harvard Divinity School graduate Chris Hedges suggests that the "engine that drives the radical Christian right in the United States, the most dangerous mass movement in American history, is not religiosity, but despair." Whereas capital, government, and suburbia were failing much of the population, the magical hereafter promised them relief and release that could not be falsified by their drab diurnal existence (2007). And one Puritan element that was never compromised? A bold and fierce nationalism that claimed for the United States something akin to predestined domination (Fessenden et al. 2001: 2).

Of course, for all these compelling sociological explanations that show why people sign up to believe, the United States constantly surprises in the fervor of its commitment to, well, magic. Evangelical Christians speak of an almost physical, trancelike transformation, from a faith based in ideas to something that resembles transubstantiation. Not surprisingly, they have powerful ties to millenarianism and the supernatural (Luhrmann 2004; Peck 1993: 8). One must ponder hard a nation where the vast majority attests to the existence of a devil and individuated angels; 45% of people say aliens have visited Earth; three times more people know there are ghosts than was the case a quarter-century ago; over one-third think houses can be haunted; 84% credit posthumous survival of the soul, up

24% from 1972; only 25% subscribe to evolution; almost two-thirds antici-
pate millennial doom and rebirth; 55% are certain that Satan exists; 44%
know there are demons (the same national proportion that has seen Mel
Gibson's anti-Semitic paean to sadomasochism, *The Passion of the Christ*
[2004], where his screen and social identities of oleaginous businessman,
vengeful messiah, anti-authoritarian larrikin, and right-wing real-estate
magnate collided); and in the South, 44% believe lightning is sent by God
to punish wrongdoers. The country has approximately 335,000 religious
congregations, and 79% of its citizens identify as Christian, with 41%
converts to fundamentalist evangelism across a bizarre array of groups,
and 18% aligned with the religious right. The latter are the most skeptical
people in the Yanqui population about environmental protection. Appar-
ently there is no future for the planet. God's design is to destroy it and
deliver true believers to safety in a kinky theological draft of wind (Hutton
2003a; Mann 2003: 103; Pew Internet & American Life Project 2004; Gallup
2002–3; O'Connor 2005: 8; Grossberg 2005: 140–41; Newport and Carroll
2003; "The God Slot" 2006; Association of Religion Data Archives 2006;
Pew Forum on Religion & Public Life 2004b; Hartford Institute for Religious Research 2007; Pew Research Center 2005a: 17; Baylor Institute for
the Study of Religion 2006; Stearns 2006: 70–71). Yet people in the United
States know almost nothing about the Bible—60% can't recite even half of
the Ten Commandments, 50% don't know the name of the first book in it
or who preached the Sermon on the Mount, 25% don't know what Easter
is, and 12% believe that Noah married Joan of Arc ("The Battle" 2007: 81).
The proportions of the Bush Cabinet covered in this survey are not available.

The population's embrace of superstition places the United States alone
amongst nations with advanced economies and educational systems.
The 96% of people who believe in a higher power, and the 59% who state
that religion is crucial to their life, represent more than twice the proportions for Japan, South Korea, Western Europe, and the former Soviet
bloc. Unlike any other First World country, most US residents connect
belief in God to morality and wealth. Unlike their fellow antisecularists in
much of the Third World, they reject state intervention to assuage social
ills, so forbiddingly individual is their account of person and deity. (In
the late 1990s, 94% of US citizens between aged 15 and 24 equated citizenship with assisting other people individually.) But they do favor state
intervention to destroy and punish others: preachers were key firebrands
in many US conflicts, perhaps most notably the War of 1812, the Civil War,
the Spanish-American War, and the oily Oedipal invasions of Iraq. Don't

bother yourself with social justice, political representation, or inequality. Just help the next person across the street, or defeat them in battle, and all will be well. It's a grotesque national smackdown, pitting Albert Camus against Norman Vincent Peale on pay-per-view in hysterical mode, with a quarter of the population sufficiently deluded to speak in tongues. Perhaps the best exemplification of this trend is the megachurch—churches with weekly attendances in excess of 2,000 people. By 2006 there were over a thousand such entities. That number has doubled since 2001, as has their average attendance. The megachurches use satellites more and more, and four megachurch pastor-authors have featured on the *New York Times'* bestseller list, with tens of millions in sales (Luhrmann 2004: 520; Pew Research Center for the People & the Press 2002b and 2003b; Kevin Phillips 2006: 122; Westheimer and Kahne 2004: 6; Pew Forum on Religion & Public Life 2006b; Baylor Institute for the Study of Religion 2006; Redden 2002: 34; Thumma et al. 2006).

This is not quite what social science predicted—neither right-wing modernization theory nor Marxist developmentalism. Secular modernity was conceived as postreligious. But we are witnessing the dread revival of superstition, its ironic triumph as a postsecular phenomenon. The United States seems to be a society where transcendence in the *hic et nunc* can be followed or trumped by deliverance (or at least persistence) after death. And true believers want to transform others, not just themselves. Faith is regarded as a sign of moral superiority that must be carried into public life. In the 1960s, 53% of the population favored no role for religion in politics. Today, 54% favor direct participation by religious organizations in government, and 60% of white Evangelicals want the Bible to guide lawmaking over the will of the population (Pace 2007; "Therapy" 2003: 13; Jeffries 2006; Pew Forum on Religion & Public Life 2006a).

The re-enchantment of politics dates from Jimmy Carter's decision to roll back special privileges accorded to Christian academies that had exempted them from federal taxes. The end to that outrageous subsidy pushed creepy Christians into the political domain. And since Richard Nixon had scored zero on political morality, post-Watergate Republicans proceeded to stress personal morality, targeting the left and social movements in areas of symbolic power. Campaigns for civil rights, feminism, and gay liberation provoked counteroffensives by fundamentalists (anti-obscenity and anti-abortion), nationalists (anti–flag burning and pro–English Only), and political conservatives (anti–affirmative action and anti–civil rights). Time-series analysis demonstrates that the last three decades have seen activist Democrats become more secular and modern, and activist Republicans more religious and antimodern (Flint and Porter 2005; Rieder 2003: 30; Schmidt 2000). Democratic partisans have favored abortion, queer rights, and women's issues, and Republicans have opposed them, from the moment they ably alliterated the 1972 Democrats as the party of "Acid, Amnesty, and Abortion" (quoted in Rieder 2003: 23). Migrating "southward down the Twisting Tail of Rhetoric," Republicans focused on "the misty-eyed flag-waving of Ronald Reagan who, while George McGovern flew bombers in World War II, took a pass and made training films in Long Beach" (Keillor 2004).

Yet Bill Clinton affiliated with a strangely fervent Christianity, his hypocrisy matched only by the righteous selfishness of reactionary US Protestants and their claims to superiority over others (Hutton 2003b: 28). Consider Clinton's two inauguration speeches—grotesque assortments of biblical and Catholic teaching plus clichés from the Gipper that signaled an ecumenical but strong religiosity indebted to conservatives. A form of "civil religion," these addresses troped the United States as a chosen land, even alluding to the Bible's claim that God changed history by referring to the end of the Cold War as a sign of "the fullness of time" (Pitney 1997; Clinton quoted in Bacevich 2003: 1). Clinton was indebted to reactionary politics, despite being animated by progressive social movements. Liberal on cultural questions and neoliberal on financial ones, but avowedly a god-botherer of the first order, he was like many progay, prochoice, antiwelfare suburbanites. In keeping with his indebtedness to this group, the economic dividend that Clinton was presented by the end of the Cold War in the form of mounting surpluses was not spent combating internal and external poverty (Falk 2004: 26)—the *secondary* moral outrage of his presidency after the failure to act in Rwanda.

But even Clinton's level of superstition was not enough for the right.

The Homeland Security Act (House of Representatives 5005, 2002) mandates bankrolling "faith-based" groups to further "civic engagement and integration." Of course, during Minor's first term, all such support went to Christians, and not a brass razoo to Sikhs, Jews, Muslims, or Buddhists (Kaplan 2004: 22). For example, "MentorKids USA" received funding until Constitutional watchdogs protested that the organization required volunteers to sign a pledge avowing that "the Bible is God's authoritative and inspired word that is without error . . . including creation, history, its originals and salvation" (quoted in Freedom from Religion 2004).

Evangelical organizations generally intervene in sex, not economics, and resolutely oppose adequate welfare and proworker policies. Instead, they fight to diminish privacy. For example, anal and oral sex and the use of vibrators remained crimes in many states until a 2003 US Supreme Court decision. In the same session, the court upheld new rules severely restricting family visits to prisoners. Only one of these decisions (decriminalizing non-procreative penetrative sex) drew the wrath of so-called family-oriented religious think tanks and lobby groups. They showed no interest in the 1.3 million children whose fathers were (and possibly still are) incarcerated. These protestors were not animated by the material well-being of the groups in whose name they spoke. There was no call to strengthen families rent asunder by prison. Protestant evangelist Pat Robertson was too busy mobilizing his Christian Broadcasting Network, calling on creepy Christians to pray for the removal of three judges who had voted to decriminalize volitional sex (he chose those with significant health problems) in order to aid Bush Minor's project of altering the court. Operation Rescue, an anti-abortion group, set up six coffins outside a federal courthouse, each one inscribed with Supreme Court decisions that displeased the organization, and proceeded to set fire to them, a reaction in keeping with two decades of terrorism by the Christian right over sex. Of course, religious attendance correlates strongly with both committing crimes and heralding punishment of others (no wonder, given the malevolent moralism and prying pressure of prelates). Those states of the union dominated by this unremitting, unforgiving, and above all hypocritical, censoriousness have the highest proportions of teenage pregnancy, out-of-wedlock births, murder, and divorce, even as bastions of morality like Chuck Colson, the Concerned Women of America, the *American Spectator,* Linda Chavez, and the Heritage Foundation blame torture at Abu Ghraib in 2003 on pornography, gay culture, feminism, and Hollywood (DiIulio Jr. 2003: 219; Jakobsen and Pellegrini 2003: 3–5; Pollard 2003: 70; Risol 2003; Rosen 2003: 48; Coltrane 2001; "Us" 2003: 12; Rich 2004; Portes and Rumbaut 2006: 329; Douglas 2004).

Despite the poll numbers, it would be wrong to regard the makeover right as an organic movement that operates from the ground up. Its ideas come from an elite of over three hundred "coin-operated" think tanks in Washington. Funded by such wealthy US foundations and families as Olin, Scaife, Koch, Castle Rock, and Smith Richardson, these organizations ideologize extravagantly on everything from sexuality to foreign policy. Ghostwriters render the prose of resident intellectuals attractive as part of a project that is concerned more with marketing opinion than with conducting research—for each "study" they fund is essentially the alibi for an op-ed piece. Their immediate audience comprises a second-tier grass-roots network stretching across the National Right to Life Committee, the

American Family Association, the Liberty Alliance, the Eagle Forum, the Family Research Council, the Christian Action Network, and the Christian Coalition. Then there is a more public audience. Progressive think tanks had just a one-sixth share of media quotations compared to reactionary institutions during the 1990s. In the decade 1995–2005, the right averaged 51% of citations, and progressives 14%. The people who appear on the three major television networks' newscasts as expert commentators on society and culture are indices of this success: 92% of such mavens are white, 85% are male, and 75% are Republican. In all, 90% of news interviewees on these networks are white men born between 1945 and 1960 (Kallick 2002; Karr 2005; Alterman 2003: 85; Dolny 2003 and 2005; Hart 2004: 52; Claussen 2004: 56; Love 2003: 246; Cohen 2004; Rendall and Broughel 2003).

These civil-society tactics, both protests and op-ed pieces, came from somewhere uncomfortably close to the left. Having learned from progressive social movements that the personal and the cultural were political, the right declared itself the ideological foe not only of subaltern groups seeking enfranchisement, but also of liberal, humanistic expressions of universality and secularism. Minorities and feminists had protested antidefamation with great impact, so why shouldn't the right protest the defamation of *its* values—fundamentalism, homophobia, and nationalism? Such methods parroted civil-rights legislation and the rhetoric of subject positions around which contemporary social movements waged their struggles. The National Rifle Association, for example, was a rather mild-mannered, Clark-Kentish advocate for field sports for a long time. Following an internal coup in the mid-1970s, it left New York City for the wilds, campaigned for people owning guns as a Constitutional right/responsibility—and overtly borrowed tactics from the civil-rights movement. The same period marked the advent of the Moral Majority, again drawing on the rhetoric and methods of civil rights. Ten years later, this indebtedness to civil-rights activism was carried forward by the United Shareholders Association, whose consumerist politics disempowered workers and turned corporations into ventures of speculation rather than generators of infrastructure. Then evangelical Christians modeled their anti–queer marriage movement on anti-tobacco activism. Today, both Stanford and UCLA feature organizations dedicated to undoing "institutional racism"—a concept long derided by the white right that is now perversely embraced by it to claim that groups such as the Movimiento Estudiantil Chicano de Aztlán, formed at the height of creative Chican@ cultural politics in the 1970s, have become so powerful on campus that they must be stopped for fear of disadvantaging white folks. In 2004, the Sierra Club fended off a takeover by anti-Latin@ candidates who opposed immigration on environmental grounds. All of these groups were underwritten by far-right think tanks and foundations—artful practitioners of an identity politics they profess to despise, rearticulated through the supposedly benign and unquestionable dogmas of faith and opportunity (Hutton 2003b: 85, 104; Coltrane 2001: 395; Lovato 2004).

Earlier battles that had been won by the left through the use of spectacle have been waged anew, with spectacle as much a tactic of reactionaries as of radicals. The umbrella term for this front, "culture war," originated toward the end of Reagan's presidency. It became media orthodoxy when Republican Congressman Henry Hyde sought to condemn flag burning as "one front in a larger culture war" in 1990 (quoted in DiMaggio 2003: 80). (A decade on, after his service as chair of the congressional committee that recommended Clinton's impeachment, Hyde further distinguished himself by writing to Bush Minor upon the election of the leftist Luiz Inácio Lula da Silva to the presidency of Brazil in 2002 that a new nation had joined the "axis of evil" purportedly formed by Iraq, North Korea, and Iran [quoted in Youngers 2003]). Grover Norquist, a key zealot and Republican apparatchik who heads an antitax front organization for the party, has summed up the times with his tasteless statement, "Bipartisanship is another form of date rape" (quoted in Keillor 2004), while public broadcasting's McLaughlin Group TV show dedicated much discussion to the notion that Clinton was Satan. This virulent think tank and social-movement anti-statism subsided once the Republicans took control of both the executive branch and Congress. A previous hostility to the state transformed into a warm embrace. Sixty-nine percent of the Republican Party soon held that government functioned for the good of all (Alterman 2003: 145; Pew Research Center for the People & the Press 2003d: 2, 8).

Here is a recent, rather secular ethno/demography of these magician-nativists:

> Hairy-backed swamp developers and corporate shills, faith-based economists, fundamentalist bullies with Bibles, Christians of convenience, free-lance racists, misanthropic frat boys, shrieking midgets of AM radio, tax cheats, nihilists in golf pants, brownshirts in pinstripes, sweatshop tycoons, hacks, fakirs, aggressive dorks, Lamborghini libertarians, people who believe Neil Armstrong's moonwalk was filmed in Roswell, New Mexico, little honkers out to diminish the rest of us.

Is this the irritated rant of an urban hipster, mercilessly mocking those beyond the world of downtown lofts and polymorphous pleasure? Did these words drop from a laptop as it hurtled across the fly-over states? No. The quotation comes from a true son of the Midwest: *Prairie Home Companion*'s Garrison Keillor (2004) was responding to the latest wave of right-wing reaction to the difference that colors US life. That politics follows many of the tenets and life forms of fundamentalism more generally in its identification of an inviolable ancient text with a contemporary sociopolitical strategy, thereby offering internal cohesion and external power. But in keeping with the traditional characteristics of reactionaries, despite the purportedly positive guidance provided by an originary text such as the Bible, it is used in a negative way, to construct an ideology known by what it opposes as much as if not more than what it supports. No wonder the distinguished former president of Argentina, Raúl Alfonsín, worried aloud that the United States was headed for neofascism because of the far-right forces unleashed by creepy Christianity (Pace 2007; Anguita and Colectivo Prometeo 2003: 43).

Pill-Poppers

The neurogenetic-industrial complex . . . becomes ever more powerful. Undeterred by the way that molecular biologists, confronted with the outputs from the Human Genome Project, are beginning to row back from genetic determinist claims, psychometricians and behavior geneticists, sometimes in combination and sometimes in competition with evolutionary psychologists, are claiming genetic roots to areas of human belief, intentions and actions long assumed to lie outside biological explanation . . . [:] political tendency, religiosity and likelihood of mid-life divorce.
—Steven Rose (2006: 6–7)

In addition to religiosity as a response to cultural and economic change, there is a more rational, less ideological, but equally far-reaching, reaction to cultural change. For nowadays, nestling alongside big faith, "'big science' and 'big technology' can sit on your desk, reside in a pillbox, or inside your body" (Clarke et al. 2003: 167, 164), offering "personalised medicine" via cosmetic pharmacology ("Billion" 2007: 71). One trend remodels belief. The other remodels the brain. The selective serotonin reuptake inhibitors (SSRIs) world of the psychological makeover through pharmacology provides a strange meeting point of the body's exterior and its interior, a site where commodities encounter emotions, mediated formally and informally through professional knowledge and intervention, and mass-produced in pill form. Pharmaceutical corporations promote fast, efficient solutions to life's problems—a call to stop reading and start swallowing.

In the quarter-century to 2003, US expenditure on pharmaceuticals grew from $12 billion to $197 billion, a seventeenfold increase at a time when spending on cars and clothes doubled and tripled respectively. Expenditure on pharmaceutical psy-drugs increased by 638% in the United States between 1990 and 2000 (as opposed to 50% in Japan and 126% in Europe), and dosages of psy-drugs increased by 70%. During that period, as a proportion of the overall market for pharmacology, the United States was more obsessed with mental health than anything or anybody else, with psy-drugs accounting for 18% of the pharmaceutical market. By the turn of the 21st century, 38 million people in the United States had tried Prozac, and over 10 million new prescriptions were written for it in 1999 alone. In 2004, 91 million people, 45% of the population, took prescription drugs regularly, and only a quarter never did so. That represents 64% of all households, filling 3 billion prescriptions a year. In the ten years to 2000, a period of minimal inflation, US expenditure on pharmaceuticals doubled, to $100 billion. A decade ago, US residents averaged seven prescriptions a year; now it is twelve (Rose 2007: 209; Erica Goode 2000; Fox 2004; Petersen 2008; Rowe 2006).

This is the era when the head of AstraZeneca can smile as he offers this tidbit of grandiose pharma-hubris: "Death is optional" (quoted in "Billion" 2007: 69). For if the self is "a cultural invention" (Kessen 1979: 815), and we are en route to a "posthuman self" (Davis 2000), then the newest "darlings of Wall Street"—pharmacorps—are its leading manufacturers (Healy 2002: 2, 353). The drug makeover experience clearly appeals to people who have decided to abandon former existences. They are living out the latest trend in a makeover nation: "SSRIs, hormones, brain boosters, neurotransmitters." Instead of old-style recreational objects that Yanquis liked to put in their mouths (alcohol, tobacco, coffee, and illegal substances), which promised instantaneous joy and release—tied in some cases to eventual death, disability, pain, contempt, or incarceration—the new substances, legal and controlled, offer a general overhaul (Davis 2000; Elliott 2003a). No huddling outside the office building, no stains on the paperwork or keyboard, no obvious need to be like others. No quick pleasure, no hangover, no nightly snoring or morning cough driving those around you to distraction, no staggering to the bathroom to be ill, no breathlessness walking up two flights of stairs, no emanations from the mouth, hair, or clothes to mark one out. Instead, a quiet daily insurance backs up the gains made the day before within one's not-so-hard drive of a body, and without the fear of employer drug testing. Rather than forming illicit, informal relationships with others through the shared experience of ingestion, new drugs "melt invisibly into the texture of the everyday" (Davis 2000). They forge a sterling relationship with the self that can be invisible to others and oneself—a preparty preparation, the perfect makeover. Or more publicly, they can be redisposed as membership badges via water-cooler discussions about whether last week's Prozac has taken hold yet, almost as per Evangelicals' seemingly insatiable need for recognition of their status as "born again" (a charming critique of mothers and birthing centers). These drugs fulfill the dream of learning the code, cracking the means of making oneself anew, leaving life as something more than when one arrived—and doing so in a seamless way that does not draw attention to itself unless desired. What may have begun as a search for authentic feelings via confession and therapy—the real me revealed—turns commodified transmogrification into authenticity itself (Elliott 2003b: 22, 29–30). For Prozac guru Peter D. Kramer, enhancement pharmacology may be "the American ideal" (2003: xi). Instead of illness cured, one type of wellness substitutes for another (Elliott 2003b: 50–51). Some say this is the corollary of a macroeconomic change, that "the scientific management of *production,* so prevalent in the early days of the twentieth century, has been displaced by a new scientific management of *consumption*" (Hansen et al. 2003: 1). What differentiates this era of enhancement technologies from others is the sense that consumer purchases displace political activism as a means of improvement. The mythic quest to "restore a lost normativity" looks modest by contrast with this hyperconsumerism (Hogle 2005; Rose 2007: 81).

Enhancement technologies have become topics of everyday conversation with the spread of brain boosters to improve concentration (Hibbert 2007).What used to be part of drug subculture—pills to transform the self—has become central to corporate capital. To quote the *New York Times,* "Big Pharma Ogles Yasgur's Farm." So we find Viagra sponsoring a tour by Earth, Wind & Fire, a '70s rhythm and blues/soul/funk group, as part of a search by its manufacturer, Pfizer, for consumers who once associated popular music with illegal, recreational drug use and who might now be open to a legal life-style equivalent (Leland 2001).

Deregulation has propelled marketing into the forefront of drug development, and pharmaceutical companies deem conventional scholarly research and education too slow for their financial rhythms. The pharmaceutical industry's proportion of US health research grew from 13% in 1980 to 52% in 1995. Marketing, not medicine, decides how to develop a new pharmacological compound once it has been uncovered, asking the following questions: Will it be announced as a counter to depression or premature ejaculation? Will it be announced in journal x or y? Which scholars will be chosen to front it and produce consensus over its benefits? Major advertising agencies that work with pharmaceutical corporations, such as Interpublic, WPP, and Omnicom, have subsidiaries like Scirex that conduct clinical trials. Known as medical education and communications companies, they aim to get "closer to the test tube." These desires for sales and speed versus protocol meet, ironically, in scholarly journals. Despite the cult of speed, scholarly legitimacy is a key part of this merchandising. Pfizer describes academic publication as a means "to support, directly or indirectly, the marketing of our product" (quoted in Moffatt and Elliott 2007). Medical education and communications companies provide ghostwriting services, paid for by corporations, that deliver copy to academics and clinicians—and then pay them for signing it. Many faculty shill for corporations by allowing their names to go on articles that they have neither researched nor written—for all the world like football players or basketballers who have not even read, let alone penned, their "autobiographies." Instead, these corporate subsidiaries write papers on behalf of academics. Such practices are increasingly common across the domain of big pharma, with few if any concessions to the notion of a conflict of interest or even to the notion of open declaration of this cash-for-research-and-comment love fest.

Thankfully, the whistle is occasionally blown by potential recruits who reject an offer (Fugh-Berman 2005). Such revelations have led the International Committee of Medical Journal Editors to establish criteria that investigate who does the research and writing that medical journals publish. Even with these criteria in place, one in ten papers in leading medical outlets is the work of ghostwriters, and an astounding 90% of articles published in the *Journal of the American Medical Association* derive from people paid by pharmacorps, which pressure medical journals to print favorable research findings in return for lucrative advertising copy (Healy et al. 2003; Moynihan 2004). The Canadian Broadcasting Corporation (2003) offers a wry column about these authorial phantoms. Entitled "Ghostwriting: The Basics," it lays out the dimensions and norms of the scam, noting the scandal of Fen-Phen as the most prominent disaster resulting from cash-register research of this kind: people shopping for weight reduction ended up with heart and lung damage. Similar investigative reports have come from ABC News, the *Wall Street Journal, Forbes,* and many other media outlets. Of course, pretend authorship is only part of the conflict of interest. Away from ghostwriting, pseudoscholars from medical schools and professional practice routinely accept monetary and travel gifts from companies in a quiet *quid pro quo* for favorable publicity. Pharmacorps' budgets for marketing to clinicians are skyrocketing (Moffatt and Elliott 2007: 19). The result? The permanently ethically and intellectually challenged oxymoronic notion of the "business school" has been overtaken by the medical academy in the collegial disgrace stakes.

The deregulatory, deprofessionalizing impulses of privatization have also been applied to the creation of drug consumers as patients, reinterpellated as sovereign consumer-citizens able to govern themselves orally. TV commercials for prescription drugs, banned for thirty years by UN protocols that restricted direct-to-consumer marketing by pharmacorps, have been washed away from US obligations (the only other nation to do this, Aotearoa/New Zealand, is rethinking the policy). In 2001, $2 billion was spent promoting pharma to Yanquis, up from $300 million three years earlier. By 2004, the figure was $4 billion; in 2006, $4.5 billion. More money is spent selling psychiatric "wonder drugs" than on medical school and residency training—in 1998, Eli Lilly and Company paid $95 million just to market Prozac. The Government Accountability Office has found the Food and Drug Administration (FDA) at fault for lack of oversight of false pharma commercials, while the Kaiser Family Foundation says that direct address of consumers in advertisements has increased prescription drug sales by 12% (Allen 2007). The key site of promotion is new diseases as much as their treatment—companies vend the problem coevally with the cure. Companies are forever developing products to deal with circumstances that have been newly defined as maladies, like baldness, obesity, and impotence: "insomnia, sadness, [and] twitchy legs" become "sleep disorder, depression [and] restless leg syndrome" as part of "the medicalization of everyday life" (Welch et al. 2007). There are also carefully orchestrated product placements undertaken by front organizations. The 2004 Academy Awards telecast saw a Boomer Coalition commercial urging adults to have their cholesterol tested, without disclosing that the coalition was invented by an advertising agency and underwritten by Pfizer. TV commercials promote pills to counter hair loss, muscle loss, and erection loss—in fact, everything bar Lacanian loss. In 2005, drug manufacturers outlaid $240 million to create and sustain erections. Republican Bob Dole, baseballer Rafael Palmeiro, race-car driver Jeff Fuller, "football"[4] coach Mike Ditka, and a National Association for Stock Car Auto Racing (NASCAR) event all

need help with their erections, and "footballer" Ricky Williams seeks alle-
viation from anxiety. Big pharma has devoted such massive proportions of
its wealth to the creation of need via promotional expenditure that approximately one-fifth of its revenue goes to research and development versus
one-third to marketing. Pfizer even stations marketers inside laboratories
to ensure that scientists don't waste time looking to create compounds
that nobody can be made to want. The corollary is a drastic drop-off in
new medications coming to market (Jaramillo 2006: 272; Scherer 2005:
72; Esposito 2006; Rose 2003: 51, 56; Healy 1997: 25; Rubin 2004: 373–74;
Gates et al. 2002; Hearn 2005; Kovac 2001; Sollisch 2000; Reitman 2003;
"Billion" 2007: 71; Jack 2006; Bloom 2000; "Beyond the Pill" 2007; Petersen
2008).[5] Even waking up is set to become easier. Drugs are planned for
the "sleep market" (Marsa 2005) and to enhance memory—matters of far
greater interest to pharmacorps than the treatment of illness (Breithaupt
and Weigmann 2004), since their military and educational market potential outstrips the temporal and spatial limitations of sickness. The *British
Medical Journal* has conducted a febrile debate over what it astringently
refers to as "non-diseases," appositely deriding such commercial projects
as "disease mongering" for profit via "an ill for every pill" (Moynihan et al.
2002; Moynihan and Smith 2002: 859). Even the always-awful *Los Angeles
Times*, located in the center of imagined disorders, wonders about the will
"to treat . . . benign personality traits" (Gottlieb 2000).

In order to ensure a neat articulation between the politics, economics,
and culture of drugs, and despite criticism from the Association of American Physicians and Surgeons, Bush Minor's administration introduced
a New Freedom Commission on Mental Health (2003), featuring former
drug-company mavens, to screen US residents for mental illness. Children
were the first targets for mandatory evaluation, because the commission's
pharmacorps members recognized schools as ideal testing venues for identifying 50 million potential customers. Their favored method was the Texas
Medication Algorithm Project, a policy adopted during Minor's disastrous
governorship. The project dressed up in mathematical discourse what
amounted to a flowchart ratcheting medical treatment up from one drug
to another, culminating in electroconvulsive therapy. Officials associated
with the project were implicated in bribes from companies whose products
they placed on the critical path. So who could be surprised when it was
recommended nationally by the president's New Freedom Commission on
Mental Health in 2003, even as the International Committee of Medical
Journal Editors and the New York Attorney General criticized the pharmaceutical sector for hiding negative clinical trials from professional and

public evaluation (Graham 2004a and 2004b; "Executive Summary" 2005; Rose 2007: 249; President's New Freedom Commission on Mental Health 2003: 68–69; Lenzer and Paul 2006; "Trials" 2004)? Or that early in 2008, a comprehensive study basically found that antidepressants are the same as placebos in their impact on what they are supposed to treat—based on unpublished studies conducted by pharma (Kirsch 2008)?

Meanwhile, cost pressures militate against complex psychotherapy, encouraging self-help software and company-sponsored electronic listeners in addition to Texas warlock craft. Corporate intranets provide around-the-clock access to cognitive-behavioral band-aid therapy through employee assistance programs. The American Psychological Association (APA) offers "Questions to Ask Your Employer's Benefits Manager" on its Web site as part of a "Consumer Help Center" (Hansen et al. 2003: 106, 123, 56), and the HSM Group's "Productivity Impact Model" (2004) estimates the cost of employee depression to company revenues. It operates from the assumption that 50% of depressed workers are "untreated" and miss between thirty and fifty days of work a year as a consequence. To start the depression evaluation/treatment process, simply log on to http://www.depressioncalculator.com, the neoliberal employer's perfect wake-up page, no doubt.

The grand industrial-era projects of land reclamation and skyscraper construction have contemporary nano- and digital equivalents in biomedicine and the Internet. The trade in spare human parts is worth hundreds of millions of dollars annually, and the United States has over a thousand firms that sell products made from dead people (who are vended for upwards of $230,000 each). Biotechnology offers the prospect of absolute control/development of people through drugs that destroy or augment memory, block or enhance fertility, create hypermusculature, and defy resistance to bacteria; and micromachines that give sight and hearing to the disabled—or take them away. The next phase, genetic engineering, promises to alter the who, what, when, where, and how of being human. *Newsweek* predicts "made-to-order, off-the-shelf personalities." The promise is "a shift from reactive to preventative and more personalized medicine" that will be at the center of economic prosperity, both as objects in themselves and as stimuli to productivity—even if the reality so far is a story of incremental development, especially in pharmaceuticals. The fact that forty cognitive-enhancing drugs were in commercial development in 2004 both excited and terrified social critics of all casts. For Jürgen Habermas, there is a sinister aspect to all this. Elements of chance and choice that characterized the meeting of genes, society, and individuality in the past are being superseded, as "the depth of the organic substrate" becomes susceptible to prenatal intervention and recoding (2003: 12–13, 23). But for the Organization for Economic Co-Operation and Development (OECD), this is part of a "transition to a more biobased economy," which all actors should welcome by removing "inappropriate barriers" and stimulating "opportunities" (Sharp 2006: 11; Kass 2003; "Supercharging" 2004; *Newsweek* quoted in DeGrandpre 2006: 57; Nightingale and Martin 2004: 564, 566; OECD 2004: 3).

This recoding appeals as much as anything because medical-enhancement technologies provide a convenient way into contemporary reinvention, at least rhetorically—and as pills, machines, and surgeries, they can easily be counted. The search for new selves is restless, imbued with cosmic ambivalence. It accompanies immigrant underclass culture as an animator of capitalist innovation and retardation and social chaos and cohesion. The next question is how to conceptualize religious and psychotropic responses to difference and economic inequality.

Conceptualization

> Suicide by race, by color, by occupation, by sex, by seasons of the year, by time of day. Suicide, how committed: by poisons, by firearms, by drowning, by leaps. Suicide by poison, subdivided by types of poison, such as corrosive, irritant, systemic, gaseous, narcotic, alkaloid, protein, and so forth. Suicide by leaps, subdivided by leaps from high places, under the wheels of trains, under the wheels of trucks, under the feet of horses, from steamboats.
> —Edward G. Robinson in his role as an insurance investigator, *Double Indemnity* (1944)

"Risk society" (*Risikogesellschaft* in German sociology of the mid-1980s) and "moral panic" (from British criminology of the early 1970s) help explain the makeover nation during this revolutionary reallocation of resources of finance, faith, and pharmacology. Unusually for sociological and cultural theories, these concepts are freely used by, for example, the mainstream UK, Australasian, and Filipino media; the British National Council for Civil Liberties; and the British Academy, while *The Lancet* has run a column called "Doctoring the Risk Society." Slow as ever, even the US media recently caught on.[6] *The New Yorker's* venerable "Talk of the Town" column, the *New York Times' Women's Fashion Magazine, Slate,* and the libertarians over at *Reason* have deployed the idea of risk society, and "risk" appeared in the title of several new magazines in the 1990s. *Risk* periodical began, aptly enough, in the 1987 stock-market crash year. Its Web site, http://www.risk.net, is for "anyone who needs to manage risk" (for which read, those in search of derivatives). Numerous professional associations advertise risky elements of their occupations, and the Centers for Disease Control and Prevention have utilized the rather ominously named "Youth Risk Behavior Surveillance System" since 1990. Academically, while risk society is mobilized in sociology and media studies through to anesthesiology and philanthropy, moral-panic discourse is prominent in critical criminology and media and cultural studies. The former is manifested almost as a technical specification from beyond ideology, while the latter is used mostly by progressive critics. The *British Medical Journal* cares enough to have attacked the moral-panic framework, while the reactionary communitarian Alan Wolfe has begrudgingly utilized it to criticize the way Republicans focus on terrorism rather than economic distress[7] (Fitzpatrick 2003; Barker 1999; Wichtel 2002; Critcher 2003: 2, 53; "An Avalanche" 2002; Tan 2001; Shafer 2005; Power 2004: 12; Gillespie 2003; Žižek 2005; Daniels 1998; Wolfe 2006; Jeffries 2006).

What do the terms "risk society" and "moral panic" mean? According to Ulrich Beck, society is characterized by "institutions of monitoring and protection" that seek to protect people from "social, political, economic and individual risks," servicing the time-discipline required by capitalism. Risk society "organises what cannot be organised." It embodies and propels the desires of capital and state to make sense of and respond to problems, whether of their own making or not. If early modernity was about producing and distributing goods in a struggle for the most effective and efficient forms of industrialization, with devil take the hindmost and no thought for the environment, risk society is about enumerating and managing those dangers. Rather than being occasional, risk is now a constitutive component of being and organization that can be sold, pooled, and redisposed. This second modernity is characterized by an ever-increasing number of sophisticated mechanisms for measuring risk, even as the range and impact of risks grow less controllable. As technologies and markets become "better," they cause greater potential and actual harm—which in turn become the object of predictive technologies and markets (Beck et al. 1994: 5; Beck 1999: 135; Power 2004: 10, 17; Smutniak 2004; Jeffries 2006).

Risk society references the psychological impact of structural economic changes and other shocks that (sometimes) accidentally accompany them. Ideological commitments to Marxism, feminism, or superstition weaken. Unlike the notion of a broad left that once infused such struggles, issues are delinked, such that a position adopted on ecology says nothing about a position on popular democracy. Through governmental knowledges that offer both aggregated and variegated statistics to define, measure, and model populations in the interest of social control, advanced industrial/postindustrial societies induce massively increased feelings of risk in people. They admit and even promote the irrationality of the economy—as a means, paradoxically, of governing populations. Risk is calculated diurnally, via finance, and registered expressively, by emotion. Feelings become metonyms of economic problems. Routine environmental despoliation, global labor competition, cyclical recession, declining life-long employment, massive international migration, developing communication technology, and the rolling back of the welfare state, alongside income redistribution toward the wealthy, have left denizens of postindustrial societies factoring costs and benefits into everyday life as never before, while their sense of being able to determine their future through choice is diminished (Latour with Kastrissianakis 2007; Rigakos and Hadden 2001; O'Malley 2001).

Risk has a storied history, generally interlaced with religious ideology. Churches ply their trade through fear, with sin leading to damnation. This is especially salient in cases where Christians have stolen and then marketed rituals from paganism, such as Halloween, or Christmas, which was traditionally a time of dread for children because they would be punished for misdeeds, until it was commodified. In the United States, radical-right Protestantism rejects the merciful aspects of Catholicism in favor of a judgmental divinity—a key recruitment device for Evangelicals since the 18th century. Away from superstition, the appearance of stock exchanges in Western Europe from the 15th to the 17th centuries, often articulated to shipping fortunes, represented new class formations and financial and governmental problems, understood as actuarial rather than accidental. From the Industrial Revolution, working people were advised to be prudent and secure their future through insurance. In the United States, the shop was set up to cater to individuals rather than companies in the 19th century. What began as a means of paying for burials led to predicting calculations of every conceivable misfortune. We can see this played out by Edward G. Robinson's maniacally recited list of the ways that people can off themselves, quoted above.

Risk became an interventionist category during the 19th-century transformation of capitalism that the economic historian Karl Polanyi called "the discovery of society." Paupers came to be marked as part of the social, and hence deserving of enumeration, inclusion, and aid. The well-being of the poor was incorporated into collective subjectivity as a right, a problem, a statistic, and a law, and juxtaposed to the well-being of the self governing worker or owner. Society was held to be simultaneously more and less than the promises and precepts of the market, with risk understood and countered as a collective problem and liability. In some sense, these formally unproductive citizens became the litmus test of society. Along came public education, mothers' pensions, and Civil War benefits. During the 20th century, this tendency was confirmed by state interventions that provided superannuation to retirees, with contributions and benefits assumed by all. Today, we find such publicly subsidized schemes criticized as drains on individual initiative, and citizens are encouraged to assume risk directly via the market. So whereas the state once underwrote export-credit insurance (in the United States via the Overseas Private Investment Corporation [OPIC] and the ExIm Bank), nowadays that service is privatized, sending risk out into the community. The result: a shift, expressed in general welfare terms but also in the particular field of insurance, away from pooling risk, the better to allocate protection. Flavors of the millennium include allocating individuals to risk groups in order to calculate their likely future—then expecting them to bet against it. The same period has seen the explosion of tort law, because poor people have come to use the legal system to obtain redress against the wealthy and corporations in ways that a mature system of income redistribution, or adequate industrial regulation, would have rendered unnecessary (Polanyi 2001: 89, 82–85; Watts 2000: 197; Skocpol 2003; Stearns 2006: 67–68, 126, 120–21, 123; Briggs and Burke 2003: 30; Rose 1999: 158–59; Rose 2007: 123; Lawrence and Herbert-Cheshire 2003; Strange 2000: 126).

Risk has long been a core advertising method. Since the 1920s and '30s, magazines, especially those directed at the proletariat, have used fear to sell products at an accelerating rate, with threats to children a particular favorite. The preferred term in the industry is "scare copy." Consider the song "In the Year 2525 (Exordium and Terminus)" by Zager and Evans. It was a worldwide success in 1969, most notably in the United States. A blend of millennial doom, environmentalism, and the Rapture, its dystopic account of technology picked up on fears of a dehumanized future programmed through machines and pills. But a few decades later, such a future gave cause for delight. What appeared to epitomize an ecumenical, equal-opportunity loss of humanness had become both a leftist rallying cry, via the passion for cyborgian self-invention, and a capitalist rallying cry, via the passion for consumer self-satisfaction. In 2007, the song was even troped in a commercial for Embarq, an Internet service provider. Such dual-faced panics and celebrations are commonplace: IBM, to name just one company, is notorious for its "FUD campaigns." Orchestrated around "Fear, Uncertainty, and Doubt," they predict dire consequences absent use of the corporation's products and services (Stearns 2006: 151, 155).

Harvard's Center for Cancer Prevention now offers a Web site which permits visitors to calculate the likelihood of various maladies entering their lives (http://www.yourdiseaserisk.harvard.edu). Fear has become "an independent variable," with "exceptional events" transformed into "normal risk" (Furedi 2005). In 2006 the Center for American Progress and *Foreign Policy* magazine launched their rather fearsomely named "Terrorism Index," which surveys "100 of America's top foreign-policy hands." It duly found that 81% "see a world that is growing more dangerous for the American people" (2007: 2). But when Inspector Jefe Javier Falcón of Sevilla suggests to the expatriate Yanquis Maddy and Marty Krugman in Robert Wilson's neo-*noir* novel *The Vanished Hands* that the United States has been a society driven by fear since September 11, 2001, he is quickly rebuked: "It's *always* been fear" (2004: 41). Of course, close to three thousand people died that day, a day that supposedly "changed everything." Yet six weeks beforehand, polls revealed that 90% of the public already feared terrorism. And that same year in the United States, 150,000 people died from lung cancer, 38,000 in cars, and 30,000 by gunshot, while 250,000 were raped. Risk society is abetted and indexed by incidents like the media hysteria over anthrax in October 2001—responses that were out of all proportion to reality, given the under-reported plenitude of industrial chemicals and organisms confronting US workers every day and the extraordinary dangers posed by chemical plants to literally millions should there be an accidental or deliberate release of their deadly product. This country is very, very unsafe, because of the immense risks generated by local commerce and masculinity—but ignored by Homeland Security. No wonder New York's Museum of Modern Art featured a 2005 exhibit entitled "The Perils of Modern Living" (Kellner 2003: 82–83; Furedi 2005). The country is physically founded on risk, with its most expensive real estate built on fault lines and hurricane sites—its wealth distributed to guarantee massive insurance premiums and gambling. This has given rise to gruesomely named and administered catastrophe bonds, which bet on avoiding these cataclysmic events. Between summer 2004 and the end of 2005, US hurricanes saw $81 billion in losses incurred by insurance companies. Meanwhile, the very US financial institutions that invent these fancy instruments for sharing risk have been shown to be incompetent, irrational, and unseemly: the subprime mortgage fiasco has seen them veer away from a love of deregulation and in favor of regulatory rescue, depending on their needs (Lewis 2007; Leonard 2007).

We might date the ideological welcome of economic risk to a 1971 report for presidential advisors that referred glowingly to "the development of flexible citizens who, as many people have already realized, are the kind of citizen the twenty-first century is going to need." No wonder, then, that by the 1990s, *Business Week* was bluntly referring to the "New Economy" as "the rise of risk capital." The idea of risk as something for which everyone became responsible had become part of the neoliberal discourse of individual mastery of one's life. As of 1997, the Federal Department of Transportation decreed that automobile "Crashes Aren't Accidents"—they are caused by human error (quoted in Mattelart 2003: 109, Hutton 2003b: 122; Stearns 2006: 131).

Today's risks are quantified by everything from earthquake modeling to actuarial estimates and share-price responses. The United States is *the* risk society, with 50% of the population participating in stock market investments. Risk is brought into the home as an everyday ritual, an almost blind faith (sometimes disappointed) in mutual funds patrolling retirement income. The insurance costs alone of September 11 have been calculated at $21 billion. In 2005, US residents spent $1.1 trillion on insurance—more than they paid for food, and more than one-third of the world's total insurance expenditure. The industry's global revenues exceed the GDP of all countries bar the top three. At one level, this represents a careful calculation of risk, its incorporation into lifelong and posthumous planning—prudence as a way of life. At another, it is a wager on hopelessness and fear that has since emerged in religion and pills, because so many risks that Yanquis worry about are *un*insurable. As dangers mount, safeguards diminish. So whether we are discussing nuclear power plants or genetically modified foods, the respective captains of industry argue that they pose no risks, but insurance companies decline to write policies on them for citizens—because they are risky. Much of this relates to the deregulatory intellectual and policy fashions of the last three decades, which have aided the historic redistribution of income upwards by opposing the universalization of Medicare, reducing labor protection, and ideologizing against collective action other than in the private sphere—at the same time as people confront spiraling health costs and multiplying economic changes (Martin 2002: 6, 12; Zorach 2003; Mann 2003: 103; Strange 2000: 127; World Trade Organization 2003: 2; Smutniak 2004; Stearns 2006: 191; "Covered" 2004; "Time for a Makeover" 2006; Beck 1999: 53, 105; Kline 2003; Bernstein 2006: 4–5; Martin 2004: 8–10).

This also connects to the financialization of the everyday and the dominance of related myths: that consumption is sovereign, labor is a problem, the economy works because of entrepreneurs and executives, meritocracy is real and omnipresent, and collective action (by progressives) is wrong. Financialization has created a surge in one sector of the economy, such that by 2004, almost 40% of all profits in the US economy were "made" by finance firms. On TV, news stories are presented in terms of their monetary significance to viewers. Neoclassical economic theory is deemed palatable in a way that theory is not accepted elsewhere. The leading sources of wholesale television and Internet news, such as Reuters, make most of their money from finance reporting, which infuses their overall delivery of news as a commodity; primarily political journalists at Reuters refer to themselves as "cavaliers," and their primarily financial counterparts as "roundheads," severe metaphors from the English Civil War (Kevin Phillips 2006: 266; Palmer et al. 1998). Business advisors dominate discussion on dedicated finance cable stations like CNBC and Bloomberg, and these advisors are granted something akin to the status of seers when they appear on MSNBC, CNN, and the networks. Former Federal Reserve Chair Alan Greenspan was filmed getting in and out of cars as if he were en route to a meeting to decide the fate of nations. Each sclerotic upturned eyebrow or wrinkled frown was subject to hyperinterpretation by a bevy of needy followers. The focus of "news" has become stock markets in Asia, Europe, and New York; reports on company earnings, profits, and stocks; and portfolio management. There is a sense of vigilant markets stalking everyday security and politics in order to punish anxieties and uncertainties or strike against political activities that might restrain capital. The veneration, the surveillance, and the reportage of the market are on notice to reveal infractions of this anthropomorphized, yet oddly subject-free, sphere as a means of constructing moral panics around the conduct of whoever raises its ire. In short, economic and labor news has been transmogrified into corporate news, and politics is measured in terms of its reception by business.

Bush Minor's presidential addresses captured political helplessness and diurnal risk very effectively, emphasizing the evils and perils of the world in ways that directly articulate to superstition. Ever ready with a phrase describing or predicting catastrophic, apocalyptic terror, Minor had a lexicon in which the ratio of pessimistic words to optimistic ones was vastly greater than in those of FDR, Reagan, Bush the Elder, or Clinton. In his first term, the word "evil" appeared over 350 times in formal speeches. The 2004 presidential election testified to the efficacy of this approach, as risk of attack was the key issue in determining voters' choices. It also made money for his apparatchiks: Paul Bremer, Minor's *patron* of Iraq after the invasion, was one of the first to profit from September 11, quickly establishing a Crisis Consulting Practice. He falls into the emergent category of "risk managers," who quantify danger and the cost of meeting it ("Congressional Report" 2005; Brooks 2003; "Faith" 2004: 27; Pew Research Center 2005: 4; Feldman 2005; Allan 2002: 90).

Media reactions to limit cases of risky-ness, played out in highly exaggerated ways and frequently projected onto scapegoats or "folk devils," amount to "moral panics," a term first coined in the early 1970s to describe media messages that announced an increase in the crime rate and the subsequent establishment of specialist police units to deal with the alleged problem. Moral panics are usually short-lived spasms that speak of ideological contradictions about economic inequality. Exaggerating a social problem, they symbolize it in certain groups, predict its future, and then conclude or change. Part of society is used to represent (and sometimes distort) a wider problem: Youth violence is a suitable case for panic about citizenship; systemic class inequality is not. Adolescent behavior and cultural style are questionable; capitalist degeneracy is not. Rap is a problem; the situation of urban youth is not. Particular kinds of individuals are labeled as dangerous to social well-being because of their "deviance" from agreed-upon norms of the general good. Once the individuals have been identified, their life-practices are then interpreted from membership of a group, and vice versa. Critics of the process rightly ask not "Why do people behave like this?" but "Why is this conduct deemed 'deviant,' and whose interest does that serve?" (Thompson 1998: 7; Erich Goode 2000; P. Cohen 1999: 192–93; Stanley Cohen 1973: 9–13; Yúdice 1990; Wichtel 2002).

Moral panics are often generated by the state or the media and then picked up by interest groups and social movements (or vice versa), and hence their impact is generally disproportionate to the "problems" they bring into being. The dual role of experts and media critics in the constitution of moral panics sees the former testifying to their existence, and the latter sensationalizing and diurnalizing them—making the risks attributed to a particular panic seem like a new, terrifying part of everyday life. The cumulative impact of this alliance between specialist and popular knowledge is a heightened, yet curiously normalized, sense of risk about and amongst the citizenry in general. When TV ratings are measured— each February, May, July, and November—news programs allocate massive space to supposed risks to viewers. The idea is to turn anxiety and sensation into spectatorship and money. The epithet once used to deride local TV journalism in the United States—"if it bleeds, it leads"—today applies to network news, where the correlation between national crime statistics and crime coverage shows no rational linkage. The drive to create "human interest" stories from blood has become a key means of generating belief in a risk society through moral panics about personal safety. Such human interest stories occupied 16% of network news in 1997, up from 8% in 1977. Even when crime rates plunge, media discourse about crime rises: as the number of murders declines, press attention to them does the opposite. Similarly, school drug use may diminish, but audiences believe that it increases. The classic case of such absurdities is the popular rhetoric about young African-American men. Rates of violence, homicide, and drug use have fallen dramatically amongst black men under age 30 in the past decade, but media panic about their conduct has headed in the opposite direction (Barker 1999; Jenkins 1999: 4–5; Shaps 1994; Thompson 1998: 3, 12, 91; Wagner 1997: 46; Hickey 2004; Lowry 2003; Glassner 1999: xi, xxi, 29; Males 2004).

Moral panics are a displacement from socioeconomic crises and fissures, a means of dealing with risk society via appeals to "values." They both contribute to, and are symptomatic of, risk society. But rather than being straightforward mechanisms of functional control that necessarily displace systemic social critique onto particular scapegoats, moral panics have themselves been transformed by the discourse of risk society. Because certain dangers seem ineradicable, moral panics are mobilized to highlight particular aspects of them that may be less intractable, but are nevertheless emblematic of wider problems in a way that deflects danger and anxiety away from their sources in the political economy. A recent example is the British Home Office's 2004–8 Strategic Plan, which focuses on "anti-social behavior" as something that just *is* on the rise. It is not articulated to the economy (Ungar 2001; Hier 2003; Thompson 1998; Critcher 2003: 164; Squires 2006).

Conclusion

Most of her life, flying, she'd felt most vulnerable right here, suspended in a void, above trackless water, but now her conscious flying-fears are about things that might be arranged to happen over populous human settlements, fears of ground-to-air, of scripted CNN moments.
—Advertising consultant Cayce Pollard in William Gibson's *Pattern Recognition* (2003: 120)

Despite the fact that the nation fails them abysmally, most of its residents embrace the United States ideologically. Why? Because the right orchestrates moral panics that explain and place blame for the risk society in which people find themselves, even as it trumpets a national capacity for effective makeovers. Whereas the left and the center focus on public policy logics, researching problems and duly, dutifully, dully coming up with reasoned recommendations, the right leaves policy proposals to its corporate masters and does not undertake rational analyses aimed at technocratic outcomes. It prefers a blend of grass-roots religious superstition and public outreach that stresses column inches and shouted seconds, not cost-benefit policy options: the politics of spectacle. The outcome? The largest technocracy in history—the United States—has re-enchanted its world, turning capitalism and statecraft into magic.

There is a special appeal to this latest Great Awakening. It is a consumerist one, with selfishness and chauvinism characterizing a revocation of traditional Christianity, as if the latter embodied Great Society liberalism. An organic link is posited between apparent logocentric opposites: church and market. Perhaps these creepy Christians hear that famous tag line from San Diego televangelism—"prosperity is your divine right"—ringing in their ears (quoted in Murdock 1997: 96). The market may have torn these people's lives apart, but the capitalistic basis to today's Great Awakening gives them ideological backing (and a choice of their superstition) in a way that formal monetary markets do not. The illogic of supporting neoliberal economic policy is of little import. The market has become "an agent of morality, rewarding good and punishing evil" (Grossberg 2005: 117), for all the world a secular fate divinely decreed by a truly invisible hand.

The New Protestantism sometimes seems like a very Old Testament form, so lacking is it in the socialist principles of love and mercy offered by Christ's teachings. Judgment, harsh and unbending, is its basis. And it makes two bizarre alliances—with pro-Zionist Jews, who might be unacceptable as neighbors, philanthropists, or intellectuals in the United States but are a good fit as custodians of Palestine until they are destroyed by the Rapture; and with corporations, which might be unacceptable as vendors of craven objects of consumption that articulate to sexual pleasure, science, and medicine but are a good fit as brutal bureaucracies that do not forgive failure and do oppose secular collectives such as unions.

The faith makeover and the drug makeover both invest in transformation through consumption. The culture industries are central to this compulsion to buy, through the double-sided nature of advertising and "the good life" of luxury: they encourage competition at the same time as they standardize processes to manufacture unity in the face of diversity. With all the pleasurable affluence suggested by material goods, the idea of people achieving transcendence has been displaced by the overwhelming force of objects. Commodities dominate a formerly human and natural landscape. The corollary is the simultaneous triumph and emptiness of the sign as a source and a measure of value. Beginning as a reflection of reality, the commodity sign is transformed into a perversion of reality, with representation of the truth displaced by false information. Then these two, delineable, phases of truth and lies become indistinct. Underlying reality is lost. Finally, the sign refers to itself, with no residual need of correspondence to the real. It has adopted the form of its own simulation (Baudrillard 1988: 10–11, 29, 170). When people embrace risk, "human needs, relationships and fears, the deepest recesses of the human psyche, become mere means for the expansion of the commodity universe" (McChesney and Foster 2003: 1).

Is there an alternative, a world where a person can "hunt in the morning, fish in the afternoon, rear cattle in the evening, criticize after dinner . . . without ever becoming hunter, fisherman, shepherd or critic" (Marx and Engels 1995: 53), consuming and producing with pleasure and politics joined? A world that will rebut dehumanizing commodity fetishism, turning instead to the Xhosa saying that "a person is a person through other persons" (quoted in Dean 2001: 502)? Where we live between the promise of cosmopolitanism and the loss of national identity (García Canclini 2002: 50) rather than as "desiccated calculators . . . rational-choice rodents moved exclusively by the short range and the quantifiable" (Nairn 2003: 7), with "freedom to choose" once "the major political, economic, and social decisions have already been made" (Mosco 2004: 60)?

Such challenges inform what I have written here. I have come neither to bury nor to praise the makeover, but to criticize it, even as I stand alternately bewildered, amused, appalled, and attracted by it. Foundational myths of the "American Dream" permeate this book. And dreams reference and distort reality. They attract and please even as they horrify and disappoint. So I look at the power of various forms of knowledge about people and their emotions applied to the US population through case studies of therapy, drug treatments, and male bodies that illustrate how sublime makeovers see people actually *become* commodities, mediated through the psy-function, capital, and culture. If we are to understand an absurdly wealthy and wasteful country, we must *question* the pleasures of reinvention as well as embrace them, teasing out as we do so the mystification of moral panics and the reality of risk society.

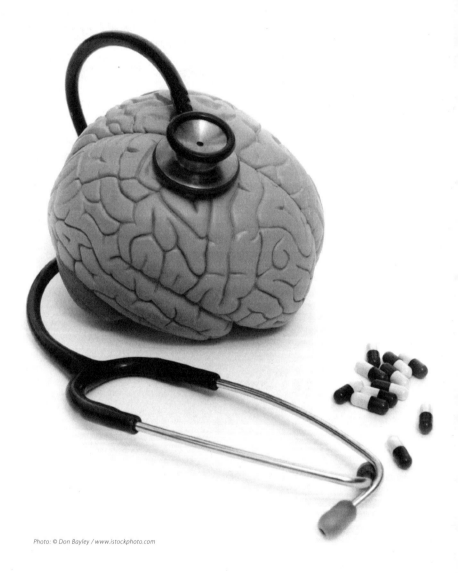

THE PSY-FUNCTION

MAKING OVER MINDS

The human condition is now so thoroughly medicalized that few people can claim to be normal.
    —*New Scientist* (quoted in Susan Hansen et al. 2003: 12)

North American psychology looked to the natural sciences for a method and concepts that would legitimate it as a science. And in order to get social position and rank, it negotiated how it would contribute to the needs of the established power structure.
    —Ignacio Martín-Baró (1996: 20)

The fundamental role of the psychological function, which historically is entirely derived from the dissemination of psychiatric power in other directions beyond the asylum, is to intensify reality as power and to intensify power by asserting it as reality.
    —Michel Foucault (2006: 190)

THIS CHAPTER addresses a key secular technique of makeovers—the "psy-function"—and how it targets potential citizens of tomorrow who must be made over: youth. The psy-function describes a shifting field of knowledge and power over the mind. It comprises psychoanalysis, psychology, psychotherapy, psychiatry, social psychology, criminology, and psycho-pharmacology, and their success in other sites of discipline—educational, military, industrial, and carceral (Foucault 2006: 85–86; also see 189–90).[1] In both its commercial and governmental forms, the psy-function references and generates makeover culture like no other form of knowledge, notably via its authority over young people, who have become key deictic pointers to shifts in cultural norms and anxieties, as per many moral panics. The psy-function trumps other forms of discourse with its dual claims to describe and manage the mind.

In 1900, the noted Swedish reformer Ellen Key predicted a forthcoming "century of childhood," with women and the young revolting against patriarchy (quoted in Ennew 2002: 339). But a hundred years later, Roy Porter looked back at what he called the "psychiatric century" (2002: 9); and Judith Ennew concluded that rather than "being a century of children," the 20th century had become "a century of child experts" (2002: 339): for the emergence of the psy-function defined young people as a group with distinct desires and needs that it could theorize and adjudicate. "Youth" references a collective mantle—the responsibility of running the country one day and making it over. So the psy-function deals both with children undergoing "normal" development toward the assumption of adult responsibilities and with those whose development is blocked by disability, race, gender, or class. The psy-function and its down-at-heel relatives in sociology, education, and communication studies construct children as future citizens unready to assume full responsibility for themselves and others. Currently incomplete projects, they must be endowed with the skills to regulate their passions and maximize their productivity.

Despite its successes, the psy-function frequently attracts controversy. Consider the antipsychiatry work of R. D. Laing and others, critiques of Freudianism, denial of public funds for therapy, negative press about both counseling and psycho-pharmacology, and battles within the psy-function itself between therapeutic and drug treatments, not to mention the Nuremberg Trial convictions of psychiatrists. Both right and left denounce the solipsistic absorption and consumerism of those derided by Bill Clinton as "the worried well." Bush Minor is renowned for boasting, "I don't spend a lot of time trying to figure me out. I'm just not into psychobabble" (quoted in Borger 2004). He is eerily reminiscent of Warren Beatty's equally idiotic Yalie from *Splendor in the Grass* (1961), who when asked if he is happy replies, "It's not a question I ask myself very often."

And no wonder. Mental health is an awkward domain for cultural politics. The psy-function is an easy mark for accusations that it generates and sustains false consciousness, bourgeois individualism, racism, and sexism, and that it implicates participants in the policing apparatuses of medicine, therapy, and thought control. Psychologizing people is said to distract attention from structural inequalities by pathologizing social issues. The taste for long-term therapy is derided as a consumerist luxury unavailable to those preoccupied with subsistence. Seen as a manifestation of middle-class guilt at the ravages of capitalism, the psy-function benefited from the

"Red Scare" of 1919, when the US government was assured that psycho-therapy could defuse the appeal of Marxism to the urban poor. Behaviorialism, a model of person-as-machine for capitalism and state socialism alike, promised to manage individual conduct on the factory floor, to "change the individual while preserving the social order." Latterly, feminist critics worry that antidepressants have kept women isolated and inchoate in domestic disappointment and oppression. In place of settling for chemical quietude, the women's movement argues that stories need to be told, rather than pills popped and lips pursed (Martín-Baró 1996: 37; Perring 1997: 228; Manne 2003). The Rolling Stones, improbable fellow-travelers, wrote a song that encapsulates this (so to speak): "Mother's Little Helper."

The right is also suspicious, because the psy-function suggests weakness, threatens productivity, and implies the use of public resources for personal "development." *Forbes* magazine, the *Wall Street Journal,* and *Investor's Business Daily* periodically rail at it (Eberstadt 1999; Murlowe 1997), and the right's formerly favorite fallen Hegelian, Francis Fukuyama (2002), fulminates at the threat to hypermasculinity of a middling personality driven by feminism and permitted by Ritalin (engaged in the next chapter). The practical philosophy movement stands in opposition to pharmacology under the slogan "Más Platón, Menos Prozac" (More Plato, Less Prozac) (Marinoff 2000). And Scientology is an implacable foe of the psy-function. The church formed a Citizens Commission on Human Rights (2003) in 1969 as part of a worldwide campaign against what it sees as pernicious social control, racism, alcoholism, sexual assault, theft, and murder. Scientology's key spokespeople, Lisa Marie Presley, Eduardo Palomo, Anne Archer, and Juliette Lewis, hand out "Human Rights Awards" and appear before congressional panels to protest "the psychotropic drugging of millions of American children." Tom Cruise has been a particularly forceful hysteric in the struggle.

But they are protesting against what seems like an unstoppable wave. The APA went from 111 members in 1900 to 83,096 a century later (http://www.apa.org/archives/yearlymembership.html), briskly populating personnel departments, universities, the military, and the bourgeois media. As part of this rent-seeking expansion, the psy-function claims the status of a science and becomes guarantor of both happiness and productivity. Its histories praise famous forefathers and their "findings," rarely problematizing the production of data in any meaningful way (Danziger 1998). It assumes that "anything that is important in its history will have been absorbed into the ongoing research tradition." This very sanguine model connects to the essentialist conceit "of an a-historical human nature" (Brock 1995) in which the self "may be donated, or housed within, a body that acts and participates in the material environment, but this aspect of it is irrelevant to—or, at best, a conduit to—the inner psychic sanctum, positive knowledge of which is psychology's (especially cognitivism's) ultimate goal" (McHoul and Rapley 2005b: 432).

But a prominent dissenting medical practitioner suggests that psychopharmacology tries to deal with culture "by avoiding it" but ends up as a "culture-thick, not science-thick, social and political endeavour" (Timimi 2002: 35, 53).[2] And the inevitably collective project of applying the psy-function to society has latterly encouraged a culturally relative perspective—mostly outside the United States (European Union Consultative Platform on Mental Health 2006; Haste 2004: 421; Hansen et al. 2003: 31; Maira and Soep 2004: 246). So rather than endorsing the psy-function's assumptions about a naturally occurring process of growing up that requires psychologization, I draw on alternative and dissident models to explain how the child has been defined, nurtured, criticized, reformed, and governed in historical and spatial terms (Tyler 1993: 35; Damon 2004: 14; Cook 2002: 2; Malkki and Martin 2003). First, we must chart an alternative to the psy-function's autohagiography.

The Psy-Function

Health itself and the proper management of chronic illnesses are becoming individual moral responsibilities to be fulfilled through improved access to knowledge, self-surveillance, prevention, risk assessment, the treatment of risk, and the consumption of appropriate self-help/biomedical goods and services.
 —Adele E. Clarke et al. (2003: 162)

While some pharmaceutical bosses admit freely that their prime motive is profit, the success of the industry derives from the fostered perception that it exists primarily as a public good. . . . Distinguished specialists and professors at prestigious institutes, in pharma-speak called "opinion leaders," are groomed for engagement. They can earn £5,000 an hour or more than £20,000 a day for delivering a specific therapeutic message, which is then accepted by the profession as gospel.
 —Margaret Cook (2004)

Foucault has been an inspiration to counterhistories of the psy-function. He sought to uncover how mental conditions came to be identified as problems in need of treatment through forms of demographic problematization that functioned as techniques, economies, social relations, and knowledges. They were the means whereby "some real existent in the world" became "the target of social regulation at a given moment" (1994: 123; 2001: 171). Foucault recognized that struggles for power take place over "the status of the individual":

> On the one hand, they assert the right to be different, and they underline everything that makes individuals truly individual. On the other hand, they attack everything which separates the individual, breaks his links with others, splits up community life, forces the individual back on himself and ties him to his own identity in a constraining way. (1982: 781, 777–78)

In the words of the great liberation psychologist Ignacio Martín-Baró, murdered by Yanqui-backed assassins: "there does not first exist a person, who then goes on to become socialized." Rather, the "individual becomes an individual, a human person, by virtue of becoming socialized" (1996: 69). The raw stuff of human beings, then, is not individuals: people *become* individuals through the discourses and institutions of culture, in an oscillation between the law, economy, and politics, with the psy-function operating as a switching point between people's proclivities and aptitudes (Foucault 2006: 58, 190). Rites of passage from traditional societies have been displaced, supplemented, or made purely symbolic in industrial and postindustrial societies by scientific accounts of personhood that are makeover coefficients of social change:

> Industrialization and urbanization created a growing number of people who could not be as readily defined by place of origin and relational ties, people who interacted with a far larger number of others than had hitherto been the norm, people who needed a "self" to present to these many others. (Healy 2002: 25)

On this account, to which I subscribe, status and ancestry joined measurement and confession, as ritual and shame met the state and guilt. Facts and interpretations derived from archivism and experimentation in addition to titular authority. The chief, prelate, and household head were no longer omniscient. But even as a looser model of power proliferated, new hegemons emerged within depersonalized social institutions like hospitals and the psy-function (Foucault called them "professionals of discipline, normality and subjection"). Today, these experts utilize knowledges to multiply and intensify the exercise of power over bodies. So we may see adults incarcerated because they lack the ability to narrate their feelings and their struggles to the satisfaction of psychologists, thereby failing the duty of disclosure and maturity that are the corollary (and test) of Enlightenment freedoms. It is the fate of "modern people," in George Orwell's words, to be "numbered, labeled, conscripted, 'co-ordinated'" (Foucault 1979a: 193, 224, 296; Foucault 1987: 23; Albee 1977: 152; Healy 2002: 29; Orwell 1982).

Of course, people were mad, and were treated as such, before the psy-function was institutionalized. Five-thousand-year-old skulls disclose signs of trepanning, suggesting holes bored to release devils, while a multitude of fables and myths of religion and other superstitions and histories refer to possession and insanity. An abiding binary of good and bad, well and ill, has characterized meditations on sanity from the earliest texts to today. The two fundamental wings of the psy-function—cognition (supposedly governed by nature) and behavior (presumptively governed by environment)—emerged from Plato's and Kant's distinctions between the bodily and behavioral sides of experience: the moral and the cognitive, expressed as a moral space that separated brain from body even as it linked them. That binary has never been undermined, and it informs the banal personality/character couplet addressed in the Introduction of this book. Philosophers writing prior to the psy-function defined lunacy and melancholy as social categories linked to obedience and self-control. Managing madness was about sustaining society. This concern helped to shift madness from a religious condition of demonic possession to a secular problem of irrational conduct (Fukuyama 2002; McHoul and Rapley 2001: 438–39; Rose 2007: 194; Porter 2002: 42–43, 10, 60; Heins 2002: 20–21). Plato understood madness as the outcome of "disease," "irritability," and "poor discipline," which could lead to conflict and threaten authority (1972: 482). In Spinoza's view, madness diminished "the body's power of activity" (1955: 217)—a concern for productivity. Locke referred to the need for each person to have sufficient reasoning capacities to abide by the law—capacities beyond the youthful and the mad alike (1990: 145). When these men proposed policies founded on their suppositions, the results were sometimes odd. Vico, for instance, was convinced that the young "may profitably occupy themselves with languages and plane geometry," but "metaphysical criticism or algebra" would leave them "incapable of any great work" (1970: 24).[3] This stimulated the desire among more rational critics for a scientific foundation to their efforts. Hume (1955: 24) and Kant (1991) longed for a Newtonian breakthrough akin to what happened in astronomy, an epistemological shift that would allow studies of the mind to transcend observation and comprehend underlying laws. Wittgenstein pointed to "something unsatisfactory" in the basic endeavor of the psy-function, because it lacked the "sort of 'metric'" found in physics (2007: 42). This desire for mathematicization has remained deeply sunken in the thinking of the psy-function as a route to the status of a science ever since. Empirical observation and categorization were never enough—artificial neologization and calculation were required (Danziger 1998: 20).

The key question for me is how people come to be subjects of the psy-function within modernity, and hence subject to psy-makeovers. Politics has been at the core of this articulation. In the United States, political links to the psy-function began with the Declaration of Independence: Benjamin Rush, a signatory and an abolitionist who nevertheless pioneered the idea that Africans were black due to leprosy, published the country's first psy-textbook, in 1812. He was decreed the "father of American psychiatry" by the American Psychiatric Association in 1965. Rush's successors in the profession were dedicated slavery supporters from the moment they founded a professional body in 1844 until the Civil War, arguing that "manumission caused insanity." Meanwhile, the psy-function was normalizing itself across public life. The US Census of 1840 calculated the national level of what it called "idiocy/insanity," which was split into seven different conditions by the 1880 version. These numbers were organized and collected not as a reflection of, or a service to, clinical work, but as a managerial tool of social order. The first US academic journal in the field, the delightfully named *American Journal of Insanity,* appeared in 1844, published by the superintendent of a state hospital after he met with thirteen colleagues to establish the Association of Medical Superintendents for the Insane. It became the American Medico-Psychological Association in 1892, admitting non-carceral specialists, and bought the *American Journal of Insanity.* In 1922, a further makeover was achieved, with the renamed American Psychiatric Association publishing the renamed *American Journal of Psychiatry.* Since then, the psy-function has undergone a shift—winding, incomplete, and frequently circular—from religious judgments and confessional norms to scientific techniques and chemical interventions, from carceral buildings and elongated couches to pill-dispensing pharmacies and returns to the social—in short, beyond lock-ups and toward shopping aisles. The psy-function has latterly completed its transformation from a highly instrumental form of government that controlled the unruly, to a site of academic legitimacy, and finally to consumer marketing. Mental illness has undergone a complex oscillation between being a danger to society, a domain of knowledge, and a sales campaign (Ozarin and McMillan 2003; Shorter 1997: 15; Kutchins and Kirk 1997: 20, 201, 208; Rose 2007: 198; Foucault 2003b: 118–19; Ozarin and McMillan 2003; Kerr 2003). How was this achieved?

Throughout the 19th century, psychiatry intervened in the legal field of Western societies, establishing its right to define individuals as sane or otherwise and claiming a role in justice and punishment. Penal law codified "dangerous individuals" as monomaniacal, degenerate, perverse, constitutionally unbalanced, and immature (Foucault 2000). Psychiatry identified, and then dismissed, alternative forms of psy-knowledge that sought to establish professional training and conduct. Several US states briefly licensed "drugless healing," such as the laying-on of hands, magnetism, and clairvoyance. But in the new century, medically qualified psychoanalysts pushed for the delegitimization of such claims, differentiating themselves from the stigmatized world of the asylum by promoting diagnosis and treatment over carceral control (Buchanan 2003: 228; David Park 2004: 112).[4] For their part, psychologists frenetically sought markets for their work with the same zeal that they pursued scientific recognition, offering to control school pupils and manage factory workers Tayloristically as a means of getting paid, even as they desired laboratories at the big end of campus (Danziger 1998: 101–3).

The state was also involved economically. In the mid-19th century, the federal government was creating business conditions that eventually generated the very pharmaceutical corporations that would surpass therapists as controllers of the psy-function. Bulk buying of medicines during the Civil War encouraged both profits and professionalization, which received further stimulus fifty years later, in the Great War, through mass purchase of aspirin and patent-breaking treatments for syphilis. Then the United States simply stole discoveries from the advanced pharmaceutical industries of a defeated Germany after the war. And whereas medicines had long been sold directly to consumers, the state came to intervene in the name of public health, shifting between regarding individual drug users as citizens and as consumers. In response to addiction, regulations mandated prescriptions for several drugs from 1914, reining in customer sovereignty and institutionalizing the power of large firms, which could mount scientific and transparent forms of research and management, and the medical profession, which profited from increased visits by patients in search of medicines. The requirement for verifiable scientific testing pushed small companies and unaccredited practitioners alike out of business. The premarket testing of drugs became part of the grand oscillation in US public culture between drugs as angelic or demonic, depending on their validation by corporations and the state (Healy 2002: 18, 20, 22, 33–34; Rasmussen 2004: 163; DeGrandpre 2006: 25).

World War I saw the creation of the position of Chief Army Psychiatrist overseas and the instantiation of numerous military disorders, as psychology offered mental measurement and testing to the army. Engineering and personnel departments began deploying the psy-function in factories after the war as a means of maximizing output and minimizing worker discontent, via both scientific-management and human-relations methods. Industrial psychology redefined anger at work as personally and professionally unproductive, diagnosing rage against capitalism as displaced private aggression. The popularity of Freudianism peaked between 1940 and 1965 after it had demonstrated efficacy with military traumas, although many "cures" may be attributable to the end of the war rather than psychoanalysis. We see these successes dramatically on display in John Huston's epic documentary, *Let There Be Light* (1946), which came out when psychology and psychiatry were combining to discredit reflexology, dianetics, and graphology, just as they had cashiered drugless healing fifty years earlier. The clinician's ear became a principal tool of analysis, and the patient's mouth a principal source of information. But the 1930s had seen the advent of somatic therapy via drugs and electroconvulsive treatment, and "big science" was about to thrive under the stimulus of Cold War rivalry. The Veterans' Administration (now the United States Department of Veterans Affairs) and the National Institute of Mental Health (NIMH) emerged as key sites for the growth of psychiatry and psychology. Congress avidly passed a Mental Health Study Act in 1955 to encourage major support for research. The National Institutes of Health (NIH) were quickly voted more money for drug development than they knew what to do with. And in 1951, the federal government mandated that all new medicines be subject to prescription, marking both a grab for professional standards and control and a new form of commodity production—collectively producing the project of a national makeover. Much of the funding also came through a desire to generate habits of mind and conduct in the postcolonial world that would elude the clutches of Marxism and Maoism. "Project Camelot" was covertly launched by the Pentagon in 1963 to finance the psy-function for such purposes. When this clandestine plan was exposed, new funding for the psy-world emerged from the State Department and the National Science Foundation. Today, the US military uses psy-function categories to deprive injured veterans of health-care and college benefits and retrieve their enlistment bonuses. It does so by defining their traumas—whether physical or psychological—as pre-existing conditions, delightfully utilized via the category of "Separation Because of Personality Disorder"—5,600 cases under Bush Minor, and rising every year (Ozarin and McMillan 2003; Hale 1995: 382; Stearns 1994: 121–25; Danziger 1998: 105; Buchanan

2003: 228–30; Musto 1995; Rose 2007: 194; Shattuc 1997: 114; Healy 1997: 24, 66; Healy 2002: 35; Herman 1998; Kors 2007; Elias 2007).

As part of this complex linkage between professionalization, governmentalization, and commodification, the psy-function required codified therapeutic explanations (which became a form of consumer education). Into this space of nosological desire and reward came the American Psychiatric Association's *Diagnostic and Statistical Manual of Mental Disorders* (*DSM*) in 1952, derived from the *Statistical Manual for the Use of Hospitals for Mental Diseases,* which had been in use since 1917 and adopted by the US Census the next year. The first *DSM* applied broad diagnostic labels, with the aim of encompassing the whole of society. Its successor, *DSM-II* (1968), embodied a psychoanalytic approach to psychiatry. The status of psychoanalysis quickly began to decline, however, because of doubts about its scientific validity (Freudianism was unable to deliver the requisite "organic correlates of its diagnoses"), a renewed interest in genetic/biological causes of mental illness (particularly with the proliferation of psychotherapeutic drugs), and the rise of alternative models. Perhaps the authors were in touch with their inner Wittgenstein (he deemed free association "queer" [2007: 42]). *DSM-III* (1980) embraced biopsychiatry (as well as discovering that homosexuality was not the disease proclaimed by its predecessors, following an intense campaign by gay activists). It focused on symptomatology and description, not etiology and theory. The purported reason for eschewing causes was to avoid controversy amongst different camps of psychiatry. Actually, this new model was directly opposed to psychoanalysis and social psychiatry—and partially underwritten by pharmacorps' subvention of the American Psychiatric Association and researchers (Rose 2007: 194; Hacking 1995: 12; Cooksey and Brown 1998: 529–30; Kutchins and Kirk 1997: 13, 39, 65–99).

As a result, serious disputes arose within the psy-function over swallowing versus speaking, none more notorious than a 1971 debate between Heinz Lehmann (for pharmacology) and Herbert Marcuse (for psychoanalysis). While Lehmann was addressing the audience, Frederick Qunes, who had helped organize the event, threw a cream cake in his face. Just as symbolically, the renowned Chestnut Lodge psychodynamic center was sued in the 1980s for malpractice because it denied drugs to a physician-patient. While the case did not set a legal precedent—terms were agreed upon among the parties—it furthered a developing discourse that juxtaposed clinically trialed drugs against impressionistic dialogues. Biopsychiatric diagnoses became dominant, and psychoanalysis fell into terminal decline (outside textual analysis and the west sides of Manhattan and Los Angeles). Since the cake fruitlessly flew and the chestnut privately settled, pharmaceutical corporations and their prescribing delegates have become hegemonic, utilizing the slogan "You can't talk to disease" (Healy 2002: 175; Rose 2003: 51; Shorter 1997: 309; Breggin 1994: 11–13, 17, 23, 122). As they have found, you *can* vend invisible goods that will disarm it. Antidepressants offer highly specific interventions, albeit with systemic impacts. Although called "magic bullets," implying precise targeting, their effect has been much wider, shifting "health to the center of Western politics and culture" (Healy 1997: 1).

The first major psychoactive drug was chlorpromazine (first sold as the brand name Thorazine). Devised in France and bought by one of the nascent Yanqui drug firms as an antiemetic, it turned Smith Kline & French into a major company. Thorazine came onto the US market in 1954 and was immediately featured in numerous print advertisements. Combined with increased governmental employment of therapists, the arrival of the new drug reversed the long-standing removal of the mentally ill from public life to an institution: two years later, the number of mental-hospital patients had declined for the first time since the previous century. The fifty years since have seen mental-hospital beds drop from 560,000 to 53,000, even as the national population has increased by well over 100 million. Patients were not the only ones to come out. Whereas almost all psychiatrists were hospital-based in 1940, by 1957 over 80% were not. The same period saw Miltown and Equanil mass-marketed as tranquilizers against suburban dross, to the point where the TV star Milton Berle renamed himself "Miltown"; in 1956, one in twenty US residents was taking what were popularly called "happy pills." The key corporations manufacturing these exit passes from asyla and *anomie*—Sandoz, Rhône-Poulenc, Geigy, Ciba, and Roche—convened many collusive meetings between 1953 and 1958. Invited to meet the Pope in 1957, participants founded the anachronistically named Collegium Internationale Neuropsychopharmacologium (nothing like some mid-20th-century Latin to confer prestige). Congress avidly passed a Mental Health Study Act in 1955 to encourage major support for research. Meanwhile, corporate sponsors were paying clinical researchers to exchange information. Merck also played a part, distributing 50,000 copies of Frank Ayd's 1961 volume *Recognizing the Depressed Patient* to doctors around the world. My copy has a page that permits the owner to sign his or her name ("Ex Libris"). It adds: "*Presented by* MERCK SHARP & DOHME"). The United Nations released an associated movie in twelve languages. This product placement successfully promoted depression as ordinary and as diagnosable in general (nonpsychiatric) medical practice. It worked: the number of depressed people in the United States grew 2,000-fold between the 1950s and the 1990s—an extraordinary development for a condition that is allegedly hereditary! From the early 1960s, advertisements in medical journals trumpeted families reuniting, men returning to work, and women embracing the home—a makeover that could be produced chemically. One famous promotion for Thorazine depicted a pill on a leather couch; it had displaced the client as well as the therapist.

With the advent of Medicare and Medicaid as part of the "Great Society" reforms of the 1960s, public hospitals lost even more patients. State governments utilized new forms of funding to shift them into nontraditional institutions, such as private nursing homes, halfway houses, and outpatient services, which were ideologized as populist by the emergent community-care movement, even though they were neoliberal triumphs that led to dreadful suffering, because deinstitutionalization occurred without the requisite expansion in community-based services and financing. This policy disaster, enshrined by the Supreme Court in *Olmstead v. L.C.* (1999), was operationalized by Bush Minor in Executive Order 13217 of 2001. The effect was to reincarcerate the mentally ill, this time in prisons rather than dedicated facilities, as more and more federal housing was dedicated to the elderly. Within six years of these decisions, the Federal Bureau of Justice Statistics disclosed that the number of mentally ill people within US jails had quadrupled, with over 50% of inmates reporting depression, a proportion five times that of the overall population. The provision of services is minimal and the situation horrendous in many circumstances (Herman 1996: 257–59; Shorter 1997: 253–54, 316; Martin 2006: 157–58; Ozarin and McMillan 2003; Rubin 2004: 370–72; DeGrandpre 2006: 52; Martinez 2005; Healy 1997: 47, 75–76; President's New Freedom Commission on Mental Health 2003: 31–32; Human Rights Watch 2006 and 2003).

These changes are both indexed and generated by the *DSM*'s stature within courts, schools, and prisons, and by health-insurance companies' insistence on its use by claimants and their physicians. The *Manual*'s impressive expansion can be measured in any number of ways, not least that it has announced 200 new mental illnesses in the past thirty years (Spiegel 2005). From its origins as a reference book, the *DSM* has become "a strange mix of social values, political compromise, scientific evidence, and material for insurance claim forms" (Kutchins and Kirk 1997: x). Of course, there have been critics. The *Manual*'s richly obsessive, seemingly unending, unbending lists bring to mind the narrator of Jerome K. Jerome's 1889 novel, *Three Men in a Boat*, who reads a medical manual and diagnoses himself with symptoms of every illness described save house-maid's knee (1938: 8–9). For Scientology, the *DSM* represents the apogee of a century in which "psychiatrists have treated man as an animal" (Citizens Commission on Human Rights 2003), and the President's Council on Bioethics (2002b) regards it as a document of finance and power as much as medicine, a "top-down approach to diagnosis" that specifies signs over society—bodily practices, not education, family, or labor. The psy-function promotes self-regulating norms, rather than offering a verifiable and absolute correspondence of physiological or behavioral signs with diseased or deviant referents. For example, in one cultural space, that of defining Obsessive-Compulsive Personality Disorder, washing one's hands frequently is a sign of illness; in another, such as working in an infectious-diseases ward, it is a sign of duty. But the *DSM* presents itself as acultural and dealing in physical universals, collocating bodily practices in order to define them as evidence of psychopathology, and fixing diagnostic truths via reification, reductionism, and synecdoche (part of one's "behavior" stands for the totality of one's personality). This drive toward a usable taxonomy may have overdetermined any underpinning in scientific knowledge. In addition, claims to a disinterested pursuit of truth were brought into question by the 2006 disclosure that 56% of the *DSM*'s authors cheerfully receive remuneration from the companies whose drugs they describe as crucial for actually existing disorders. And when the *DSM* is avowedly in use to diagnose patients, evidence suggests that its criteria are frequently interpreted by doctors in terms of their own presuppositions about race and gender (McHoul and Rapley 2001: 434; Hansen et al. 2003: 12; Spiegel 2005; Santostefano 1999: 322–23; Aldhous 2006; Loring and Powell 1988).

But in 1990, Bush the Elder declared a "Decade of the Brain" (perhaps preparing the nation for being led by his son). The nomenclature represented the triumph of "New Psychiatry" as per the *DSM*. Psychosurgery and drug treatments were in the ascendant. Congress and the NIH devoted large amounts of money to research of cognition and recollection via molecular biology, genetics, and brain-imaging technology. Identifying the brain as the etiological site of educational, social, personal, and even political problems, psychiatrists have gone on to medicalize misery to the point where ideas of early childhood trauma appear outmoded, moves are being made to erase psychotherapy from psychiatric education, and popular culture has turned against it: *Time* published a 1993 cover story asking, "What If Freud Was Wrong?" A gathering body of case law covering murder defenses is constructed around diminished responsibility, as illustrated by brain scans and genetic maps. All in all, the brain is getting larger and more powerful: the American Society for Neuroscience attracts upwards of thirty thousand academics to its annual conference, and the American Psychiatric Association formed its very own political action committee in 2000. In the decade to 2007, the number of mainstream-press references to neuroscience grew by 33%, providing new oracular accounts of everything from ideological proclivities to merchandising preferences. These "diagnoses" are based on snapshots of a moment in time in terms of brain activity, as opposed to the power of history to display continuities and discontinuities, individual preferences, and cultural practices (Maslin 2000; "Supercharging" 2004; Rose 2007: 232–33; Rose 2006: 3; Ozarin and McMillan 2003; Cass 2007).

In shifting its tasks from naked control to generative, productive power, the psy-function has engaged in a systematic and purposive discrediting of aberrant mental phenomena as somehow beyond "discursive acts, meaningful performances by skilled human actors" (Harré 2004: 4). It models government at a distance that aims to improve "discipline in domestic life" (Rafavolich 2001: 373). This is part of a departure from law and toward medicine as a means of handling middle-class problems with alcohol, sexuality, and other stormy topics where superstition/religion can only do so much (Clarke et al. 2003: 164). The trend is accompanied by an increasingly consumer-oriented address of both public culture and professionalism. In keeping with many self-legislating professional associations, the APA once opposed advertising therapeutic services, for ethical reasons. But in the early 1970s, the Federal Trade Commission objected to this stance on the ground that it was denying consumers the perfect knowledge required to choose between providers. The APA changed gears, welcoming what was suddenly redefined as an economic stimulus. Today, it even describes itself as a "consumer advocacy organization" (Hansen et al. 2003: 41, 45, 25). Possessive individualism had long been the touchstone of ego psychology; now it was an ideological price point, too. (By 2007, the association boasted 100,000 members "bringing you" National Public Radio via sponsorship.)

The Young

Psychiatry would dearly love to have a rational material basis to its theories and practices, but has yet to manage this. Instead, psychiatrists have tried to replace spiritual, moral, political and folk understandings of distress and madness with the technological framework of psychopathology and neuroscience.
—Sami Timimi (2002: 51)

Young people occupy a privileged location in the psy-function, in the context of risk society and moral panic. Positioned between birth and adulthood, holding keys to both the promise of the future and its potential corruption, youth are both "at risk" and "a source of risk." Moral panics about them have abounded and continue to abound, from British protests against the Industrial Revolution via child-abduction stories, through US worries about lost generations after the Great War, movements *contra* fascist "disappearances" of children in Argentina, and postindustrial Yanqui concerns over Satanism (Durham 2004: 589, 591). The young must be protected from harm inflicted by self, family, society, and education. At the same time, young people embody a threat to order and stability as defined and provided by those same entities, for they are shaky makeovers still underway. From characterizations of hedonistic consumption to associations with subcultures and resistance—in the form of popular culture, antiwar activism, extralegal recreational drug use, antiglobalization movements, and alternatives to traditional life styles—panics about youth and safety are also panics about moral and social order, about defining and policing unacceptable conduct (Thompson 1998: 1). Young people "are always available to serve for the time being as the immediate signifier of the general need for governability," the ultimate sanctioned makeover (Hartley 1998: 14).

This governability is achieved through an array of techniques. Today's "positive psychology" movement is popular within academia, the volunteer sector, and public policy. It seeks to ensure "positive youth development" by focusing on spirituality, god-bothering, volunteerism, and sport, abjuring legal and illegal recreational drugs in order to "build a better kid" who is self-reliant, which translates as obedient to state, religious, and commercial norms rather than subcultural ones (Peterson 2004a: 7, 9; Damon 2004: 21; also see Peterson 2004b and Nansook Park 2004a and 2004b). These triumphs are encapsulated in the claim that "*personal responsibility* and *high standards* have been universally adopted by professionals and policy makers of all ideological persuasions" in the last decade. The psy-function encourages children to monitor themselves against values preferred by the psy-function, and it urges parents to see themselves as "helicopters," hovering over the impending disasters known as their offspring. The psy-function has massive exposure across tertiary education. Virtually every student in US colleges can take classes in it, and more than half a million people across the population work inside it (Damon 2004: 21; Stearns 2006: 42; Sloan et al. 2006).

Youth-oriented nongovernmental organizations (NGOs) and state programs roll on and on in the antiwelfare era of neoliberalism: the Character Counts! Coalition, the Aspen Declaration on Character Education, the Character Education Partnership, the Character Education Network (Nansook Park 2004b: 41); and so it goes. They embrace "The Golden Rule" and resolutely work for "good manners" (Westheimer and Kahne 2004a: 242). Such people simply cannot stop their restless quest for power, a quest undertaken via a methodological individualism exemplified in the notion that civil society is a collocation of atomized subjects seeking personalities (Youniss et al. 1997: 620). At the level of education, there is an ever-increasing, and increasingly perverse, ratchet effect, whereby state aid diminishes as the link between economic success and schooling grows more intense. Risk is now distributed across society in a way that militates against class mobility, even as young people in the United States are audited along a success-failure horizon (Jeffrey and McDowell 2004: 132, 135; Maira and Soep 2004: 247). Who, apart from those of us in cultural studies, will stand up for personal *ir*responsibility and *low* standards?

The psy-function and public policy tend to essentialize childhood as timeless, creating and sustaining moral panics that assume children have been denied the innocence that comes from a state of grace. Echoing the philosopher William Whewell's challenge of a century and a half ago that "anyone can make true assertions about a dog, but who can define a dog?" (1840: 8.1.4), a wisely bemused APA president in his 1978 plenary address noted of young people that "no other species has been catalogued by responsible scholars in so many widely discrepant forms, forms that a perceptive extraterrestrial could never see as reflecting the same beast" (Kessen 1979: 815). Youth remains "a term without its own center" (Grossberg 1994: 26). So what is it? Can we even define it before we circle and control it?

Preindustrial European societies seem to have had very permeable categories of age. They lacked social or biological concepts of adolescence or a natural subjectivity that was weak yet pure. Edenic fantasies about innocence and opportunities for collective change were absent from Ancient Greek pedagogy and philosophy through Descartes, while Plato argued that the young should be respected rather than criticized, in order to encourage modesty as they grew up. Such ideas were predicated on children as transitional forms whose essence and value awaited their maturity. Hegel regarded them as creatures with "sensory emotions" who needed to attain "empirical consciousness" of themselves and the world in order to transcend their "immediate and lawless character" through a transition to ethical self-sufficiency (Descartes 1977: 192–93; Canguilhem 1994: 358; Hegel 1988: 129, 198). Natural law emphasized the right of the young to parental development, protection, and aid, in return for obedience and respect. In medieval Europe, children were organically embedded in collective culture, including work. But this did not mean that what are laughably termed "family values" in today's United States were prominent. In feudal times, the young were fetishized through the role of their families in the economy. Most parents abandoned their children (Rousseau dispensed with five), and as recently as the 19th century, youth routinely worked from the age of 7 and left home between 10 and 15 to become servants. Until the 16th century, European girls could marry of their own volition at age 12, and boys at 14. Far from being a distinct cohort, children were thought of as "miniature adults," lacking autonomy or distinctiveness (Pufendorf 2000: 124–28; Hobbes 2002: 107–14; Locke 1990: 142–43; Acocella, 2003; Heins 2002: 20; Mazzarella 2003: 28; Kline 1993: 46; World Economic Forum 2004: 68).

Ideologies of privacy, domesticity, individuality, and family that developed in Europe and then the United States between the 15th and 18th centuries slowly spread to include the young, whose sexual purity and vulnerability were announced and dithered over as part of 19th-century evangelization, urbanization, and industrialization. With the emergence of capitalism and Protestantism and the decline of self-sufficiency, new social priorities were adopted: dividing labor, restricting workers' wages, and centralizing organizational power. Urban migration dramatically increased as factories displaced domestic industries. Young people left the countryside to join city life, attracting new forms of knowledge and governance as they went. Managing them through religion was crucial to securing their everyday obedience. Between 1870 and 1910, the *family-wage economy* appeared, as both production and producers departed the home. Factories spread across the United States, along with labor organization and public schooling, which channeled workers' unrest into active citizenship rather than economic upheaval, instilling a paradoxical blend of knowledge and obedience. Wealthy children were increasingly defined in relation to family power structures. They were represented apart from public life in art and writing and at the core of a new utopianism about childhood fantasy, as expressed by such writers as Victor Hugo, Charles Dickens, and Charles Baudelaire (Heins 2002: 8; Stephens 1995: 5; Griffin 1993: 12–13; Sommerville 1982: 97, 112; Liljeström 1983: 128; Canguilhem 1994: 359).

Late-19th-century urbanization in the United States was accompanied by newly freed labor—black workers—and the subsequent adoption of an ideology of adolescence via a religious fervor that privileged Puritan norms. An emergent middle class endorsed restraint and deferred gratification, norms that could be inculcated in children by minimizing affection and maximizing surveillance, thereby prohibiting undue pleasure. The psy-function offered a systematic doctrine of child rearing along these lines. At the same time, the states enacted legislation to protect children from alcohol and work and guarantee them milk and school. Religious, academic, and reform intellectuals allied around the idea of adolescence as a critical phase in subject formation, a moment when spiritual maturity and behavioral obedience could be ensured or forever lost. The ideology of church and factory countered and channeled sexual urges. At the same time, a new literature of parental advice emerged, distilling religious and medical superstitions and knowledges into guidance manuals and steering clear of Soviet theory, which argued that children were basically social creatures who later underwent individuation (Griffin 1993: 13–15; Ehrenreich 1990: 85; Getis 1998: 21; Heins 2002: 20; Staiger 2005: 28).

Education for boys provided a means of class differentiation away from physical skill and toward managerial calculation. Adolescence was a convenient alibi for the middle class to lobby for public subsidy of its offspring's educational capital, based on a psychologization that supposedly rendered the latter emotionally vulnerable absent years of schooling. In short, the discovery of "immaturity" cross-subsidized upward mobility. Kant rang the school bell and said it was time to come in from play-lunch. By the 1890s, US public education had developed a "good citizenship" system that mimicked responsibilities to come. Schools were cities, classrooms were wards, pupils were voters, and student councils were governments. This mirror of the social world became an endless process of innovation, for despite ongoing mimetic pedagogic success, new threats and opportunities were identified. So the developing capacity to write good English was only a temporary elevation, as risks emerged to imperil the shaping of future citizens (Ruddick 2003: 336; Ruddick 1996: 16; Thelen 2000: 553).

Problematic conduct among children at this time was attributed to defects of authority and self-discipline, evident in unruly bodily motions and inattentiveness, which Social Darwinism attributed to class differences (Sandberg and Barton 1996: 1, 5–6). Moral and medical discourses blurred on their way past one another, with each affected by the transaction. "Behavior" came to displace "morality." But the latter heavily coded the former, if in a scientist manner that treated norms as necessary for social cohesion and individual advancement on a secular rather than a

God-given basis. Knowledge, business, and the state were borrowing religion's methods, even as they challenged its authority

The expansion of public education, both demographically and chronologically, put people of the same age together for increasing amounts of time. Peers displaced parents as key points of identification. The freedom and obligation to learn and work independently turned into the freedom and obligation to consume and enjoy independently. Across the 19th century, English children progressively gained protection from being treated as chattel by factory owners, attaining the same guarantees against cruelty as animals, in addition to certain property rights. As part of a new Edenic mythology, children were encouraged to adopt the personae of animals while playing. The spread of kindergartens (children's gardens) emphasized the notion of children existing in a state of nature, before the Fall—a weird reverse anthropomorphism. These reforms recognized, *inter alia,* young people's cultural distinctiveness and emergent economic power, which were coevally registered through a new popular culture: toys and other domestic objects, plus sections of the new department stores designed specifically for them, offering both sales and child care. Children soon became indices of the changes wrought by industrialization, thanks to the musings and innovations of critics, reformers, politicians, priests, and manufacturers who formed a "child-saving" movement to end child labor. In addition to controlling and channeling youthful urges, these agents sought to inculcate liberal self-reliance at the heart of childhood, even as mass recreational consumption was emerging as a seeming counter to Puritan restraint. This also encouraged a recoding of clothing and gender: following a US debate over the right colors to associate with boys versus girls, baby boys were dressed in blue and baby girls in pink by the first quarter of the 20th century. Children were given individual toys and required to sleep alone in order to develop strong senses of self, while training in consumption was theorized and promoted to alleviate unpleasant emotions. Removal from factory life brought with it a new sanctification of childhood, a sentimentality that was quickly codified. Hence the historical emergence of what the President's Council on Bioethics blithely renders today as a timeless drive: "deep and familiar human desires . . . for better children" (Mazzarella 2003: 229; Kline 1993: 46–49, 51–52; Cook, 2007; Kimmel 1997; Stearns 1994: 208, 210, 212; Levine 2007: 248; Mickenberg 2006: 1218; President's Council on Bioethics 2003: xix).

The psy-function was crucial to these processes. Based on studies in France, Jacques Donzelot found that child psychiatry was not originally concerned with psychological particularities amongst children per se. The early physicians who directed mental asyla, and the alienists and neu-rologists who restricted their expertise to a small group composed of the severely insane, were interested in childhood insanity in the light of future adult health. For example, vagabonds became the focus of psychiatric atten-tion in the last decade of the 19th century. Problematic children were seen as potential future vagabonds—"bad" citizens—who must be subjected to a policy of "preselect and . . . pretreat" (Donzelot 1979: 131). The school became a site for observing signs of disorders in children, with the family the originary site of mental illness, and the law aligned with the psy-func-tion in favoring "a court of perversity and danger" over "a criminal court" (Foucault 2003b: 40).

In the United States at this time, juvenile law shifted from punishment and repression to education and prevention, alongside new public-health measures such as better domestic hygiene, pasteurized milk, and puri-fied water. The psy-function played a major role as the state transformed itself from a disciplinarian to a foster parent, and there was a reaction against the evangelical taste for instilling fear in the young. Children were medicalized through not only ideas but also practices, through the labor of janitors, pharmacists, nurses, teachers, architects, gym instructors, hygienists, philanthropists, and social workers as well as the usual psy-function suspects. Juvenile courts were founded in 1899 on the premise that an adult-oriented system was doling out sentences that were not therapeutic for the young. These reforms featured leadership and ideas from middle-class, educated women, as per Jane Addams, who articu-lated psy-intervention with campaigns against child labor. By the late 19th century, the "nervous child" had been identified and typified, with treatment available from patent medicines and vivisection. Freud arrived in the United States in 1909, the same year as the Juvenile Psychopathic Institute was founded in Chicago, while the American Psychoanalytic Association was formed in 1910. Within a decade, Freudianism and child guidance had found much in common as they marched into the class-room together to treat the normal alongside the aberrant. At the same time, the federal government set up a Children's Bureau to coordinate programs aimed at young people and make psy-insight a cornerstone of justice, because not all the animals in the garden were easily civilized. The "dangerous individual" ran around looking up little girls' skirts, stealing public signs, and disrupting class. He was a future problem citizen, and his existence posed several puzzles: were there intrinsically dangerous people, could they be recognized, how should one react to their presence, and was gender a key variable? The search to solve these puzzles shifted from a focus on heredity as a cause of deviance to an emphasis on families of origin, repression, and sexuality.

Institutions took fallen children off the street and into legal, pedagogic, and therapeutic contexts where they could be diagnosed, punished, treated, directed, and taught, blending new rights (protecting them from state violence) with new responsibilities (indoctrinating them into self-governance). Through this union of child law, child psychiatry, and child bureaucracy, progressives hoped to uncover the causes of juvenile crimes and ultimately eradicate delinquency, frequently siding with children and blaming parents. Medical science gained in popularity as infant mortality dropped spectacularly between 1880 and 1920. Children were no longer expected to die but to become problems in other ways, and fields allied to doctoring that emerged to manage them attained some of medicine's glow. The turn of the century was an auspicious time to garner public support, as the media were filled with moral-panic reports of rising crime. Pressure to enact special legislation and establish treatment facilities for youth came from an array of civil-society activists in schools and clubs. The Juvenile Psychopathic Institute suggested that delinquents were "normal" children, not feebleminded or psychopathic. Its findings were praised by welfare and prison reformers and inspired a national child-guidance movement, which created more court-affiliated clinics. In 1910, a US National Committee for Mental Hygiene was founded to counter mental illness and delinquency, with grants from the Rockefeller Foundation and the Commonwealth Fund. In 1922, the committee provided seed money to establish child-guidance clinics. By 1936, there were 235 such clinics across the nation, embraced by politicians as a means of avoiding a costly welfare system (Ruddick 1996: 18–19; Levine 2007: 248; Foucault 2003b: 110; Skocpol 2003: 191; McCallum 1993: 142–43; Petrina 2006: 505, 508; Hale 1995: 7, 85, 87; Garfinkle 2006: 71; Stearns 2006: 82, 96, 99; Herman 2001: 304–6; Jones 1999: 4, 15, 37–38, 43, 56–57, 58–60; Getis 1998: 21).

The child-guidance clinics' first patients were delinquents, mostly from immigrant, poverty-stricken families. But the shift from irredeemability toward educability—the perfect makeover—saw US child psychiatry more and more concerned with "ordinary" children and their parents and how to promote correct child raising. Over the next few decades, child psychiatry's clientele grew to encompass middle-class children, brought in by mothers concerned about their children's educational performance and sexual behavior. By the early decades of the 20th century, psychiatry was interested in "normal" children of all ages and classes, not just the criminally insane. Families, suburbs, and schools were targeted as sites of intervention and were rapidly medicalized. Medicalization as a concept came into use among school hygienists to account for the way medicine defined and responded to an ever-widening array of social issues. US developmental psychology effectively began at the turn of the 20th century with major studies into adolescence that focused on developing/preserving autonomy, in keeping with the methodological individualism characteristic of Yanqui social-science rhetoric. Such inquiries frequently neglected the underlying moral panic animating them—how to instill national- and world-leadership qualities into a local and imperial class in the face of popular temptations toward social democracy, isolationism, or lassitude. By the 1920s and '30s, child guidance had begun to take an interest in the "problem child," who was "normal" in comparison with 19th-century psychiatric subjects but deviant with respect to authority, such as the family or school. The psy-function had transcended an initial association with immigrant and proletarian youth to encompass all those who might be "developed." Problem children could come from any social class. Their future capacity to monitor their conduct and be good citizens was at stake (Jones 1999: 9; Herman 2001: 299; Lunbeck 1994: 22–24; Foucault 2003b: 150, 250; Petrina 2006: 504, 522; Maira and Soep 2004: 248–49; Mickenberg 2006: 1218).

In the hundred years to 1950, the school displaced the factory as a key site for disciplining children, and popular culture became identified as risky. Parents in the evolving nuclear family were held responsible for their children's welfare and punishable by the state for failing to be so. Child psychologists emerged to theorize and treat children in terms of "natural" forms and stages of development into adulthood, even as the child was constituted as a future citizen whose loyalty and security were imperiled by Sovietism. After World War II, child psychiatrists associated more with the medical community than with social workers and reformers. In the 1950s, the "privatized nuclear household with its male breadwinner, female homemaker, and dependent children" shifted from an "insurgent ideal" of the 19th-century white middle class to a tentatively achieved, but ideologically naturalized, norm—80% of children grew up with their married, biological parents. But they were being circled by the psy-function just the same. The American Academy of Child Psychiatry was founded in 1952, restricting affiliation to medically trained members of the American Psychiatric Association. In 1959, child psychiatry became a formal medical subspecialty. Meanwhile, in 1958, the National Defense Education Act invented the school guidance counselor, funding 60,000 jobs. Almost overnight, children were subject to external testing and self-monitoring.

Norms of scholastic and occupational achievement derived from the psy-professions were deployed to invigilate adherence to and deviation from managerial norms. The obsessive desire to explicate, enumerate, legislate, and codify childhood is nowhere better expressed than the thousands of mental-hygiene films made between 1945 and 1970 that maniacally detailed how to date, destroy, develop, drive, drug, eat, fail, feminize, sub-urbanize, and succeed (Jones 1999: 7, 217–18; Herman 1996: 257–59; Rose 2007: 119; Smith 1999).

An additional factor was crucial to the psy-function and young people over this period and beyond: the media played a critical role in the cre-ation, circulation, and subject matter of moral panics about a childhood/future citizenry at risk. Of course, baleful attitudes toward popular culture have a distinguished lineage. Theatre, for example, has long been plagued with the sense of an ungodly public sphere of secular make-believe that can dupe its audience. Plutarch, for example, recounts the following story about Solon. Having enjoyed what later became known as a tragedy, he asked the play's author, Thespis, "whether he was not ashamed to tell such lies in front of so many people":

> When Thespis replied that there was no harm in speaking or acting in this way in make-believe, Solon struck the ground angrily with his staff and exclaimed, "Yes, but if we allow ourselves to praise and honour make-believe like this, the next thing will be to find it creeping into our serious business." (Plutarch 1976: 73)

In the 12th century, John of Salisbury warned of the negative impact of juggling, mimicry, and acting on "unoccupied minds . . . pampered by the solace of some pleasure . . . to their greater harm" (quoted in Zyvatkauskas 2007). On the other side of the ledger, active interpretation was assumed to be a crucial component of media consumption. Socrates was the first of many to argue that what we would now call media effects could occur only by touching on already-extant proclivities in people. Away from the public sphere, the emergence of private, silent reading in the 9th century was criticized as an invitation to idleness, but it was also welcomed as an invitation to intertextual meaning-making by readers. In the 18th century, Denis Diderot asked, "Who shall be the master? The writer or the reader?" And up to the early 19th century, it was mostly taken as read that audi-ences were active interpreters, given their unruly and overtly engaged con-duct at cultural events (Kline 1993: 52–53, 55; Manguel 1996: n. p., 51, 63, 71, 86).

With the Industrial Revolution, the psy-function became both an enabler of commercial targeting and a guardian of correct conduct in the textual sphere. The telegraph was connected with the dissociabilities and insensitivities of industrial life, its permissive connection to the production and circulation of truth brought into question. Telegraph cable's capacity to produce truth before breakfast was accused of exhausting newspaper readers' emotional energies at the wrong time of day. Neurological experts attributed their increased business to it, alongside the expansion of steam, periodical literature, science, and educated women. The telegraph's presence in saloons expanded working-class betting on sporting events. At the same time, its messages of goodwill became highly marketable and standardized, the prospect of individual marks—seemingly enhanced through popular education—devastated by the very industrialization that had produced it. The extension through societies of the capacity to read had as its corollary the possibility of a public forming beyond a group of people physically gathered together. With mass literacy came industrial turmoil. When unionists in the Cuban cigar industry organized mass readings of news and current affairs to workers on the line, management and the state responded brutally. White slave-owners terrorized African Americans who taught themselves and their colleagues to read along with their white collaborators: Nat Turner's Rebellion of 1831 was attributed by many to his literacy. The advent of outdoor reading and of the train as a site of public culture generated anxieties about open knowledge and debate. Nineteenth-century US society saw spirited debates over whether new popular genres such as newspapers, crime stories, and novels would breed anarchic readers lacking respect for the traditionally literate classes. The media posed a threat to established elites by enabling working people to become independently minded and informed, distracting them from the one true path of servitude (Manguel 1996: 110–11, 141, 280, 284; Stearns 2006: 65; Miller 1998).

A gendered side to the new openness through mass literacy became the heart of numerous campaigns against public sex and its representation, most notably the 1873 Comstock Law, which policed sex beginning in the late 19th century. The law was named for the noted Post Office moralist Anthony Comstock, who organized and ran the NGO the New York Society for the Suppression of Vice. Comstock was exercised by "EVIL READING" and avowed that before the Fall, reading was unknown. In the early 20th century, opera, Shakespeare, and romance fiction were censored for their immodest impact on the young. Media regulation since that time has been colored by both governments and courts policing sexual material based on its alleged impact on young people, all the way from the uptake of Britain's 1868 *Regina v Hicklin* decision and its anxieties about vulnerable youth through to the US Supreme Court's 1978 *Federal Communications Commission v. Pacifica* (Heins 2002: 9, 29–32, 23).

By the early 20th century, academic experts had decreed media audiences to be passive consumers, thanks to the missions of literary criticism (distinguishing the cultivated from others) and psychology (distinguishing the competent from others) (Butsch 2000: 3). The origins of social psychology can be traced to anxieties about "the crowd" in a suddenly urbanized and educated Western Europe that raised the prospect that a long-feared "ochlocracy" of "the worthless mob" (Pufendorf 2000: 144) would be able to share popular texts. In the wake of the French Revolution, Edmund Burke was animated by the need to limit popular exuberance via "restraint upon . . . passions" (1994: 122). Elite theorists emerged from both right and left, notably Vilfredo Pareto (1976), Gaetano Mosca (1939), Gustave Le Bon (1899), and Robert Michels (1915), arguing that newly literate publics were vulnerable to manipulation by demagogues. The founder of the "American Dream" saw "the mob mentality of the city crowd" as "one of the menaces to modern civilization," and he disparaged "the prostitution of the moving-picture industry" (Adams 1941: 404, 413). These critics were frightened of socialism; they were frightened of democracy; and they were frightened of popular reason (Wallas 1967: 137). With civil society growing restive, the wealth of radical associations was explained away in social-psychological terms rather than political-economic ones, as the psy-function warmed itself by campus fires: Harvard took charge of the theory, Chicago the task of meeting and greeting the great unwashed, and Columbia the statistical manipulation (Staiger 2005: 21–22).

Throughout this history, the young were the special focus of the moral panics. As working-class immigrants and their children learned to read in the United States, the middle class sought to manage the population. Tests of beauty and truth found popular culture wanting and promulgated the notion of the suddenly enfranchised being bamboozled by the unscrupulously fluent. Such tendencies moved into high gear with the Payne Fund studies of the 1930s, which juxtaposed the impact of films on "'superior' adults—young college professors, graduate students and their wives" with children, notably in juvenile centers, easily corralled due to what were thought of as "'regular régimes of living.'" These studies inaugurated mass social-science panic about young people at the cinema through the collection of "AUTHORITATIVE AND IMPERSONAL DATA WHICH WOULD MAKE POSSIBLE A MORE COMPLETE EVALUATION

OF MOTION PICTURES AND THEIR SOCIAL POTENTIALITIES" to answer the question, "What effect do motion pictures have upon children of different ages?," especially on the many young people who were "retarded" (Charters 1933: 8, iv–v, 12–13, 31; see May and Shuttleworth 1933; Dale 1933; Blumer 1933; Blumer and Hauser 1933; Forman 1933; Mitchell 1929). These pioneering scholars boldly set out to see whether "the onset of puberty is or is not affected by motion pictures," especially given what were called "The Big Three" narrative themes: love, crime, and sex. They gauged reactions through "autobiographical case studies" that asked questions such as whether "All Most Many Some Few No Chinese are cunning and underhand." They also investigated "demonstrations of satisfying love techniques" for fear that "sexual passions are aroused and amateur prostitution . . . aggravated." This was done, *inter alia*, by assessing a viewer's "skin response." "Laboratory techniques" used such sensational machinery as the psychogalvanometer and beds wired with hypnographs and polygraphs (Charters 1933: 4, 10, 15, 25, 32, 49, 54, 60; Wartella 1996: 173; Staiger 2005: 25).

This example has led to seven more decades of obsessive attempts to correlate youthful consumption of popular culture with antisocial conduct, emphasizing the number and conduct of audiences to audiovisual entertainment: where individuals in the audiences came from, how many there were, and what they did as a consequence of being present. Moral panics and the psy-function combine in media critique to create what Harold Garfinkel calls a "cultural dope," a mythic figure who "produces the stable features of the society by acting in compliance with pre-established and legitimate alternatives of action that the common culture provides." The "common sense rationalities . . . of here and now situations" used by ordinary people are obscured and derided by such categorizations (1992: 68). The pattern is that whenever new communications technologies emerge, children are immediately identified as both pioneers and victims, simultaneously endowed by manufacturers and critics with immense power and immense vulnerability—early adopters/early *naifs*. They are held to be the first to know and the last to understand the media—the grand paradox of youth, latterly on display in the "digital sublime" of technological determinism, as always with the superadded valence of a future citizenship in peril (Mosco 2004: 80).

Congressional hearings into juvenile delinquency in the 1950s heard again and again from social scientists, police, parents, and others that popular culture was dividing families by diverting offspring from their elders' values. The hearings promoted psychiatric denunciations of comic books as causes of nightmares, juvenile delinquency, and even murder. To elude regulation, publishers developed codes of conduct that embodied "respect for parents" and "honorable behavior" in their precepts of self-governance (Steinberg and Kincheloe 1997: 1–2; Mazzarella 2003: 230; Malkki and Martin 2003: 217–18; Gilbert 1986: 3; David Park 2004: 114; Heins 2002: 52–54).

The Payne Fund studies were animated by the realization that "motion pictures are not understood by the present generation of adults" but "appeal to children" (Charters 1933: v). And each communications technology and genre has brought with it a raft of marketing techniques focused on young people, even as concerns about supposedly unprecedented and unholy new risks to youth recur: cheap novels during the early 1900s; silent, then sound, film during the 1920s; radio in the 1930s; comic books of the 1940s and '50s; pop music and television from the 1950s and '60s; satanic rock as per the 1970s and '80s; video cassette recorders in the 1980s; and rap music, video games, and the Internet since the 1990s. Recent studies totalize eight- to eighteen-year-olds as "Generation M," for "media." The satirical paper *The Onion* cleverly mocked the interdependent phenomena of moral panic and commodification via a faux 2005 study of the impact on US youth of seeing Janet Jackson's breast in a Super Bowl broadcast the year before (Kline 1993: 57; Mazzarella 2003: 228; Roberts et al. 2005; "U.S. Children" 2005).

As Bob Dylan puts it, recalling the '60s in Greenwich Village, "Sociologists were saying that TV had deadly intentions and was destroying the minds and imaginations of the young—that their attention span was being dragged down." The other dominant site of knowledge was the "psychology professor, a good performer, but originality not his long suit" (2004: 55, 67). They still cast a shadow across that village, and across many others. Consider Dorothy G. Singer and Jerome L. Singer's febrile 21st-century call for centering media effects within the study of child development: "can we ignore the impact on children of their exposure through television and films or, more recently, to computer games and arcade video games that involve vast amounts of violent actions?" (2001: xv).

Effects studies suffer all the disadvantages of ideal-typical psychological reasoning. They rely on methodological individualism, failing to account for cultural norms and politics, let alone the arcs of history that establish patterns of text and response inside politics, war, ideology, and discourse. Each massively costly laboratory test of media effects, based on, as the refrain goes, "a large university in the mid-West," is countered by a similar experiment, with conflicting results. As politicians, grant-givers, and jeremiad-wielding pundits call for more and more research to prove that the media make you stupid, violent, and apathetic—or the opposite—academics line up at the trough to indulge their contempt for popular culture and ordinary life, and their rent-seeking urge for public money. The model never interrogates its own conditions of existence—namely, that governments, religious groups, and the media themselves use it to account for social problems, and that broadcasting's capacity for private viewing troubles those authorities who desire surveillance of popular culture.

Of course, things *have* changed for young people, thanks to the commercial media—though not in the way the psy-function's epistemology allows it to address. John Hartley refers to a process of "juvenation," which simultaneously positions the young as sources and targets of the media. An early example was 1930s radio clubs. They encouraged programming directly attuned to children's interests in order to develop loyalty to brands as well as stories, providing listeners with clandestine codes that made them feel privileged to possess secret knowledges (Hartley 1998: 15; Mickenberg 2006: 1223; Cook 2007). Youth became simultaneously a "mass movement and [a] mass market" in the postwar period. *Popular Science* magazine coined the word "teenager" in 1941, and *Seventeen* magazine appeared on newsstands three years later ("teen" clothing sizes had been named in the previous decade, but things moved into full swing after the war, with cosmetics aimed at training girls for teenage life by 1946). The "subteen" was identified as a consumer in the mid-1950s. Both left and right were susceptible to panic about this (Lewis 1992: 3; Hindess 1993: 320–21; Cook and Kaiser 2004: 207), alarmed by the "commercial child" (Liljeström 1983: 144–46).[5] By the 1950s, identification through marketing and protection through policing were the norm, with the white-faced family and white-picket-fenced home seemingly under threat from this newly enfranchised shopper and worker, who communed with other readers rather than parents. Earlier forms of literature for young people, which were didactic and largely restricted to economic and militaristic advice, had been supplanted by pleasure and "life directions" (Riesman et al. 1953: 122, 175–76). With jobs emerging from marketers trained in psychology and advertising departments, the psy-function was infiltrating the very genres it drew strength from denouncing.

Before this period, toys were advertised to the trade, with 80% of sales made each December. But "children began their training as consumers" at the age of four or five during that decade. When Disney introduced the *Mickey Mouse Club* on TV in 1955, product placement and commercials centered them as consumers on a year-round basis for the first time (via what became known in the '80s as the "Shortcake Strategy," named by Tom Engelhardt after the popular "Strawberry Shortcake" doll). This innovation picked up on Disney's promise from its earliest cartoons of beneficial consumption, not unprincipled exploitation. Within a decade, market researchers began spying on children via dedicated academic instruments of surveillance to elicit their desires. By 1999, children were estimated to account for $300 billion a year in expenditures by parents across the United States, while direct targeting worked with the slogan "Kids Getting Older Younger" (young people themselves were spending upwards of $20 billion). In 2004, US industry spent twice as much on targeting sales to children as a decade earlier. Viacom, Time Warner, and Disney identify children as key sources of TV profit, because advertising, programming, and merchandising have such an effortless, organic connection. In 2003, Nickelodeon sold $3 billion of consumer products, up one-fifth from the previous year. That made it the fastest-growing part of Viacom. PBS launched Sprout for two- to five-year-olds in 2005, and BabyFirstTV, aimed at six-month-old viewers, began in 2006. Companies like Posh Tots offer a bewildering array of personalized bedroom furnishings and ambience for the billion-dollar child via http://poshtots.com. No wonder that when the "stars" come to life in *Toy Story* (1995) and *Toy Story 2* (1999), they converse about their "parent" companies and brand identities. While pop parts of the psy-function aid consumer targeting, they also feed anxieties about lost innocence via a raft of Olympian literature denouncing child commerce, finding fellow traveling media-panickers in bodies such as Action for Children's Television, founded in the 1960s (Riesman et al. 1953: 120; Mickenberg 2006: 1221; Kapur 2005: 33, 31, 29, 2; Stephens 1995: 14; Watson 2004: 14; "Kids & Cash" 2004; "Children's Television" 2004; Cook 2007; DeFao 2006; Cook and Kaiser 2004: 215).

Meanwhile, for reasons entirely unrelated to comic-book consumption, VCR absorption, or chromosomal misconduct, the supposedly idyllic world of the bourgeois US family was simply not working by the 1980s. Just 12% of children lived with their biological parents at the end of eight years of Reagan as president, and 7% lived with employed fathers and "home-duties" mothers. The 2000 Census disclosed that married couples with children were just 25% of the population. To the horror of creepy Christianity, this history reveals the family to be "a contingent form of association with unstable boundaries and varying structures" (Shapiro 2001: 2). Ideologies, institutions, and policies predicated and structured on "tradition" fell under the threat of major social change, often indexed by the media. On the one hand, children had to cope with the extended working hours and diminished spending power of harried, often single, parents. On the other, they were interpellated by corporate advertising and entertainment as competent, knowledgeable consumers who should not be cowed into submission by authoritarian parental or educational will. Meanwhile, problems such as child abuse, which correlate quite clearly with poverty, were scrupulously defined by the state and the psy-function as unrelated to the economy. The response was to psychologize rather than politicize: The Centers for Disease Control and Prevention estimate that at least 40% of parents seeking aid for their disturbed children emerge from doctors' offices with prescriptions in hand (Healy 2007). By 2003, more money was being spent on stimulants and antidepressants for children than antibiotics or asthma medication. And Minor's New Freedom Commission on Mental Health recommended surveillance of all preschoolers for mental disorders and called for a consumerist ethos to mental health that focused on clients as customers (Steinberg and Kincheloe 1997: 2–3, 16–17; Reeves and Campbell 1994: 186–89; Coltrane 2001: 390; Hacking 1995: 64–65; Albright 2006: 170; Lenzer and Paul 2006; President's New Freedom Commission on Mental Health 2003).

For their part, right-wing front organizations such as the Parents Television Council undertake obsessive content analyses of media texts. The council's Entertainment Tracking System (2005) seeks to "ensure that children are not constantly assaulted by sex, violence and profanity on television and in other media . . . along with stories and dialogue that create disdain for authority figures, patriotism, and religion." Hence the bizarre sight of state, church, and commerce governmentalizing, demonizing, and commodifying youth culture (Hartley 1998: 14).

Jacques Gansler, Clinton's Assistant Secretary of Defense for Acquisition and Technology, declared that teen hackers posed a "real threat environment" to national security (quoted in Bendrath 2003: 53). However ridiculous this assessment may be, it neatly indexes the state's contempt for its young and the symbolic power of popular culture—the makeover out of control. Young people incarnate adult terror in the face of the popular. They provide a *tabula rasa* onto which can be placed every manner of anxiety about new knowledges, technologies, and tastes (Hartley 1998: 15). So we find Clinton announcing in 1997 that the nation had "about six years to turn this juvenile crime thing around or our country is going to be living in chaos," even as youth crime had dropped by almost 10% in a year. And a decade later, the press was lapping up a spurious claim by the American Automobile Association that castigated young drivers for accidents. Meanwhile, psychiatry blamed the failure to manage "this recalcitrant and difficult-to-access population" (juvenile delinquents) on faith in criminology, when the resources of the world should go to viewing "criminality as a form of psychopathology." William Bratton, the much-heralded former Chief of Police in New York City, celebrated his first term in charge of the Los Angeles Police Department by denouncing "a youthful population that is largely disassociated from the mainstream of America," even as the average age of violent criminals in his city was well on the increase and arrests of local youth had plummeted. No wonder the United Nations Children's Fund (UNICEF) warns that childhood is "under threat" at the same time as it is deemed threatening (Males 2006a; Glassner 1999: xiv; Males 2006b; Steiner and Karnik 2006; The Children's Society 2006: 5–6).

Moral panics about the young and the popular have displaced attention from the horrific impact on children of deregulation and the cessation of vital social services that characterized the catastrophic presidencies of Reagan and the Bushes. The data on youth welfare demonstrate the centrality of big government to the family solidity that these hegemons rhetorically pined for but programmatically undermined through massively eroded expenditures on health, nutrition, foster care, and a raft of other services for young people, notably the State Children's Health Insurance Program. In the 1960s, young people lost free-speech protection when the Supreme Court differentiated them, permitting state governments to legislate in ways that would be unconstitutional if applied to adults (*Ginsberg v. New York* 390 US 629). In 1968, the court established that young people could be arrested if they "didn't look right" to officials (Davis et al. 2002). (The FBI and the Customs Service use this decision to justify body-language profiling as a means of identifying potential terrorists, with agents trained to notice "exceptional nervousness" via visible carotid arteries, chapped lips, "fleeting smiles," "darting eyes[,] and hand tremors.") Such protocols establish that "the individual already resembles his crime before he has committed it" (Foucault 2003b: 19). And while the court shields adults from being treated with psychotropic drugs against their will, this protection does not exist for the young in most US jurisdictions. The young have also been subject to genetic testing, on the ground that it can predict classroom disobedience (Albright 2006: 171; Rose 2007: 119). For 700 years, the British legal doctrine of *doli incapax* decreed that people under the age of 10 could not distinguish wrong from right. It has been rescinded. Conservative justices are contemptuous of privacy rights for children, and the United States repeatedly establishes new records amongst developed countries for the execution of people under age 18, with the longstanding support of the Supreme Court, half of which, until a 2005 decision, favored killing those aged under 15. Only two nations deny children rights in criminal cases, other than to counsel and due process. One is Somalia. You are encouraged to guess the identity of the other. A handy hint is that the Kansas Juvenile Code incorporates parental rights as part of creepy Christianity's horror in the face of children's citizenship. This is in keeping with Evangelicals' support for violence against children, which has characterized their methods of family domination for more than three centuries. Let's not even discuss the implications of future parents reprogramming their future progeny genetically (Males 1996: 7, 35; Watson 2004: 5, 18n5; The Children's Society 2006: 6; Minow 2002: 262; Stearns 2006: 68–69; Habermas 2003: 76).

The outcome of decades of policies exacting a toll upon the young is that US citizens over age 40 are the wealthiest group in world history, with the lowest tax payments in the First World. Child poverty is at unprecedented levels—18.6% for Yanquis and 28.2% for immigrants. In each case, the proportion is massively greater than for any other age group (Pew Hispanic Center 2008). This is three times the figure for Northern Europe; and half of all US children experience poverty at some point, with black children suffering at twice the rate of whites, in addition to the burden of having twice the rate of teen unemployment. Whereas very few teenaged children in the United States worked for money in the first half of the 20th century, almost half had to do so by its end, while one in eight children has no health coverage today. Using an index of material wealth, health and safety, education, relationships, and conduct that draws, *inter alia*, on the World Health Organization and the OECD, UNICEF judged the wellbeing of young people in the United States in 2007 to be second-worst among wealthy nations, at number twenty—bested only by its neoliberal partner in experimentation, the UK, and far behind its nearest point of comparison, Hungary. Suicide is the eleventh largest cause of death in the United States, but third amongst the young. As suicide levels fell across the population between 1950 and 1995, the rate for fifteen- to nineteen-year-olds quadrupled, notably among males. Key social measures of unhappiness correlate with youth today in a way they did not up to the mid-1970s, beyond even the concerns of the elderly. The psy-function argues that adolescents are ten times more likely to suffer depression today than they were one hundred years ago. To cope with feelings of helplessness, 135,000 teenagers packed a gun with their sandwiches and school books in 1990, while by 2004, eight children/teenagers died by gunshot each day. Perhaps this incidence actually has something to do with marketing. When the white-male market in firearms became saturated, and attempts to sell to women fell short of the desired numbers, manufacturers turned to young people in the 1990s. At the same time, powerful antipsychotic drugs were being used on them as never before, increasing five times between 1993 and 2002, with white boys a particular target/beneficiary, depending on your perspective; and the *DSM* was invoked in the courts and schools to classify, exculpate, and indict them (Romer and Jamieson 2003; Putnam 2000: 261–63; Gillham and Reivich 2004: 152; Lewis 1992: 41; Children's Defense Fund 2004; UNICEF 2007; Glassner 1999: xxi, 55; Ruddick 2003: 337, 348; DeNavas-Walt et al. 2006: 13; Hacker 2006: 32; Foundation for Child Development 2004; Black Youth Project 2007: 4; Liebel 2004: 151; Ivins 2005; Carey 2006a; Kutchins and Kirk 1997: 11–12).

For all this disenfranchisement and peril, the little beasts must be prevailed upon for yet more sacrifices: Reagan education bureaucrat, pop philosopher, and secret serial gambler William Bennett called for young people to respect the law and the individual, and Bush Minor introduced a "Lessons of Liberty" schools program to ideologize them into militarism. In 2004, 83% of US high schools ran community-service programs, up from 27% two decades earlier. For all the world a throwback to Soviet-era Yanqui drills that involved scurrying under school desks to elude radiation, Minor's administration announced a "Ready for Kids" initiative in 2004, hailing children in emergency responses to terrorism (Westheimer and Kahne 2004a; "Kid's" 2004). In 2002, Minor promulgated policies to "improve students' knowledge of American history, increase their civic involvement, and deepen their love for our great country." He went on to require that children learn that "America is a force for good in the world, bringing hope and freedom to other people." Senator Lamar Alexander, previously federal head of education and a university bureaucrat, sponsored the American History and Civics Education Act "so our children can grow up learning what it means to be an American" (Bush and Alexander quoted in Westheimer 2004: 231). Meanwhile, progressive political activism by young people led to sanctions. In West Virginia, a high-school pupil was suspended for inviting her colleagues to join an antiwar club in 2002, as were a ninth-grader in Maryland for marching against the invasion of Iraq in 2003 and a high-schooler in Colorado for posting peace flyers (Westheimer 2004: 232): wrong knowledge of "American history"; wrong type of "civic involvement."

Despite the propaganda masquerading as education in this country, whereas three-quarters of school-leavers thought the United States was the best country in the world in 1977, only half were sufficiently narcissistic and deluded to believe this in 2000. They are less likely than their self-satis-fied elders to proclaim US culture superior to all others or to oppose immi-gration. Globally, preferences for European over US influence on interna-tional relations see young people appalled by Yanqui imperialism. In the 2004 presidential contest, the young were the only age group that favored Democrats, and they were solidly Democratic in the 2006 midterms. Plus they are by far the least religious sector among the US population (Center for Information & Research on Civic Learning & Engagement 2004; Pew Research Center for the People & the Press 2004a; Globescan/Program on International Policy Attitudes 2005; Baylor Institute for the Study of Reli-gion 2006).

These mild-mannered signs of a critical, skeptical attitude are interpreted by their elders and betters with shock and awe, in keeping with the latter's belief in severe moral decline among the young. A 1997 Public Agenda Report disclosed that two-thirds of US adults regarded young people as out of control and irresponsible, and parents sought to shield children from news that reflects world and domestic social conflict. And whereas half the adult population in 1952 was convinced that young people knew the difference between good and evil, only 19% believed so fifty years later. US political science decreed the political views of young people unimportant because they often changed en route to adulthood. The discipline basically ceased addressing youth interests from the 1980s (Giroux 2000: 15; Galston 2002: 280–81; Lemish 2007: 13; Black Youth Project 2007: 7). Youth's grand paradox had fully emerged, its fate to be simultaneously "the most silenced population in society" and "the noisiest" (Grossberg 1994: 25), caught between the psy-function's "production and marketing of the idea that the inevitable alienation, dispossession and injustice inherent in consumer capitalism is an individual and personal . . . problem" (Hansen et al. 2003: 15) and the national loathing of children, summed up in *Time*'s denuncia-tion of "half-pint hellions who drive parents and teachers to distraction" (quoted in Schmitz et al. 2003: 399).

The next chapter focuses on what happens when the governance and commodity functions of the psy-function meet and offer the young a pill to make themselves over, leading to a contradictory rush of panic and risk as different fractions of the psy-function, capital, the family, and the state struggle over how to reinvent people.

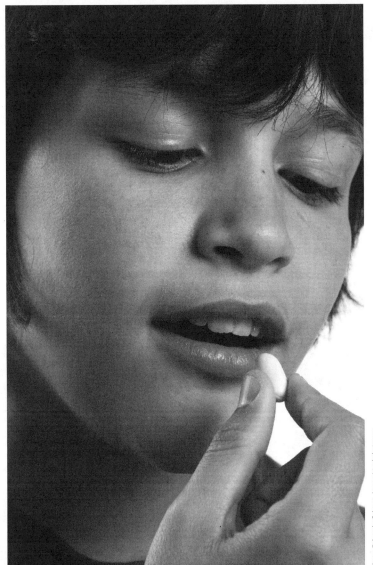

RITALIN

MAKING OVER YOUTH

How did we—or at least those of us who live in the United States—come to code children's inattentiveness, difficulties with organizing tasks, fidgetiness, squirming, excessive talkativity and noisiness, impatience and the like as Attention Deficit Hyperactivity Disorder?
  —Nikolas Rose (2003: 46)

Carol Sutherland knew something was seriously wrong when her husband tried to baptize the parakeet.
  —Dale Brazao and Patricia Orwen (2001b)

Don't be surprised if it turns into a big new feminist cause all over the world: the plight of women who say they have trouble focusing their attention—and can't get anybody else's attention for long enough to deal with their problem.
  —*The Economist* ("Really Desperate Housewives" 2006)

THIS CHAPTER picks up the dual themes of managing and selling make-overs that were introduced in the analysis of the psy-function and youth. It focuses on the nexus of education and pharmacology, specifically controversies about Attention Deficit Hyperactivity Disorder (ADHD) and Ritalin, an amphetamine-related pill that has been prescribed over three decades for children diagnosed with the disorder.[1] ADHD and Ritalin offer a means of identifying, naming, curtailing, and channeling unproductive, uncontrolled, disruptive exuberance, such that "troubled" young people lead disciplined lives, making them over without allocating vast human resources to monitor and direct them.

Many thanks to Marie Leger, with whom I wrote a paper that formed the basis for much of this chapter.

In 1999, almost 2.98 million pharmaceutical prescriptions were written for US adolescents—over eleven thousand new scripts each weekday—and in 2000, 37% of US residents aged 15 to 24 were diagnosed as mentally ill (Waters 2000; Berman et al. 2000). So just as young people are identified as problems in ever more sophisticated ways, so they are more and more likely to be treated via consumption, in the shape of a pill. Thanks to such medical interventions, classroom conduct and scholastic results are made over by an invisible and inexpensive device; Ritalin is, as per the wider designer-drug phenomenon, central to US upward-mobility fantasies of transcendence through purchase. It is a sign of how commodified forms of generational transcendence characterize the United States and its niche fetish—identity for sale.

I do not argue that ADHD is arbitrarily "made up," even though it was a politically correct construction by pharmaceutical corporations to replace the less palatable "minimal brain damage" (Gottlieb 2000). Nor do I negate the necessity of social formations decreeing certain forms of conduct (and suffering) unacceptable. I acknowledge the efficacy and legitimacy of democratically derived and policed norms of life. But to regard definitions (for example, of what is mad or sane) as timeless, spaceless, absolute accounts of interiority that explain and match exteriority is to miss the temporal and spatial contingency and discursive and institutional politics of the occasions when suffering becomes illness (Halasz et al. 2002: 1). So rather than endorsing or debunking ADHD, or promoting or condemning Ritalin, I suggest that the moral panic associated with them is a routine, generic event that emanates from today's risk society via a political economy and political technology of personhood that invest contradictorily in the national makeover.

Attention Deficit Hyperactivity Disorder

Within the last few years scientific studies have shown . . . that ADHD probably is not primarily a disorder of paying attention but one of *self-regulation;* how the self comes to manage itself within the larger realm of social behavior.
—Russell A. Barkley (1995: viii)

Initially intended for classroom use, the MotivAider ($90.00 retail cost) is a pocket-sized, battery-operated device that can be set to provide a gentle vibration at determined intervals for the ADHD child and/or parent. The *ADD Warehouse* on-line catalog states, "The MotivAider sees to it that a child receives enough of the right reminders to make a specific improvement in behavior."
—Adam Rafavolich (2001: 380)

The first quotation above comes not from some loopy Foucauldian, social constructionist, or risk sociologist, but a pro-Ritalin clinician. Yet despite his insight, Barkley and others still desire scientific correlations between conduct they are keen to control and a somatic problem. ADHD provides the psy-function with reasons to make Ritalin "the cornerstone of therapy" (Steinberg 1999: 223). And treatment is acceptable only as part of medicalization. There must be a physiological underpinning to these disorders, lest they be dismissed as malingering by patients; as quick and easy explanations for parents, teachers, and doctors; or as self-interest on the part of the psy-function and the pharmaceutical and educational establishments (Conrad 1975). The American Medical Association asserts that each year, $77 billion of national income is lost due to educational underattainment caused by ADHD (2004), and the American Academy of Pediatrics (2005) has no doubt that the disorder exists. In 1990, an NIMH study included colorful pictures of brain scans, suggesting that a number of adults with a history of ADHD in childhood had decreased brain metabolism. These images circulated widely in the media, and the research was used to assert a biological basis for the disorder: brain lesions that affected dopamine (Breggin 1998; Steven Rose 2006: 261). In the words of prominent academic Harold Koplewicz, "It is not that your mother got divorces, or that your father didn't wipe you the right way. . . . It really is DNA roulette" (quoted in Waters 2000). In 2003, a study funded by the NIH suggesting that people with ADHD had small brains led to debate over whether brain size was a function of the disorder or of its treatment; the author declined to make underlying data freely available. Not surprisingly, many mothers welcomed medical diagnoses and drugs for dealing with their children in order to elude the patriarchal blame of psychoanalytic explanations and the intrusive child-guidance movement—a classic case of competing forms of rent-seeking within the psy-function, with neurology and pharmacology triumphing over the talking cure. True believers were delighted when the diagnosis globalized in the 21st century, as the globalization was taken to prove that ADHD was not the creature of pharmacological hubris, medical gullibility, or national specificity—though it was subaltern white-settler colonies that fell most fully into line (AKA Canada and Australia) (Singh 2002; Lenzer 2006; Oak 2004; Carey 2006b; Herman 2001: 307; Anwar 2007; Scheffler et al. 2007).

ADHD adherents express alarm at "a discipline known as the sociology of medicine," claiming that its "politicization of neuropsychopharmacology undercuts everything for which evidence-based medicine stands" via "a recurring wave of anti-medication hysteria" (Accardo and Blondis 2001). The "International Consensus Statement on ADHD" rails at "media reports" relying on "wholly unscientific . . . social critics" whose concerns are "tantamount to declaring the earth flat, the laws of gravity debatable, and the periodic table in chemistry a fraud" (2002: 89–90; also see Carey and Diller 2001 and Ginther 1996). But should these self-anointed successors to Galileo, Newton, and Mendeleyev be so confident? The "International Consensus Statement on ADHD" drew sturdy repudiation from authors of equivalent eminence—but without equivalent ties to pharmafunding (Timimi et al. 2004).

The medical literature on ADHD displays a strong preference for what is described, almost in base-superstructure terms, as "underlying physiology." Yet even subscribers lament the weak correlation of "brain damage with attentional dysfunction" (Lock and Bender 2000: 30–31), and many admit that "definitions of learning disabilities are astoundingly plastic," depending on "one's choice of boundaries" (Hinshaw 2000: xv). This dilemma is euphemized as "the heterogeneity of ADHD," a function of combining "a cluster of several behavioral deficits, each with a specific physiologic substrate" (Sieg 2000: 111). There seems to be a rather puzzled search in physicians' offices, laboratories, classrooms, and recreational facilities for a singular truth about ADHD that either coheres logically, or corresponds to empirical observation. The *Journal of Attention Disorders* has dedicated a decade to it (Messinger 1978: 67; Sandberg and Garralda 1996: 281–82; Tait 2005).

Five attempts have been mounted to provide a biological basis to the disorder:

- The first takes the efficacy of treatment as proof of the existence of disease: since Ritalin works like a neurotransmitter, reducing disruptive conduct and increasing concentration, there must have been a problem with neurotransmission in the first place. This reasoning neglects the fact that Ritalin used by "healthy" children also leads to greater obedience and focus.
- The second removes the blame from neurotransmitters and places it on pregnancy and birth. Prenatal and perinatal traumas are held responsible for early behavioral difficulties. Research validates such claims only up to the age of three years, so they are rarely used to justify Ritalin prescription.
- The third turns to retarded maturation, "soft signs" of neurolog-

ical function; but again, they are encountered in normal children as well.

- The fourth looks in the direction of physical abnormalities, but there are weak correlations between these difficulties and hyper-activity.
- Last, the inevitable appeal to genetics has produced no absolute proof; concordance of ADHD among monozygotic twins is only 51%, compared to 100% concordance of eye color, which suggests only a partial genetic link, although an ADHD Molecular Genetics Network continues the hunt.

(Rubinstein et al. 2000: 42–43; Livingstone 1997; Kent 2004; Howlett et al. 2005: 95)

These five forms of thought offer less than compelling evidence that ADHD exists independently of its diagnosis and treatment. The credulous *New York Times Magazine* is reduced to arguing that at the end of the day, "doctors know it when they see it" (Belkin 2004). When and where have they seen it? The American Academy of Pediatrics' treatment guidelines for children aged 6 to 12 emphasize that symptoms may not be apparent during an appointment, so doctors should ask parents, caregivers, and teachers about conduct at home and at school. The symptoms must be present for six months in at least two of the child's social settings (for example, home and school), and other conditions should be ruled out (or diagnosed as coexisting disorders); it can get crowded in those brains. Endless studies that find children are hyperactive at home but not at school, or at summer camp (where 40% of the population was on chronic prescription drugs in 2006) but not in clinicians' rooms, do serious disservice to biological claims. The NIH Consensus Conference has not established any basis for ADHD in brain functioning. So when parents, encouraged by television commercials that warn of youth violence and/or educational failure absent psy-intervention (Welch et al. 2007; Glassner 1999: 78), present professionals with such queries as "Do you test for ADD [Attention Deficit Disorder]?," they are reifying a cluster of symptoms and signs into a biological-neurological condition (Diller 1998: 3). Perhaps there is no "objectively discoverable pathogen" and "ADHD is a purely *hypothetical* construct" that lacks an incontrovertible clinical test, relying instead on symptomatology (Schubert et al. 2005: 151, 155). In the words of the *British Journal of Psychiatry*, it may be "best understood as . . . cultural" (Timimi and Taylor 2004).

But that is not the hegemonic account: both therapy and drugs are recommended forms of treatment once extensive surveillance has done its work. This is no surprise, given that clinical discussion of unruly conduct amongst children has a long history: mania and melancholy were identified as distractions two millennia years go. The NIMH (which, like the American Psychiatric Association, is unable to spell the word "principal" or correctly parse "well-qualified" in its publication on ADHD, a document full of imprecations and incantations to do with "impulsivity" that nevertheless appear not to have constrained its rush to publish) dates discovery of the disorder from 1845, when Heinrich Hoffman (1999) wrote "The Story of Fidgety Philip" for children. George Still, who had been "collecting observations . . . of defective moral control as a morbid condition . . . in association with idiocy or imbecility" for some time, described ADHD-like symptoms in 1902. He attributed them to an inherited neurological disorder that produced "defects of inhibitory volition" leading to an "abnormal defect of moral control" via theft, sex, violence, mendacity, hyperactivity, and an "abnormal incapacity for sustained attention" (Hall 2000; "New" 2001; Accardo and Blondis 2000b: 4–5; Porter 2002: 48; Breggin 1998: 179; National Institute of Mental Health 2006: 2; Ozarin and McMillan 2003; Still 1902 and quoted in Lakoff 2000: 149–50).

It took the 1917–18 encephalitis epidemic to stimulate this discourse more thoroughly. Clinicians were presented with numerous young patients who behaved oddly, which suggested a link between lively but unfocused conduct and brain damage or disease. Hyperactivity was first declared in the late 1950s by European researchers. The 1960s witnessed a grand Atlantic bifurcation over the disorder(s). European clinicians began, and have largely continued, to define the problem narrowly, in terms of "excessive motor activity," probably caused by damage to the brain. In the United States, by contrast, hyperactivity has been viewed as part of the problem, with brain damage part of the cause. Things shifted in 2003, when a review of research that alleged correlations between ADHD and brain damage revealed that these studies had not disclosed that their subjects had been using a variety of drugs prior to the brain images, which may have produced the injuries depicted (Sandberg and Barton 1996: 2–3, 8; O'Meara 2003).

As per these key differences of opinion over defining the disorder, its diagnosis has remained controversial and may even appear ludicrous to the non-initiate. The very word "disorder" is preferred *DSM* nomenclature, "code for a vision of the world that ought to be orderly" (Hacking 1995: 17). Successive *DSMs* differ radically in their definitions of ADHD: *DSM-*

II offers hyperactivity, impulsiveness, and inattention as three cores, supposedly diminishing in adolescence; *DSM-III* divides these cores into their own groups, with minimal disorders within each one to qualify (it rapidly doubled US diagnoses); and *DSM-IV* clusters the cores into one multifaceted problem while criticizing previous rules of inclusion and exclusion. This version requires a minimum of six forms of inattention/hyperactivity in order for children to be diagnosed as sufferers, and it offers some rather sinister-sounding variations, such as "Conduct Disorder" and "Oppositional Defiant Disorder." The latter comes complete with the splendid acronym "ODD." It is applied to children who "argue with adults or refuse to obey," in the approving words of the NIMH, and is often diagnosed among gay adolescents. Hmm. And the Brown Scale urges parents to watch over their charges lest they "act smart," a sure sign of the condition. The text revision of *DSM-IV-TR* devotes eight pages to ADHD, compared to eight lines three decades earlier, with the disorder now divided between problems with "executive functions" versus "selective attention." The one thing not in doubt is ADHD and its treatment. No surprise here, when a cool 62% of the 2006 *DSM* panel concerned with the disorder have ties to pharmacorps (McBurnett et al. 2000: 229–31; Perring 1997: 230–31; National Institute of Mental Health 2006: 17; Albright 2006: 186; Conrad and Potter 2000: 564; Glassner 1999: 79; "The Role" 2006; Hari 2007; Aldhous 2006).[2]

The casual reader of the *DSM*'s list of ADHD signifiers may be inclined to identify with such "symptoms" as: easily distracted, clumsy, impatient, explosive, always on the go, fidgety, talking loudly, moving a lot during sleep, immature, and a loner. I plead interpellated, and I am not alone. The power of the Protestant work ethic to require productivity and erase failure is clearly evident in the NIMH's concern that ADHD sufferers "impulsively choose to do things that have an immediate but small payoff rather than engage in activities that may take more effort yet provide much greater but delayed rewards" (Hacking 1995: 145; National Institute of Mental Health 2006: 4). *New York Times* columnist Maureen Dowd (2003) went on-line to self-administer "Dr. Grohol's PsychCentral Adult A.D.D. Quiz" and immediately found herself hailed by the available signage and symptomatology. Edward M. Hallowell and John J. Ratey's Random House–published, auto-diagnostic questionnaire of one hundred tests for ADHD asks whether potential adult sufferers "laugh a lot" or "love to travel" (quoted in Eberstadt 1999) (surely reminiscent in its "craziness" of Vico's other-worldly distinctions between plane geometry versus algebra's impact on children's fitness for work). The questionnaire gained legitimacy because Hallowell and Ratey are psychiatrists who have decreed themselves to be ADHD sufferers, although neither is a researcher in the field and self-diagnosis is highly dubious. The Adult ADHD Self-Report Scale encourages participants to note any tendencies to "fidget or squirm" when undertaking dull tasks or confronted by background noise; to misplace objects; or to finish others' sentences. Right. For those especially keen to be the fourth man or first woman in Jerome K. Jerome's boat, TV commercials encourage viewers to consult http://www.adhd.com/adults/adults.jsp, and *Vogue* magazine directs readers to the World Health Organization's 2003 instrument for screening adult ADHD, to help sufferers avoid speeding tickets, multiple sexual partners, alcohol, recreational drugs, and philandering scoundrels. There is also advice for those who might be able to achieve the diagnosis of "executive dysfunction," a related problem identifiable through compulsive emailing. To help recruit patients/consumers, drug companies use a variety of techniques: Strattera (Eli Lilly) offers the Self-Report Scale on its site; Lilly has purchased http://adhd.com/index.jsp; and Shire (maker of Vyvanse) dispatches an ADHD Progress Kit from http://www.vyvanse.com. *Time* magazine suggests that prominent sufferers include Bill Clinton, Benjamin Franklin, Albert Einstein, and Winston Churchill (Lee 2003: 316, 318; Conrad and Potter 2000: 566–67; "Are You Living?" 2006).

No wonder the disorder was the most-diagnosed psychiatric problem for US children by the mid-1970s (Conrad and Potter 2000: 563). The rush to identify it becomes rather sinister (and anthropometric) when physiological forms of diagnosis extend to associating a "double posterior hair whorl," an "anterior cow lick," or "electric hair" with a proclivity toward ADHD (Accardo and Blondis 2000a: 153). Such articulations connect to a long history of attributing deviance to anatomy. Take, for example, Cesare Lombroso's examinations of prostitutes in late-19th-century Italy for signs of physical "degeneracy," or the sex-variance study carried out in New York City between 1935 and 1941, in which Robert Dickinson compared the genitals of women traced on a glass plate covering their vulvas to differentiate lesbians from nonlesbians. Such research became a model for understanding delinquent conduct as hereditary, sometimes alongside and sometimes in competition with schools of thought that focused on feeblemindedness (Terry 1998; Horn 1995; Griffin 1993: 17; Getis 1998: 24; Gray 2003: 37).

Foucault usefully identifies three key qualities of the psy-function that can guide us through this conceptual thicket: "the power to determine, directly or indirectly, a decision of justice that ultimately concerns a person's freedom or detention"; "discourses with a scientific status"; and "discourses of truth that provoke laughter" (2003b: 6). This remarkable amalgam of state power, academic legitimacy, and popular whimsy sees an almost unprecedented blend of control, authority, and pleasure. When Dowd or *Vogue* link concerns with conduct and status to humor, the sense of ADHD as something that can be normalized becomes all the stronger. The very epistemological weaknesses of the psy-function allow it to serve as a "switch point" between government, commerce, and jocularity (Foucault 2003b: 33).

Once more, children are both *at risk,* and are *themselves risks,* with popular culture a folk devil. Parents are urged by the psy-function to control children's interaction with television and computer games, lest they become dupes at the console. TV is blamed for making them unable "to sit still," leading to ADHD. Researchers probing the minds of people aged between one and three decree that watching television produces ADHD at seven, because it encourages impulsiveness. The American Academy of Pediatrics recommends no "screen time" for this group, and just an hour or two a day of "quality television and video" for older preteens, as ADHD is articulated to the fast pace of *Rugrats, The Wiggles,* and *Sesame Street,* with Disney's *Baby Einstein* products a supposed corrective (Malacrida 2002: 369; Malacrida 2003; Malkki and Martin 2003: 219; Rafavolich 2001: 388; Gillam 2004; Christakis et al. 2004; Jane Healy 2004; Melissa Healy 2004). ADHD and its prescription drug of choice are crucial in juvenation. The psy-function has rarely had such success circling the young.

The "true" prevalence of ADHD across gender, geographic, class, and racial lines has generated many conflicting opinions, yet certain groups of people are more frequently circled than others. Boys are four times more likely than girls to receive a diagnosis of ADHD and be prescribed stimulant medication (Woodworth 2000). Based on US Census data and other studies, it has been proposed that in 1994, 5.8% of boys and 1.5% of girls aged between 5 and 17 had ADHD. *DSM-IV* suggests that 6.8% to 7.5% of children are sufferers. In the UK, the gender ratio is three to one. Epidemiological studies vary in reported prevalence between 0.5% and 26% of all children, and the NIMH estimates from 3% to 5% of, or 2 million, US residents. Gender differences have been explained as an outcome of the less violent ways of girls, which lead to fewer referrals than the attention-getting conduct of bratty boys and to the assumption that boys are more unruly, so they are more closely evaluated. Only in the area of sex do girls draw an equivalent gaze of the medical police: twenty-five years ago, the National Association of Private Psychiatric Hospitals recommended "immediate acute-care hospitalization" for girls who embark on "sexual promiscuity" (quoted in Glassner 1999: 79). Recent feminist scholarship and activism, such as Australia's ADDventurous Women electronic community, regard the association of males with ADHD as largely mythic, proposing that the clinical imbalance derives from underdiagnosis amongst girls and older women, such that there is said to be a "hidden epidemic." But the tendency equally originates in the 1970 Isle of Wight studies and some behavioral checklists, which divide disorders between those of conduct, among boys, and emotion, among girls. This bifurcation, as per the Platonic/Kantian binary mentioned in the previous chapter, informs the *DSM* and the *International Classification of Diseases*. It constructs children as "miniature adults" open to adult syndromes, even as their specific disorders may achieve mature onset or recognition (Quinn and Nadeau 2000: 216–17; "Really Desperate" 2006; Timimi and Taylor 2004; Steele et al. 2006: 1893; National Institute of Mental Health 2006: 1; Rogers 2001; Staller and Faraone 2006; Timimi 2002: 34–35).

ADHD is mostly found amongst upper-middle-class white people living in the suburban Northeast, South, and West of the United States. African-American families use Ritalin at one-half to one-quarter the rate of their white socioeconomic equals, while the drug's uptake is virtually zero amongst Asian Americans. Black Yanqui communities are flooded with antipsychiatric materials alleging every manner of conspiracy—for example, that ADHD and Ritalin form a "genocidal plot." This may account for the low prevalence/credulity/uptake among African Americans, along with a tendency to incarcerate African Americans or diagnose them as in need of remediation as part of racist moral panics. There is conflicting evidence about the impact of class and family background on ADHD diagnoses. Some studies propose a link between disadvantaged families; some do not. There has been little sustained research into this disparity. Outside the United States, as well as within, ADHD is less prevalent in rural areas, while in Canada there is a relationship between poverty and diagnosis. Certain findings suggest that cultural differences have zero impact on the problem once the diagnosis is in play, though this claim has caused controversy among medical and educational anthropologists. By 2004, it was suggested that 8 million US adults had the disorder, putting it second only to depression in prevalence (Diller 2000; Sandberg and Garralda 1996: 283–84; Williams 2003; Barry 2002; Bender 2006; Diller 1998: 35–36; Hepstintall and Taylor 1996: 330; Luk 1996: 358; Cantwell 1999: 4; Brownell et al. 2006; Brewis et al. 2000; Brewis 2002; Caldararo 2002; Jacobson 2002; Belkin 2004). Diagnosis continues. And once a diagnosis is secured, it generally leads to one outcome—prescription drugs, classically Ritalin, an education/fun/social-control makeover rolled into one.

Ritalin

> How has it come to pass that in *fin-de-siècle* America, where every child from preschool onward can recite the "anti-drug" catechism by heart, millions of middle- and upper-middle class children are being legally drugged with a substance so similar to cocaine that, as one journalist accurately summarized the science, "it takes a chemist to tell the difference"?
> —Mary Eberstadt (1999)

> 7-year old Douglas Castellano's unbridled energy and creativity are no longer a problem thanks to Ritalin. . . . "After years of failed attempts to stop Douglas' uncontrollable bouts of self-expression, we have finally found success with Ritalin," Dr. Irwin Schraeger said.
> —*The Onion* ("Ritalin Cures Next Picasso" 1999)

Ritalin is related to amphetamines, a class of chemicals first synthesized in the 1880s that replicates neurotransmitters to arouse the nervous system. Since the 1920s, their capacity to stimulate activity has been widely appreciated as a source of both recreational pleasure and occupational effectiveness, with the first recorded prescription against hyperactivity in 1937 and later use by fighter pilots and JFK. Children diagnosed as educational underachievers participated in clinical trials from 1930, with Benzedrine tested as a counter to nerves and wildness and a stimulus to academic success. As of 1970, fifteen different pharmaceutical corporations manufactured over thirty kinds, amounting to 12 billion pills annually. Under the chemical name of methylphenidate, Ritalin is within this group. Methylphenidate was created in 1944 as part of a search for a nonaddictive stimulant. Ten years later, it was endorsed by the FDA to treat narcolepsy, depression, and lethargy. Reborn as Ritalin in the early 1960s by the pharmaceutical company Ciba-Geigy (later called Novartis following a merger with Sandoz) as a memory aid for seniors and treatment for chronic fatigue syndrome after tests on the wife of a researcher named Rita (who said it improved her tennis), the drug was soon redisposed yet again, for use on children (Petrina 2006: 521; Jenkins 1999: 30–31; Perring 1997: 231; President's Council on Bioethics 2002b; Steinberg 1999: 225; Breggin 1998: 180; Diller 1998: 21–22, 25; DeGrandpre 2006: 4; Blech 2006: 65).

Ritalin has been enormously popular since its introduction. By the mid-1960s, it was the drug of choice for treating performance and behavioral issues in US children—perhaps an early sign that psychoanalysis was on the wane. In 1970, 150,000 children were using it, increasing to 900,000 in 1990. Across the 1990s, the number of US children and adults diagnosed with ADD/ADHD rose, with most patients taking Ritalin and some using Dexedrine. Between 1990 and 2005, methylphenidate production increased seventeenfold, and amphetamine production thirtyfold. Sales went from $109 million in 1992 to $336 million four years later. Eleven million prescriptions are now written in the United States each year. These figures are astonishing for controlled substances (Sandberg and Barton 1996: 11–12; Marshall 2000; Healy 2006; Russell 1997).

Studies suggest that Ritalin increases adherence to polite, restrained social norms and encourages strong academic performance, calm conduct in class, pacific public behavior, intersubjective pleasure, and participation in organized sports (Trapani 2000: 201; Powers 2000: 486; Cantwell 1999: 16). Such effects register the ideal makeover, encouraging government at a distance via consumption that transforms the self. We might translate these correlations between Ritalin and conduct by a few degrees, such that they are viewed as preparation for a conservative role in the labor pool, via the suppression of disgruntled responses to oppressive institutions and norms and via the diversion of energy into recreational pastimes rather than politics. A healthier, fitter, more polite population reduces the cost of public health and guarantees a functioning and pliable workforce. It even helps tourism by delivering a ready supply of happy, smiling people ready to welcome strangers and their money.

Just as ADHD has its skeptics, so does its treatment. Peter Breggin, one of the most visible contemporary critics of pharmacological psychiatry, stigmatizes Ritalin as an "Iatrogenic Drug Epidemic" that generates mindless obedience, suppresses emotions and ideas, and diminishes self-esteem (1994: 303–5, 309). Other medical professionals/populist authors who dissent from the mainstream cast doubt on the drug's long-term safety, its role in facilitating or obstructing long-term cures for ADHD, and its capacity to treat-without-understanding—changing behavior by masking biological, familial, or institutional problems (Diller 1998: 13). Richard DeGrandpre (1999) does not question the existence of the disorder. He takes reports of its increasing incidence literally but claims that ADHD is prompted by a speedy society in which rapid-fire culture, rather than abnormal biology, produces addictions to newness and change. DeGrandpre uses the amount of money poured into pop-culture moments—such as *Titanic* (1997)—to advance this hypothesis. His recommendation is not medication—providing stimulants to sensory addicts just compounds the problem, he says—but slowing society down to a "natural speed and rhythm" to challenge "the dominant paradigm of work work work . . . [and] overcome cynicism through hope and action" (DeGrandpre 1999; also see Rafavolich 2001: 387–88). Psychiatrist Paul Steinberg (2006) believes ADHD to be just one of many disorders that are artifacts of a knowledge economy. There are clear ties in such analyses to prayer-and-care communitarian anxieties about the impact of neoliberalism on atomized social relations, and the Margaret Mead school of anthropology, which argued that the United States imposed quite specific stresses on young people (Maira and Soep 2004: 249). For his part, Ratey argues that contemporary office life creates problems for executives because they lack secretaries to maintain their calendars and expense accounts (cited in Belkin 2004). Put another way, he is referring, in distinctly gendered terms, to the impact of self-governing and multiskilling on the middle class.

Some critics suggest that the psychologization and therapization of teaching have produced the rush to Ritalin, because schools, now viewed as mental-health institutions, often threaten parents with removal of their children from classes absent medication. The right attributes this trend to egalitarian educational philosophy, alleging that it makes teachers responsible for students' performance against a presumed *tabula rasa* of equal innate ability. Such conservatives contend that this tendency, along with pharmacology's displacement of old-style physical sanctions as a means of disciplining children, has encouraged educators to put their charges on Ritalin. Alternatively, it has been suggested that the introduction of "high-stakes" testing into many states—with funds allocated to school districts on the basis of improved student test scores—has compelled counselors, teachers, and principals to recommend Ritalin to parents to heighten students' performance. Indeed, property values, jobs, and salaries can depend upon grades. Meanwhile, critics accuse the federal government of exacerbating the trend by creating incentives to define pupils as disabled, via special-education programs that support low-income parents and schools once children are diagnosed with ADHD. This becomes a concern of progressives, too, as they note the medicalization of education and the advent of "Teachers as Sickness Brokers for ADHD" via a formal role allotted by *DSM-IV,* something duly exploited by pharmacorps' assiduous use of Web sites to promote products in ways that masquerade as disinterested informational clearinghouses. It can be excruciatingly difficult for parents from non-psy backgrounds to master and counter the discourse of such environments. The Ohio State Board of Pharmacy worries that these programs heighten stimulant prescriptions, while both CBS's *Eye on America* and the Drug Enforcement Administration (DEA) disparage Ritalin as "the fourth R in schools" (Diller 2000; Livingstone 1997; Sax 2000; Murlowe 1997; Phillips 2006; Tait 2001; McHoul and Rapley 2005b: 442–44; McHoul and Rapley 2005a; House of Representatives, Subcommittee 2000: 11; Woodworth 2000). Would that such critics had it within them to tie these concerns to the way contemporary capitalism devalues equity and social justice in comparison with efficiency and effectiveness—to see that Ritalin is the risk-society additive par excellence, as evidenced in the moral panics which ensue when its proliferation attains levels that trouble ideas of nature and godliness.

Bush Minor's Council on Bioethics has conducted far-reaching discussions on drugs as cures to illness versus aids to performance (2002a, 2003). One key point is the ethical distinction between "therapeutic" and "enhancement" uses of Ritalin. Broadly put, many people and institutions, most importantly Health Maintenance Organizations (HMOs), accept the former but reject the latter. They endorse medical intervention to enable people to achieve a potential that has been diminished by some disability, but abjure attempts to excel beyond the norm through biochemical intervention—so mad people may control themselves with lithium, but athletes should not use stimulants to improve their performance; treating pupils' "severe hyperactivity" is acceptable, but improving "the concentration of Ivy League test-takers" is out of order. Medicine should enable factor endowments to flourish in the face of obstacles, but equalizing the distribution of endowments reduces self-esteem, with subsequent achievements devalued as "cosmetic enhancements." This is "fitting in" versus "fitting in too well" (President's Council on Bioethics 2002a; Kass 2003; Elliott 2003b: xv). It is equally a meeting point of neoliberalism, Social Darwinism, and religiosity.

The distinction between therapy and enhancement becomes difficult to sustain, with ADHD's classroom impairment and Ritalin's classroom improvement mutually defining one another, in ways described by staff of the Council on Bioethics as "subjective" and "fuzzy." And the entire diagnostic and biochemical setting is colored by contradiction and capital. Such topics became a matter of legal redress when some US medical students who failed their National Board of Medical Examiners tests claimed their failure was due to ADHD and sued the board, asking for additional exam time—unsuccessfully, because the Courts found that their completion of medical school indicated they could perform above-average intellectually. Many litigants have used the Americans with Disabilities Act (ADA) against dismissal for poor work performance caused by ADHD, but they have lost virtually every court case. The National Collegiate Athletic Association, on the other hand, allows athletes with proof of ADHD to take stimulants. In other words, the distinction is cultural: when medicalized, these drugs are legitimate; when claimed as pathways to transcendence (or eugenics), they are not. Meanwhile, colleges across the United States ponder the statistics estimating that anywhere between 65,000 and 650,000 students have ADHD; the Federal Rehabilitation Act that prima facie requires them to offer special services to sufferers, so they often seek exemption from it; and the evidence that more and more co-eds are using prescription drugs as study aids (President's Council on Bioethics 2002b; Elliott 2003b: xvi–xvii; Belkin 2004; Farrell 2003; Nichols 2004).

In 1999, the Colorado Board of Education resolved to discourage teachers from recommending Ritalin. In 2000, a five-year, $6 million federal government study of its effects began. That same year, the drug's manufacturer, Novartis, the 20,000-strong parents' rights group Children and Adults with Attention Deficit/Hyperactivity Disorder (CHADD), and the American Psychiatric Association faced class-action lawsuits in Florida, New Jersey, California, and Texas, charging that they conspired to drive up demand for Ritalin and did not publicize warnings about its risks to the nervous and cardiovascular systems. The lawsuits were all subsequently dismissed or withdrawn (Leibowitz 2000; Diller 2000; Layton and Washburn 2000; Wilce 2000; Rogers 2001; "Doctors, Lawyers" 2001; Hausman 2002).

Part of this panic derived from a challenge to the psy-function. Pediatricians and family practitioners write most prescriptions for Ritalin in the United States, thus removing it from the exclusive clutches of psychiatrists, the traditional gatekeepers of mind-altering drugs, who argue that the ability of pediatricians and psychiatrists to prescribe the drug leads to overprescription. Of adolescents treated for depression in Oregon in 1998, 60% were prescribed drugs not by psychiatrists but by pediatricians; in North Carolina in 1999, the figure was 72%. It comes as no surprise that old conflicts over credentialism are raging anew, with psychologists seeking the right to prescribe medication, and psychiatrists seeking to discredit them. While the AMA and the American Psychiatric Association ban members from participating in US torture, the APA does not, on the advice of its Task Force on Psychological Ethics and National Security. For much of the 1990s, the military had granted psychologists the right to prescribe medication, and they hope to have this right renewed by participating in interrogations. The American Psychiatric Association lobbies with all its might against this dispensation. These conflicts are occurring in a context where

HMOs have undermined previously hegemonic power brokers through a discourse of bureaucratic-managerial commodification. Insurance-company support for family therapy has rapidly declined since the mid-1990s advent of wholesale managed care versus fee-for-service. HMOs want to erase symptoms and reduce long-term, face-to-face, and in-patient treatment. They will fund only four to six therapeutic visits before the use of pharmacology, paying psychiatrists much more for follow-up visits to evaluate the impact of drugs than to meet a child's family. Lance Clawson, a Fellow at the American Academy of Child and Adolescent Psychiatry, suggested on C-SPAN in 2003 that the refusal of HMOs to fund sufficient meetings with physicians encouraged the early prescription of Ritalin. The drug has had its own makeover as a cost-cutting policy technology, a substitution effect for what had become an annual hospital cost to insurance firms of $30 billion for children (Schachar et al. 1996: 435–36; "Doctors, Lawyers" 2001; Gaus 2007: 28; Kory 2007; Shorter 1997: 295; Waters 2000; Hyman 2000; Woodworth 2000; Daly 2006).

Meanwhile, alternative ADHD therapies are also being governmentalized and commodified via support groups, counseling, biofeedback, and vitamin supplements ("nutraceuticals"). In many cases, this "alternative" (but equally corporate) discourse blames mothers for causing their children's mental problems, notably through breast-feeding (Scheid 2000; Waters 2000; President's Council on Bioethics 2002b; Glassner 1999: 78, 80; "Nutraceuticals" 2003; Malacrida 2002: 373, 379). Here we see deregulatory health-care policies and alternative health movements generating new forms of consumerism and self-government that both criticize and mirror prescription drugs.

Apart from questions of prevalence, and in whose hands prescription lies, some important issues surround the ethics and the physiological impact of Ritalin. True believers argue that moral panics over the drug are driven by illegitimate anxieties about the number and rate of diagnoses. They point to its high therapeutic safety index, a figure derived from dividing a toxic dose by a therapeutic one. But Ritalin may produce anorexia; "intermittent drug holidays" are recommended to ensure normal growth; and there are concerns over its role in the etiology of tics and Tourette Syndrome. Long-term use (beyond fourteen months) has not been studied, as the pharmaceutical industry is primarily interested in the short-term effects of medications. In the period between 1990 and 2004, of the 2,353 drugs that the FDA approved and required pharmacorps to study via postsales research, just 6% were scheduled for further study (Powers 2000: 477, 483, 489–90; Hyman 2000; Chen 2007).

Conflict-of-interest concerns have also caused controversy for the disorder and its drug. In reaction to organic, bottom-up patient groups that have been successful in goading and criticizing medical capital, big pharma has established and sponsored pseudo-civil-society arms of their publicity campaigns (Rose 2007: 142). CHADD is one of many front organizations masquerading as organic consumer groups that lobby on behalf of their key substructural base—in this case the pharmaceutical sector—by claiming to deliver "science-based, evidence-based information" (Children and Adults with Attention Deficit/Hyperactivity Disorder 2005). In the words of the *British Medical Journal*, the reality is that entities "ostensibly engaged in raising public awareness about underdiagnosed and undertreated problems" are really part of corporate marketing and surveillance campaigns, creating comprehensive media platforms of experts, victims, and advocates. The United Nations International Narcotics Board has issued a warning about CHADD's responsibility for the rate of Ritalin consumption (Moynihan et al. 2002: 886; also see Conrad and Potter 2000: 560; Singh 2002: 593).

In the 1990s, pharmacorps gave CHADD 9% of its annual revenue. Despite adverse publicity and a stern reprimand from the DEA, the organization continued to secure funding from the industry: for the period 2002–3, 17% of its operating funds; in 2005, 22%; and in 2006, 28%, from such friends as Pfizer, Shire, New River, UCB Pharma, Cephalon, McNeil, Novartis, and Lilly. In 2005, CHADD activists and staffers appeared on almost nine hundred radio shows to spread the word. CHADD's arresting magazine *Attention!* has a print run of 141,000—with 65,000 copies bought by Shire and UCB Pharma for product placement in doctors' waiting rooms. The glossy *ADDitude* magazine comes out six times a year. Featuring inspiring stories of social, educational, and financial success, *ADDitude* is underwritten by advertising drug regimes and financial programs that guarantee a profitable life for sufferers, and it offers information on academic scholarships thoughtfully provided by drug companies. For customers who want their diagnostic acronyms personalized or credentialed, CHADD offers its own Visa card, and one can study on-line at the ADD Coach Academy, where $3,695 for nine months of instruction qualifies graduates to charge $400 an hour for listening to adult sufferers on the telephone. Astonishingly, CHADD was attacked by Republican Congressman Dan Burton on the grounds that this constituted a conflict of interest—staggering hypocrisy from a US political party, but in keeping with its denizens' terror in the face of ungodly mental intervention. More typical was the double-declutching of Representative James Greenwood, who shifted directly from chairing a House subcommittee charged with monitoring pharmaceuticals to running the Biotechnology Industry Organization, a lobby group for firms he had supposedly just been interrogating, such as Pfizer, Bristol-Myers Squibb, Eli Lilly and Company, and GlaxoSmithKline (Russell 1997; House of Representatives, Subcommittee 2000: 43; Children and Adults with Attention Deficit/Hyperactivity Disorder 2005; Children and Adults with Attention Deficit/Hyperactivity Disorder 2006; Hearn 2004; Hansen et al. 2003: 51; Phillips 2006; Belkin 2004; Montero 2002; Gettelman 2004). For patients interested in a more organic site of shared experience, http://www.adhdnews.com provides many hair-raising as well as reassuring stories of medical competence and incompetence and what it is like taking this stuff.

Pediatrician Michael Ruff has found the use of stimulant medications "a blessing" in his practice but is appalled by the hidden financial/pharma self-interest that underwrites much ADHD research. Here is his account of going through the morning mail:

> Almost everything I received had something to do with ADHD. There was a magazine entitled "The ADHD Podium" (sponsored by Shire and Adderall), which contained an article on how to use the DSM IV criteria to diagnose and treat children with ADHD. Next was a brochure and video-tape from the University of Florida and Lilly (Straterra) on how to diagnose ADD in adults. Additionally, there were several faxes and letters offering to teach me more about the genetics, neurochemistry, and pharmacotherapeutics of ADD via dinner meetings and telephone conferences.
>
> Finally, there were 3 magazines of different genres for my waiting room; all of which contained cover ads for Straterra, boldly proclaiming "Welcome to Ordinary" (via medication). (2005: 557)

In addition to this overdetermined political economy, Ritalin is also liable to induce moral apoplexy. It works similarly to cocaine, though more slowly because it is a pill. A link has been established between its medical applications and recreational drug use, starting in 1960s Sweden. The drug was subsequently removed from distribution there. The DEA designates it as a Schedule II substance, a categorization that stigmatizes drugs as liable to lead to abuse.[3] In 1995, when CHADD, the American Academy of Pediatrics, and others petitioned the DEA to lower regulatory controls, on the grounds that Ritalin had minimal recreational potential, the DEA refused, aware of the drug's capacity to suppress appetite, induce wakefulness, and make people happy (Vastag 2001; Poulin 2001; Diller 1998: 348n86;

DeGrandpre 2006: 11; Woodworth 2000; National Institute on Drug Abuse 2006).

Street names for Ritalin include some clever coinages: Vitamin R, Skippy, the smart drug, R-ball, JIF, and MPH. Dealers in the United Kingdom call it "kiddie coke." In 1994, a national high-school survey found that 1% of all seniors had taken it the year before without a prescription, and five years later the figure was 3%. In 1990, there were 271 emergency-room reports of Ritalin overdoses, and 1,727 in 1998. By 2005, the figure was 3,212. From January 1990 to May 1995, methylphenidate ranked in the top-ten controlled drugs stolen from Registrants, and about seven hundred thousand dosage units were reported to the DEA's drug-theft database in 1996 and 1997. One in ten US teens reported recreational use of Ritalin and its kind in 2005. School nurses, "teachers of the year," and principals are among those found "liberating" Ritalin from school coffers (Lynette Scavo in *Desperate Housewives* uses her son's supply). Use of Ritalin was banned from the professional golf tour in 2008 ("Generation Rx" 2005; "Behave" 2004; Kolek 2006; Jarboe 2006; Leinwand 2007; Teter et al. 2006; Bonk 2007). DEA and UN evidence presents grim findings on prescription/use (see figures 1–3).

All of this has, of course, attracted major media attention as part of an emergent moral panic, contradictorily tied to neoliberal media marketing struggles over youth that parallel Ritalin's chronology: for by the late 1960s and early '70s, popular magazines were locked in a contest with color tele-

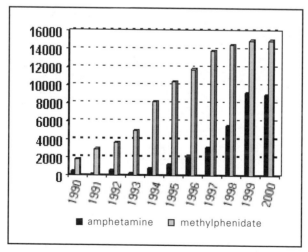

Figure 1. Aggregate production quota (in kilograms), DEA data (*Source:* Woodworth [2000]).

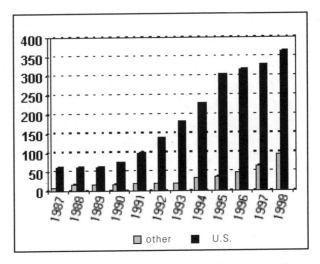

Figure 2. United Nations data, methylphenidate consumption (defined daily dose in millions) (*Source:* Woodworth [2000])

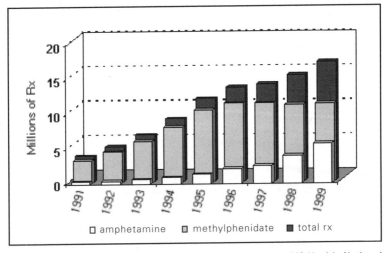

Figure 3. Amphetamine and methylphenidate prescriptions, IMS Health, National Prescription Audit Plus (*Source:* Woodworth [2000])

vision for audiences. They reacted by addressing young people both as readers (through stories on popular culture) and as problems (through generational stereotyping). This practice continued as the cultural industries promoted the existence of catchy-sounding generational cohorts to advertisers ("the Greatest Generation," "Baby Boomers," "Generation X," "Generation Y," and "Generation Rx") with supposedly universal tendencies and failings. When the Partnership for a Drug-Free America (free of recreational drugs, not corporate ones) released a report on teens in 2005, the bourgeois media leaped at the neologism "Generation Rx" as part of an emergent moral panic over prescription abuse—without noting this was just the second occasion such substances had been included in the national survey (Kitch 2003b: 188; Shreve 1997; "Generation Rx" 2005; Szalavitz 2005).

Recognizing the media's power, Ciba-Geigy spreads the gospel of brain disorders as the key to depression and other abnormalities wherever possible—for example, by financing Public Television's series *The Brain* (Breggin 1994: 122) during Bush the Elder's celebration of the brain, when ADHD became known as the "diagnosis of the decade." Media attention has since been "unprecedented" in terms of "national magazine covers, science features in daily newspapers, broadcast television highlights, talk radio topics, and local-news spots" (Hinshaw 2000: xiii). Positive popular literature about the phenomenon also appeared around this time, via a flurry of populist parental and adult-sufferer guidebooks, many written by clinicians and academics. Notable examples include Barbara Ingersoll's *Your Hyperactive Child* (1988); Hallowell and Ratey's *Driven to Distraction: Recognizing and Coping with Attention Deficit Disorder from Childhood to Adulthood* (1994); Barkley's *Taking Charge of ADHD* (1995): Colleen Alexander-Roberts's *ADHD and Teens* (1995); Grad L. Flick's *Power Parenting for Children with ADD/ADHD* (1996); Edward H. Jacobs' *Fathering the ADHD Child* (1998); and Paul Weingartner's *ADHD Handbook for Families* (1999). There was a veritable explosion of stories, mostly credulous, in popular periodicals during the 1990s, from *Better Homes and Gardens* to *Seventeen*. As well as favoring biological and genetic explanations for ADHD and providing tips on diagnosis and treatment, such texts function as behavioral guides, offering recommendations on managing children so they learn to govern themselves through token economies and other rewards and punishments (Eberstadt 1999; Rafavolich 2001: 375; Schmitz et al. 2003).

At the same time, popular culture has picked up on anxieties from the antipsychiatry movement, represented by the tragic heroics of Jack Nicholson's character in *One Flew Over the Cuckoo's Nest* (1976), to embark on such pop-psy-function denunciations of Ritalin as *The Myth of the Hyperactive Child, and Other Means of Child Control* by Peter Schrag; Diane Divoky and Gerald Coles' *The Learning Mystique* (1987); and Scientology founder and science-fiction writer L. Ron Hubbard's repeated attacks (Diller 1998: 31). In the wake of Prozac's popularization and associated debates about antidepressants, the genre drew new strength in the 1990s via Breggin's *Toxic Psychiatry* (first published in 1991) and *Ritalin Nation* (1998); Lawrence Diller's *Running on Ritalin* (1998); Thomas Armstrong's *The Myth of the ADD Child* (1995); and DeGrandpre's *Ritalin Nation* (1999). The debate has trickled into popular literature as well through Robin Cook's 1994 novel *Acceptable Risk* (Stookey 1996: 163, 172–73, 175, 18n1).

Not surprisingly, from the 1970s, horror stories about Ritalin began appearing in the bourgeois US press as part of its drive to identify appealing topics unrelated to old definitions of news. In the late 1980s, articles critical of ADHD and Ritalin were published in the *New York Times,* the *Wall Street Journal,* the *Washington Post,* and the *Los Angeles Times;* and a segment was aired on ABC's *Nightline* (Singh 2002: 579; Breggin 1998: 180, 183). *Good Housekeeping* magazine queried "the rush to Ritalin," dubbing it "kiddie cocaine" and suggesting that "at the slightest sign of trouble—a child keeps running back and forth to the water fountain, has an unruly week pushing other kids on the playground, or plays drums on his desk with pencils—parents are circled by the school's teachers, psychologists, and even principals, all pushing Ritalin" (Russell 1997). Activist Jim Hightower referred to "Babies on Drugs" (2001). Other critics called it the "chemical cosh" or "a cane-for-the-brain" (Midgley 2003; Hari 2007). The "'War on Drugs' slogan" was accused of transmogrifying into "not medicating your child is unethical" (Schubert et al. 2005: 152). And *Newsweek* went from an unfortunately worded endorsement of Ritalin as "one of the raving successes in psychiatry" to warning that it "may be causing some hidden havoc . . . in an impatient culture" (quoted in Schmitz et al. 2003: 394).

The first Congressional report on behavior-modification drugs and children was inspired by Ritalin as far back as 1970, while hearings were prompted in 2000 by a story in the *Washington Post* entitled "Omaha Pupils Given 'Behavior' Drugs," which raised the specter of mind control and merged with popular concerns about diet to suggest a more "natural" treatment. Over the next three years, Ritalin made guest appearances on

Dateline NBC; CNN's *Larry King Live* (featuring Bush Minor's dyslexic brother and ADHD-diagnosed nephew explaining why Ritalin must be abjured); *48 Hours* and *Eye on America* from CBS; and Cleveland's WKYC-TV. These programs screened investigative reports and idiot punditry on Ivy League Ritalin abuse and drug dealing, emergency-room visits, and school complicity. PBS and A&E ran documentaries, with "journalist" Bill Kurtis intoning that Ritalin was challenging "the very essence of childhood itself" (Singh 2002: 579; Leo 2002: 58; House of Representatives, Subcommittee 2000: 14; Kurtis quoted in McDonald 2001). The *New York Post* headlined CHADD as a "Ritalin Pusher" and the *New York Times* noted the panic (Diller 1998: 30–31; Sandberg and Barton 1996: 3, 18–19; Montero 2002; Zernike and Petersen 2001). The House of Representatives Subcommittee on Early Childhood, Youth and Families, Committee on Education and the Workforce (2000: 7) queried whether the problems of accurate diagnosis meant that "youthful rambunctiousness" or "serious stressors like divorce or neglect" saw Ritalin erroneously prescribed. Congressman Bill Goodling said, "Ritalin may be the biggest drug problem we have in the country, and it drives me up the wall to see little children get hooked so early" (House of Representatives, Subcommittee 2000: 9).

The biggest flurry of media attention devoted to children and Ritalin was set off in 2000 by a study stating that in the previous decade, the prescription of stimulants as treatment of ADHD in US children aged 5 to 14 had increased dramatically, with use by those aged 2 to 4 growing three-fold between 1991 and 1995. These findings were confirmed by subsequent research (Zito et al. 2000; Goode 2003). The NIMH reacted strongly, rejecting prescription to large numbers of preschoolers (which the DEA had never approved) and funding a large research project to evaluate that group. Skeptics argued that their findings would eventually legitimate the practice. Major media attention was also paid to state intervention against parents who took their children off Ritalin. In one New York case, a local school district informed the Child Protective Services Unit, which accused some parents of child abuse—a charge that was not sustained in court and led to eleven states insisting teachers not mention Ritalin or ADHD to families. Then the House's Government Reform Committee heard testimony from Lisa Marie Presley on behalf of Scientology that children were being "drugged" and ADHD was an invention that obscured the real problems of allergies, lead exposure, hearing, and eyesight. It was, in the words of the church's Citizens Commission on Human Rights, "psychiatry's cash cow diagnosis" and had helped to kill Kurt Cobain. In 2003, the House Committee on Education and Labor introduced a Child Medication Safety Act to protect parents from schools requiring them to have their children medicated. It was sponsored by several leading Republicans, including then-Speaker Dennis Hastert. All this was much to the chagrin of true believers in Ritalin ("Scandal!" 2000; Leo 2002: 53; Leibowitz 2000; President's Council on Bioethics 2002b; Citizens Commission on Human Rights 2003; Titus 2004; Barkley et al. 2003).

USA Today proposed a national debate on the growing gender gap in educational attainment, under the headline "Girls Get Extra Help While Boys Get Ritalin" (2003), blaming the decline in male scholastic performance on the preponderance of female teachers, the absence of "advocates," and the easy availability of Ritalin as opposed to holistic, pedagogical answers to their difficulties. This was part of a clever reversal of arguments for gender equity, a standard move by the right to reassert patriarchy by deconstructive sleight of hand and a return to long-standing anxieties about the impact of female role models on young men. At the same time, the science in support of therapeutic rather than pharmacological interventions was gathering strength—with the APA and the American Academy of Child and Adolescent Psychiatry favoring behavior modification as first steps in 2006 and clinicians blaming "permissive or uncertain child-rearing" for ADHD (Kimmel 1997; Carey 2006b).

Meanwhile, Neil Bush, the officially intellectually disabled Bush brother, appeared on ABC's modestly named *Good Morning America* in 2002, blaming dull textbooks and a lack of engagement in school for ADHD, while thoughtfully taking the opportunity to promote his investment in pedagogic courseware—but this conflict of interest was not noted by the network or by fellow Republicans. By 2006, Neil's big brother's No Child Left Behind Act had provided a means of profit for his Ignite Learning firm. Partly owned by their parents, the company's product is purchased through uncompetitive bidding by school districts utilizing federal, Saudi, and Moonie funds, despite widely variant evaluations of its value. Their mother, Barbara, made purchase of it a condition of her "charity" to school districts after Hurricane Katrina (Roche 2006). Perhaps this was familial synergy, not sharp practice. Sometimes it's hard to tell them apart.

Conclusion

Upon reflection, I think a combination of prayer and Ritalin could eliminate her excess energy.
—Head priest at Catholic school to a mother

How dare you! You may call her hyperactive, but if the good Lord gave her excess energy then by God no one is taking it from her.
—Mother (*Superstar* 1999)

The increasing number of children diagnosed with ADHD is deemed objectionable because the public is worried about harm done to the young in a hyperspeedy age of hypercompetitive parents, and because the diagnosis pathologizes children who were previously viewed as normal or mischievous. Critiques of Ritalin evoke nostalgia for a less technological era when "boys were boys" and that was all there was to say about the topic. Today's fuzzy boundaries differentiating the feisty child from the ill one are viewed as problematic; they help explain fervent searches for signs of ADHD displayed on the body, in the hope such signs may clearly distinguish children who need treatment from those who do not. Hair, toes, and brains are categorized and evaluated in the expectation that they will lead to a concrete, unitary diagnosis acceptable to scholars, clinicians, parents, teachers, and the public. But the absence of incontrovertibly objectifiable signs linked to an underlying cause remains matched by symptoms that are always liable to redefinition. The twin objectives of the applied sciences—to understand causes and to master interventions—are only partially met. Any notion of "pure" medicine is compromised by forces of management, education, government, and capital (Hacking 1995: 12). Drugs answer the question of the disorder's "realness" by sidestepping it. Who can identify authenticity or distinguish illness from factor endowments when pills make people comport themselves differently from before they were ingested? In the process, pharmacology partially lifts psychiatry out of its ascientific mire (Reznek 1998: 214, 220) and advances makeovers through government at a distance. A pill is a commodity and governmental form par excellence—truly "consumed," genuinely material and measurable, utterly standard, and infinitely repeatable. It adheres to bureaucratic norms of reliability, efficiency, and substitutability, thus enabling the actuarialization and financialization of the sick mind—perfect Yanqui-makeover material.

For therapists, the pharmacological threat to talking cures has encouraged collective action to preserve analysis (Lerner 2000). For pharmaceutical corporations, it has encouraged competition. Shire, the extraordinary new company that is a developer and marketer of drugs rather than their researcher and manufacturer, expanded at unprecedented pace in the new century via Adderall. Long a weight-loss pill and now an alternative to Ritalin, it offers three kinds of amphetamine instead of one, and it lasts longer. Shire bought the rights to Adderall in 1997 and "repositioned" it from anti-obesity to anti-ADHD. The company also purchased data on the 180,000 US doctors who had prescribed drugs for the disorder; then it mapped national sales strategies around the areas with the highest numbers of prescribers. Adderall rapidly attained 36% of the US market, with $758 million in US sales by 2000. Compared in its effects and toxicity to the demonized Ecstasy, the drug is banned in Europe and was abruptly outlawed in Canada in 2005 after links were drawn to twenty deaths and its use led to the acquittal of a man who killed his daughter because the drug made him psychotic. In the United States, it is approved for three-year-olds. Meanwhile, Shire developed a patch, Daytrana, to disseminate a generic form of Ritalin that would supposedly avoid abuse. It was approved by the FDA in 2006, even as the administration issued a strong warning about Ritalin's potentially fatal impact on the heart and its hallucinatory side effects. Other "new" treatments (almost generics, they are known as "me-too drugs") include Concerta, based on methylphenidate; Atomextine, which is marketed as Strattera (a nonstimulant); Dexedrine; Cylert (which is toxic to the liver); Ritadex, Novartis's kinder, gentler Ritalin; and Modafinil, sold as Alertec and Provigil as a nonaddictive alternative and used illegally by US athletes and legally by high-altitude bombers. The fact that Strattera targets noradrenaline, not dopamine, compromises the claim that ADHD is all about brain lesions affecting dopamine, but this fact is rarely, if ever, commented on (Clark 2000a; Clark 2000b; Zernike and Petersen 2001; Cox et al. 2003; Phalen 2000; Oliver 2000; "Shire" 2003; "Drug Withdrawal" 2005; Steven Rose 2006: 260–61; Hearn 2005; President's Council on Bioethics 2002b; Spartos 2001; Gardiner Harris 2005; Gardiner Harris 2006; National Institute of Mental Health 2006: 22; Krauskopf 2001; Heavey 2006; Wallis 2006; "Supercharging" 2004; Eccleston 2006).

When sales of Ritalin slumped in 2002 in the face of longer-acting rivals, Novartis sought to strike back via extended-release Ritalin LA, which supposedly lasted the length of a school day. The one drawback was that the comparative advantage that the corporation claimed over competitors had no research to support it. WPP's subsidiary Intramed commissioned faculty to author a paper filling that gap. Intramed wrote it and the professors signed it, based on the guarantee that the piece would be "quick, down and dirty." A ghostwriter with a doctorate in anatomy and a dozen years of experience in penning such deceits was hired to produce the required outcome. It was approved by Novartis and published in a journal (Moffatt and Elliott 2007; Petersen 2002). The next task of these unscrupulous cash-register intellectuals would be to deal with a 2007 government order requiring

ADHD drug producers to tell patients about adverse cardiovascular and psychiatric responses to their medicines ("FDA Directs" 2007).

The *New York Times Magazine* had a large, glossy series of "articles" and advertisements in 2002, paid for and produced by pharmacorps, entitled *From Cause to Cure: Mental Health and Nervous System Conditions*. It offered a "case study" of an adult ADHD sufferer who, once diagnosed and treated, increased his salary by $10,000. Thus shall we know them. There is no shame: after September 11, 2001, promotions for Zoloft associated the drug with firefighters, flags, and the corporation's relief fund, noting its sorrow, "We wish we could make a medicine that could take away the heartache." Lilly lined up to market Strattera to what it hoped were 8 million adults across the United States, and Concerta appeared in commercials on A&E and the Discovery Channel. Meanwhile, the FDA warned Shire that its advertising claims were unsubstantiated. But while most people believed that the administration approved all such texts prior to their going to air, its capacity to do so had been undermined by Minor. Physicians are beginning to depart the picture, just as psychoanalysts had done, eclipsed by the drugs they broker. Next, it will be the turn of the FDA to disappear as an independent watchdog—its Center for Drug Evaluation and Research is now virtually half-funded by corporations, in order to hasten approval of new medications (Jaramillo 2006: 277; Pfizer quoted in Rubin 2004: 377; Rosenthal et al. 2003; Zarembo 2005; Zernike and Petersen 2001; Diller 2001). All this direct-to-consumer advertising had clear effects on treatment, as patients and their caregivers read misleading claims for the curative powers of medications through slogans such as "an idea that a kid with ADHD can believe in," "the science behind ADHD and self-esteem," and "life stopped being about ADHD and started to be about staying in the game" (quoted in Goldstein 2006). Children are important targets for Novartis, which has produced a picture book about Hippihopp, an octopus who is "everywhere and nowhere," suffering the trials and tribulations of adult scolds until a turtle medico diagnoses him with ADHD and proffers the cure: "a small white tablet" (Blech 2006: 64).

By 2004, ADHD medication sales added up to over $2.7 billion, with more than 33 million prescriptions. Sales rose to $3 billion in 2006. Novartis might assert that Ritalin holds only 20% of the US market in methylphenidate, but prescriptions for those aged between 20 and 44 rose by 139% in the five years to 2005 (Jarboe 2006; "Really Desperate" 2006; Barry 2002). And the drug's name represents more than sales; it stands for recalibrating a new generation—the triumph of psy-drug treatments. For example, the Riddlin' Kids (2002), a postpunk Texas band with a homonym to avoid legal action and a debut album entitled *Hurry Up and Wait*, were promoted as "fired-up energy balls" with a "hyped-up stage antic." They featured in *Orange County* (2002) and the video game *ATV Offroad Fury 2*. The Ritalin Reading Series on New York City's Lower East Side restricted writers to four-minute performances, while the founder of JetBlue Airways boasted that staying off medication enabled "his" ADD to differentiate him from ordinary workers, and Novartis referred to the disorder as "a life-long loyal companion." The Cyberathlete Professional League decided to test participants in e-sports for use of Ritalin. True believers estimated that as many as 25% of US children suffered from "communication disorders." Perhaps this made Bush Minor more legitimately representative of the nation than was often thought. And as more and more pharma drugs were blamed for violence, GlaxoSmithKline, Pfizer, and Lilly provided prosecutors with information and even special manuals for use against defense teams whose clients claimed they were driven to kill by a pill—a somewhat more sinister outcome than baptizing a parakeet (Tavernise 2004; Belkin 2004; Accardo and Blondis 2001; Blech 2006: 64; "CPL to Test" 2006; Waters 2004). Product placement had migrated from doctors' offices to prosecutors' briefs.

In late 2007, the Multimodal Treatment Study of Children found that Ritalin and Concerta were effective in the short term; but over three years, they had no discernible impact on conduct and could diminish physical growth. The NIMH advised that those diagnosed with ADHD simply "grew out of it" and caught up with their age group academically. At that moment, 4.4 million school pupils across the country were deemed to be sufferers, with half of them prescribed stimulants. But have no fear—providential new territory had been unveiled. Bipolar disorder, long assumed not to exist amongst children, was announced as a sleeper, with a fortyfold increase in diagnoses over the previous decade—though the NIMH was skeptical (Stratton 2007; Gellene 2007; Healy 2007).

New best-selling drugs used on hundreds of thousands of children in the United States to counter "behavior problems" have often not been approved or adequately tested for these populations. These "atypicals" are frequently prescribed by doctors who receive direct financial inducements from pharmaceutical companies. Minnesota, the one state that requires disclosure of such arrangements, reports that such graft increased sixfold in the five years to 2005, a period during which Medicaid prescriptions of atypicals to children increased by a factor of nine, with a dramatic correlation between psychiatrists receiving money from companies and urging patients to spend it on related brands (Harris et al. 2007). Along the way, a grand project of bringing the mentally ill out into the light of day was accomplished, and a new way of seeing the world modeled upon, and in turn modeling, madeover citizens. The moral panics over ADHD and Ritalin veer in "diametrically opposed directions"—one finds overtreatment, the other discerns undertreatment; one disavows ADHD as an invention, the other demonizes its critics as unscientific (Lewis 2006: 85). Perhaps the panics about Ritalin will die off once it is recognized as one more cosmopolitan investment in human capital, in a risk society that wagers its future on the very people about whom it is most worried. As pharmaceutical companies market their wares more and more effectively to parents, doctors, and teachers—and forces mount in opposition—all participants must make peace with the tension between promises of new applications and fears of doping the future. The moral panic may become as hidden as the disease and the drug that birthed it.

Young people are a canvas for painting contradictory images of social life. As the noted pharmacological researcher Julie Zito asks, "How do you even know who the kid is anymore?" when multiple prescriptions expose children to "a potpourri of target symptoms and side effects" (quoted in Carey 2006a). Onto their bodies are projected the foibles of adulthood and the mythologies of the makeover, from all sides. The latest jag for pharma is paying doctors to talk up the likelihood of bipolar disorder amongst children—a bold untapped market/diagnosis. At the same time, the Child Medication Safety Act of 2003 is meant to "protect children and their parents from being coerced into administering a controlled substance" (Harris et al. 2007; Act quoted in Petrina 2006: 531n42). Can there ever be a sphere for discussing these topics from beyond diagnosis and prescription, outside the *DSM*'s reach (Harwood 2006: 144)?

So swallow and blink—*then* talk. As you do so, recall the words of David Healy, a former Secretary of the Royal College of Psychiatry: the pills on your tongue "lie midway between magic bullets and snake oil" (1997: 4). And note that the culture-jamming group *Adbusters* sells sugar placebos as antidepressants, given their favorable results in clinical trials (Greenberg 2005)! Concerns about mental health, educational success, drug use, and corporate commodification have joined left and right in a bipartisan panic culture, all orchestrated around a little pill and its impact on turning little people into big citizens. Unless the nature of corporate-state relations is fundamentally questioned as part of the debate about the disorder and its treatment, this panic will prove unproductive.

METROSEXUALITY

MAKING OVER MEN

A metrosexual is a man who wants to be looked at . . . a collector of fantasies about the male, sold to him by advertising.
  —Mark Simpson (quoted in Andrew Williams 2005)

The lines are blurring between men who work with their hands and men who have their hands worked on.
  —Jim Rendon (2004)

All the complicated material conditions [dandies] subject themselves to, from the most flawless dress at any time of day or night to the most risky sporting feats, are no more than a series of gymnastic exercises suitable to strengthen the will and school the soul.
  —Charles Baudelaire (1972)

MOVING BEYOND the psy-function and young people, this chapter argues that US secular commodity transcendence is undergoing renewal through a major change in the political economy of masculinity, allied to the deregulation of television. Together, these forces have created the conditions for a new address of men as commodity goods, sexual objects, sexual subjects, workers, and viewers, thanks to neoliberal policies that facilitate media businesses targeting specific cultures. Viewers are urged to govern themselves through orderly preparation, style, and pleasure—the transformation of potential drudgery into a special event, and the incorporation of difference into a makeover treat rather than a social threat.

Of course, men have been prone to primp for a very long time. Recent archaeology has unearthed sophisticated male grooming twenty-five hundred years ago. German Romanticism of the 1800s conceived of men as sensuous, emotional creatures, as per Friedrich Schlegel's "tender manhood." The Enlightenment era of rationality had its double in *Empfindsamkeit,* or spiritual sensitivity amongst intellectuals of both sexes. It called for the expression of feelings and for attention to the passional. Men were encouraged to record their emotions in diaries and discuss the results with others. The sybarite/bon vivant is a familiar figure in fashion history, and the New York Public Library's famous "Rakish History of Men's Wear" show detailed the way that clothing made the man across time and space ("Metrosexual Man" 2006; Trepp 1994: 13n25; Jauffred 2006; Irizarry 2007). Baudelaire (1972) dates dandyism as far back as Alicibiades, with further links to Lucius Sergius Catilina and Julius Caesar, and locates it as far afield as the wilds of the New World. The early-19th-century dandy was preoccupied with style and pleasure juxtaposed against depth and responsibility. A figure for whom creativity was all and work anathema, he favored art over nature (Elsaesser 1999: 4–5). The severe Calvinist prelate Thomas Carlyle called the dandy "a Clothes-wearing Man, a Man whose trade, office and existence consists in the wearing of Clothes," sacrificing "the Immortal to the Perishable" in the name of "Self-worship." In *Sartor Resartus,* Carlyle typified the 1830s "DANDIACAL HOUSEHOLD" as:

> A Dressing-room splendidly furnished; violet-colored curtains, chairs and ottomans of the same hue. Two full-length Mirrors are placed, one on each side of a table, which supports the luxuries of the Toilet. Several Bottles of Perfumes, arranged in a peculiar fashion, stand upon a smaller table of mother-of-pearl; opposite to these are placed the appurtenances of Lavation richly wrought in frosted silver. A Wardrobe of Buhl is on the left; the doors of which, being partly open, discover a profusion of Clothes; Shoes of a singularly small size monopolize the lower shelves. (1999; also see 1837)

Baudelaire classified dandies as men with "no profession other than elegance" who lived under "a rigorous code of laws" despite standing outside formal legal institutions. However "ardent and independent their individual characters" may have been, their search for "a personal form of originality" took place "within the external limits of social conventions." The dandies' "cult of the ego" took pleasure in the surprise others showed when they appeared. Nevertheless, Baudelaire saw them disappearing with the rise of democracy, because patrician attitudes and aristocratic wealth would be rhetorically and materially compromised (1972). His prediction was instantiated in subsequent histories that refer to the "Great Masculine Renunciation," which supposedly saw men shy away from consumption as women's business. But traces of Bohemian culture are found in the consumption booms of the 1890s, 1920s, and 1960s. The fashion industry broadened its means of production and communication to encompass men with the proliferation of the department store and retail catalogs at the end of the 19th century. Then the interwar period's revised marketing systems ushered in a new acceptability of men as clothes horses via the notion of their rationality in purchasing, as opposed to the emotion-driven wastefulness of women consumers, and via the association of goods and services with soldiers and sportsmen. This trend countered the link of effeminacy to homosexuality, which had intensified following Oscar Wilde's 1895 trial for gross indecency (Sedden 2002: 48; Shannon 2004; Honeyman and Godley 2003: 105).

Even so, despite François de Chateaubriand finding rural dandies in North America, the United States has a male tradition that has frequently defined itself in a hypermasculinist and specifically Francophobic way. Early Puritanism stood alongside the frontier as a defining characteristic of the New World, via the careful calibration of conduct through devotion to a higher being who transcended base human desires—a blend of rugged individuality and collective piety. As per the personality/character dialectic noted in the Introduction, men who wrestled with their hungers and drives could attain a life-world of the spiritual through proper behavior, which would compensate for secular privations. They might even feel liberated by establishing and maintaining an alternative universe to the secular. Puritanism's ethical technology took on a deeply pre- and proscriptive form that ramified and intensified secular law with a duty to obey God's (heavily interpreted) word. It also became a monetary technology, an index and guide to thrift and self-actualization via utilitarian calculation. Late-18th-century Yanqui theater parodied British men, unfavorably contrasting their supposedly effete, foppish display with putatively courageous, rugged nativism. The Old World was associated with a feminizing influence that had to be resisted/infiltrated in order to restore and institutionalize hypermasculinism. Misogyny, xenophobia, machismo, and cultural nation building were bound together. At a time when 80% of men worked in agriculture, John Adams wrote to Thomas Jefferson in 1819 that he feared that economic growth would generate "effeminacy, intoxication, extravagance, vice and folly," while Washington Irving favored keeping young men as ignorant of the world beyond as possible, lest they "grow luxurious and effeminate in Europe." There was great anxiety about avoiding not just luxury, but the *look* of luxury; one had to appear frugal

(Baudelaire 1972; Susman 1984: 41–45; Motley 2006: 90–91; Adams and Irving quoted in Kimmel 1997: 19). Adams and Irving clearly never took a cultural-studies course, where we admire such things.

This decidedly material mode of salvation stressed the male propensity—nay, imperative—to work, save, and invest rather than consume, in accord with the uptake of John Locke's ideas on private property and the role of the state. It supported the formation of capital and the disciplining of the workforce, even as it rhapsodized about self-sufficiency. In the hands of heralds and apologists for 19th-century capitalism, Puritanism endorsed labor and savings as keys to building an earthly heaven, ordering individuals through the material rule of law and the interpersonal rule of belief. In 1832, Senator Henry Clay coined what became a famous neologism: "self-made men." These heroic figures attained trust in the business world by contrasting their lack of personal style with demonstrative European aristocrats. Woe betide would-be leaders who did not adopt this look. Despite being described on today's White House Web site as "trim and erect," Martin Van Buren was criticized in his 1836 and 1840 presidential campaigns for wearing ruffled shirts and failing to embody frontier masculinity. Davy Crockett accused him of being "laced up in corsets," which perhaps explains the Bush Minor White House's admiration for his tumescence. This was also the period when Great-Awakening preachers mocked men without facial hair or who wore glasses, while the Civil War became a moment for the reassertion of the North as a place of manly industry contrasted with the South's mannered racism. The term "sissy" entered Yanqui English at this time to describe men who cowered in the face of peril (Clay and Crockett quoted in Kimmel 1997: 26, 38; http://www.whitehouse.gov/history/presidents/mb8.html; Kimmel 1997: 60, 73; Stearns 2006: 98).

But between 1870 and 1910, a middle class formed comprising folk who were not agricultural, proletarian, or capitalist. In the two decades to 1890, the number of professionals in the US labor force went from below 350,000 to almost 880,000, and subordinate white-collar workers grew from 80,000 to 470,000. Urbanization and Eastern European and Asian immigration accelerated, rural whiteness receded, more and more women entered the labor force, and queer culture emerged. Intellectuals with managerial and scientific knowledge appeared on the scene. Science favored truths that could be tested, rather than magically revealed. The corollary to the intense rationalism of science was an aesthetic notion of human quintessences that would emerge in art: desires were not to be denied or displaced. Puritanism was held responsible for the personal and social alienation experienced by intellectuals. Writers began to wonder about other forms of self-expression than those mandated in the narrow corridors of the Puritan mind. H. L. Mencken famously defined Puritanism as "the haunting fear that someone, somewhere, may be happy" (1956: 233). Freudian discourse made desire an inevitable and valuable corrective to the anal retentiveness of prevailing ideology. Aesthetic discourse privileged expressive totality and sensuous response over tightly buttoned shirts. Temperance and censorship were seen to favor certain categories of person over others. The duel between these tendencies has continued, along with the xenophobic nativism that attaches to men who have a sense of style.

Meanwhile, the emergent psy-function began to worry about the impact of modernization on men by the mid-1850s. The 19th century also saw the proliferation of advice manuals to boys on preparation for business success. By the end of the First World War, when so many Yanquis faltered under fire through shell shock, mental illness had begun its process of normalization (Schiller 1996: 17; Susman 1984: 41–48; Kimmel 1997: 82, 85, 87, 98, 132–33; Heller 2006: 3). And the centrality of hypermaleness to the economy had been fatally compromised via a shift away from the foundational mythology of masculinity in agrarian life and then factory life. Even as the economy was undergoing dramatic agricultural and manufacturing growth in the 19th and 20th centuries, the services area, too, expanded. Services were not theorized as such at the time, but we can discern their significance for some time prior to the Depression. The countinghouse was transformed into the modern office, as new technologies, educational investments, and systems of labor emerged, helping the United States to overtake Britain as the key center of world productivity via a shift from customized, low-volume production to standardized, high-volume manufacture. These transformations began in communications and transport, before widening to finance and culture (Broadberry and Ghosal 2002). As George Orwell put it, with reference to belated but similar changes in Britain, the corollary was "a general softening of manners" as industrial technology relied less and less on the "old-style 'proletarian'—collarless, unshaven and with muscles warped by heavy labour"—and helped to produce a "common culture" of "tastes, habits, manners and outlook" that veered toward the middle class (1982). This sector of the economy was feminized, at both an occupational and a stylistic level, with appearance often an important part of work (Sarah Berry 2000: xiii). The devastation wrought by the Great Depression expressed itself as violent irruptions on domestic landscapes. Herbert I. Schiller recalls his family's "frequent quarrels, most of which had an economic origin." His "father's continuing joblessness was viewed by my mother as weakness and inadequacy" (2000:

12). The return of soldiers from the subsequent World War appeared to reinstate male power along with male employment. Then the rise of feminism and civil rights increased pressure on violently achieved and preserved male antiquities. Through all these changes, a severe Puritanism often revived its cranky self, with culturally libertarian conduct obsessively chronicled and decried. But the political economy has largely militated against this worldview.

All this amounted to what Barbara Ehrenreich views as a "masculinity crisis that gripped middle-class men in the late fifties," with traditional jobs changing and advertisers focusing more and more on female consumers as key decision makers. By 1960, about 40% of jobs outside farming were in manufacturing. That figure was 14% in 2002, when the service industries accounted for 80% of employment beyond agriculture. By the mid-1980s, 36% of corporate purchases were of high-technology products. Factory machinery had been dropping steadily as a factor since the war. The United States today has 86 million private-sector jobs in services. Well over half of US employment growth between 1988 and 2000 was in the service sector. The corollary of such changes is increased credentialism and internationalism—since the only things people want to buy from the United States are military-related manufactures and cultural, legal, financial, medical, and psy-function texts, technologies, and techniques. The outcome, alongside the deregulatory outcomes explained in the Introduction, has been atrocious for the material underpinnings to working-class masculinity: between 1973 and 2005 the economy grew by 150%, and productivity by 80%, while the hourly wage of the male worker, adjusted for price shifts, went from $15.76 to $15.62. Over the same period, the proportion of women's income to heterosexual household incomes has increased dramatically. In 1970, men brought in all the earnings in 50% of Yanqui homes; by 2000 it was 20%. Men have become less central to the material survival and comfort of those they live with, and women have developed the independence necessary to love them or leave them. Divorce rates correlate with female earnings to reflect that shift in autonomy (Ehrenreich 1990: 33; Hacker 2006: 80, 88, 105; Office of the US Trade Representative 2001: 1, 10, 15; Schiller 2000: 101; Schiller 2007: 12; Goodman and Steadman 2002; Bernstein 2006: 73).

As if to blend these contradictory lineages, the new masculinists of the 1970s and beyond appeared to go forward and build culture anew via an appeal to supposedly ancient verities. The "development and integration of body, mind, and emotions" would result from consulting such pop-psy-function literature as *Accessing the King in the Male Psyche* and *The Warrior*

Athlete. Newsweek announced "the first postmodern social movement" in 1991: poet and tree-hugger Robert Bly's followers looking within for the lost monarch. This tendency was rooted in Carl Jung's uptake of Greek and Roman mythology as a universal, transhistorical truth about masculine and feminine bases to personality, a "collective unconscious" that animates everyone. Other accounts derived from middle-class reactions against feminist challenges to male authority and privilege. Sometimes these reactions have been misogynistic and antifeminist; at other moments, they have expressed envy at women's "feelings" discourse, their unity, and their claims to expressive totality. One wing became "Father's Rights," the other "Men Against Sexism." Both sides stressed the difficulties of being a man, the pain of leadership, the confusion of roles "under" feminism, the vacuum of authority and direction, and the need to "share." Carol Gilligan notes that where the "feminist movement has held men responsible for their violence and privilege," the "mythopoetic men's movement has embraced men as wounded" (Moore and Gillette 1992: 25–27; Millman 1979: viii; Ross 1980: 118; *Newsweek* quoted in Boscagli 1992–93: 71; Gilligan 1997).

There were much more interesting contributions from 1960s and 1970s television and glam rock. *The Man from U.N.C.L.E.* added a touch of the feminized male to the banality of dyadic male action-adventure TV drama, for example. Whereas its predecessors certainly targeted male viewers keen on action and women keen on bodily display, this series cast men of ordinary physique and soft features as its heroes after the show's producer met a woman who pointed out that "there were other types of people in the world" than vast hunks (Miller 2003). And in music, androgynous/queer personae of that decade and the next three—Mick Jagger, Jimi Hendrix, David Bowie, Marc Bolan, Elton John, Brian Eno, Peter Gabriel, Lou Reed, Mick Ronson, Todd Rundgren, Alice Cooper, Slade, Sweet, Freddy Mercury, Boy George, Michael Jackson, Robert Smith, Morrissey, Prince, Ricky Martin, and others—led to an androgyny that welcomed queerness, a "cavalier feminizing" that envied girls' monopoly on "pretty, floaty nonaggressive free spirit[s]" (Doonan 2007). While the blaxploitation film genre of the period may have emphasized violence, it also stressed conspicuous consumption via the superfly figure, who placed great value on stylish, effervescent personal appearance.

As part of a gathering critique across the human sciences and social movements over the last thirty years, we have also seen a burst of scholarly writing and thinking about men from feminist and queer theory (Kimmel 1992; Connell 1992: 735). The critical arm of this research draws much of its inspiration from the idea that we live in an era of "hegemonic masculinity" (HM). The concept's lineage is in Antonio Gramsci's theorization of hegemony, as picked up and redisposed by RW/Bob/Raewyn Connell. For Gramsci, an Italian Marxist writing from jail in the mid-1930s, hegemony is a contest of meanings in which a ruling class gains consent to the social order by making its power appear normal and natural. Ordinary people give "'spontaneous' consent" to the "general direction imposed on social life by the dominant fundamental group" as a consequence of education and entertainment. Society contains old cultural meanings and practices, no longer dominant but still influential, and emergent ones, either propagated by an upcoming class or incorporated by the ruling elite. These discourses are carried by intellectuals, who work at "superstructural 'levels'" to forge the "hegemony which the dominant group exercises throughout society" (Gramsci 1971: 12).

Connell, an Australian Marxist writing from Australian and US research universities in the '80s, '90s, and today, applies this notion of consent-through-incorporation to gender relations, especially masculinity. Combining theories of imperialism with feminism, he/she[1] articulates the history of North Atlantic commercial republics expanding into the rest of the world with contemporary anthropological study. The result makes Western European and North American white male sexuality isomorphic with power: men seek global dominion and desire, orchestrated to oppress women. HM encompasses obvious sexism—rape, domestic violence, and obstacles to female occupational advancement—and more subtle domination, such as excluding women from social environments and sports teams, and lopsided media interest in men. Connell calls for critical investigations of masculinity across the state, work, the family, sex, and organizational life (1987, 1995, 1998, 2001).

Of course, HM (straight, strong, domineering) oppresses the many men excluded from it, while even "subscribers" often find its norms unattainable. HM's articulation against women and queers makes it unpopular with vast numbers of people. While men who feel socially weak (the working class, minorities, and many immigrants) may find the hegemonic model appealing, the real sources of their powerlessness lie in the monetary and racial economy, not struggles against women and gays (Messner 1997: 7–8, 12; Rowe 1997: 124). Connell acknowledges that male identity is complex and polyvalent, with no singular set of qualities consistently marked as masculine; masculinity and men's bodies (symbolically conceived as unitary) are contested sites, fraught with contradictions (1998). But the work sometimes reads like neat, ideal types overlying messy evidence. Counterexamples to a narrative of Western domination abound in the Third World, and significant aspects of everyday male conduct are about the desire to share and build, not control and shutter. Francesca M. Cancian argues that what counts as loving conduct has been erroneously feminized in the United States by identifying it with expressing feelings rather than, for example, helping or fucking. She favors equal value being placed on all sides to love (1986: 692). For his part, Wil Coleman (1990) calls for a focus on masculinity in use—not as a term freighted-in from ideal types, as per Connell, but when maleness appears as such in the vocabulary of everyday life.

Those contradictions became manifest and manifold beyond the expectations of HM in the most recent Yanqui makeover. In the 1990s, traditional ways of dividing First World consumers—by age, race, gender, and class—were supplemented by cultural categories, with market researchers proclaiming a decade of the "new man." Life-style and psychographic research sliced and diced consumers into "moralists," "trendies," "the indifferent," "working-class puritans," "sociable spenders," and "pleasure seekers." Men were further subdivided into "pontificators," "self-admirers," "self-exploiters," "token triers," "chameleons," "avant-gardicians," "sleep-walkers," and "passive endurers" (Fox 1989). Something was changing in the landscape of Yanqui masculinity, as part of a general turn in employment from manufacturing to culture.

Consider Clinton. *The Economist* looks back on him as "the first androgynous president," and he was identified early as a "classic metrosexual" (with ADHD, as we saw earlier) (Lexington 2004; "Real Men" 2003). When lapsed-leftist Christopher Hitchens mocked Clinton with Paula Jones's implication that "it would have taken two of his phalluses to make one normal one" (1999: 50), he referenced quite precisely the discourse long-used to find fault with women's bodies. OK, Bill's is "five inches long when erect, as big around as a quarter, and bent" (Paley 1999: 222). That I could so boast. This information is clearly an objectification of his body. It indicates that the commodity fetish has moved on to men. A similar process problematizing masculinity took place during the 1992 elections, when Bush the Elder accused Clinton of being influenced by "the tassel-loafered lawyer crowd." Reform Party candidate Ross Perot forbade his staff from wearing the offending shoe, and the Elder's press secretary, Toni Clarke, compared Clinton to Woody Allen (Kimmel 1997: 297). A big girl, Clinton is described by friends former and current, psychoanalysts, and poly-sci mavens as desperate to please, "seductive," and eager to hear differing points of view (Wayne 1999: 559–61). He is both the new man of advertising—flawed, sexy, priapic, sensitive—and the publicly humiliated adulterous woman of misogyny. This replays issues close to Augustine, the Ancient Greeks and Romans, and Burke. Clinton looked back on his impeachment as something akin to a Du Boisian/Aristotelian moment, referring to the split he experienced between public and private selves, between duty and desire, as "parallel lives" that return "with a vengeance" via a duel of "outer life" versus "old demons" (Clinton 2004: 775, 811, 923). This was a combat between "personality" and "character."

During Clinton's presidency, the variegated male body was up for grabs as both sexual icon and commodity consumer, in ways that borrowed from but also exceeded earlier commodification of the male form. The most obvious sign was the emergence of the "metrosexual," a term coined in the mid-1990s by queer critic Mark Simpson after encountering "the real future. . . . [and finding that] it had moisturised." Key metrosexuals included Spiderman, Brad Pitt, and David Beckham (Miller 2001; Simpson 2002; Simpson 2004; Simpson quoted in Williams 2005).

Historically, male desire for women has been *over*legitimized, while female and male desire for men has been *under*legitimized.[2] The metrosexual represents a major shift in relations of power, with men subjected to new forms of governance and commodification. Simpson calls his discourse of metrosexuality "snarky sociology, which is no good to anyone." But it has been taken up and deployed—as a *pre*scription as much as a *de*scription—because it promises "highly profitable demography" guaranteed to stimulate any "advertiser's wet dream" (Simpson 2003; Simpson 2004). The metrosexual has been joyfully embraced by Western European, Australian, South Asian, Latin American, East Asian, and US marketers, who regard it as "about having the strength to be true to oneself," rather than a sign of being a vain cat. Based on its rapid diffusion, acceptance, and national usage, "metrosexual" was declared word of the year for 2003 by the American Dialect Society, ahead of "weapons of," "embed," and "preemptive self-defense." Euromonitor's 2006 report on the phenomenon was entitled *The Male Shopping Giant Awakes*. He even gave his name to a prominent 2006 Thai film (St. John 2003; Casqueiro 2003; Álvarez 2006; Nixon 2003: 6; Euromonitor 2006; Deepti 2005; Chan 2006; Salzman et al. 2005: 55; Barboza 2007; "Bangladesh" 2006; Poblete 2007; American Dialect Society 2004; Diego 2006).

The metrosexual "might be officially gay, straight or bisexual, but this is utterly immaterial because he has clearly taken himself as his own love object and pleasure as his sexual preference" (Simpson 2004). He endorses equal-opportunity vanity, through cosmetics, softness, women, hair-care products, wine bars, gyms, designer fashion, wealth, the culture industries, finance, cities, cosmetic surgery, and deodorants. Happy to be the object of queer erotics, and committed to exfoliation and Web surfing, this newly feminized male blurs the visual style of straight and gay (St. John 2003) in a restless search "to spend, shop and deep-condition." He is supposed to be every fifth man in major US cities (Fenley 2004), despite the hysterical right's claim that metrosexuality "reaches nary an iota of the general populace outside of sushi-sick San Francisco and nightlife-nauseous New York," and despite *American Chronicle*'s divining that it falls outside "True masculinity" (Manes 2003; Austria-del Rosario 2006). Single straight men now embark on what the *New York Times* calls "man dates," nights out together without the alibis of work and sport or the props of televisions and bar stools—although Yanquis shy away from ordering bottles of wine together. (That would be going too far, other than perhaps in a steak house [Lee 2005].) The last refuge of male-separatist brawn and flailing manbags at two paces (the Canadian ice-hockey changing room) has become a site for swapping recipes and swooning over dining ambience (Brown 2006). And in a triumph of nurture over nature, testosterone "has somehow been supplanted by urban living arrangements" (Williams 2006). Even avowedly antimetrosexual men swarm to Web sites such as basenotes.com in search of comparison tips on fragrances (Petridis 2006).

Summed up by *Jet* magazine as "aesthetically savvy," the metrosexual appeared 25,000 times on google.com in mid-2002; three years later, the number was 212,000; by the end of 2005, close to a million; and by mid-2007, almost 1.5 million. He even managed to transform characters on *South Park*, which devoted an episode to the phenomenon through a conversion narrative of its mildly amusing, banally offensive kind. And in case men aren't sure they rate, an on-line metrosexual quiz is available. The average grade of the one hundred thousand who took it in its first year was 36.5%. I scored 54%, and qualified. ESPN, the sports cable network, also offered a quiz (Yarborough 2004; Sender 2006: 132; Simpson 2004; Bachelor 2004; Gladden 2005).

In 2003, Californian gubernatorial candidate Arnold Schwarzenegger told *Vanity Fair* he was "a major shoe queen." *The Metrosexual Guide to Style* suggests that such a remark would have been "unthinkable ten years ago" but is now "deeply in touch with the Zeitgeist," because the "new man" needs to display "style, sophistication and self-awareness" (Flocker 2003). The *New York Times*'s "Cultural Studies" section discerns a full-fledged "democratization of desire" (Trebay 2003), because men are increasingly key objects of pleasure for female and gay audiences. Male striptease shows, for example, reference not only changes in the gender of power and money but also a public site where "women have come to see exposed male genitalia . . . to treat male bodies as objects only." During the 1998 men's World Cup of association football, the French Sexy Boys Band, who had been performing in Paris since 1993 to sellout crowds, offered strip shows for "les filles sans foot" (girls without soccer/girls who couldn't care less). The US Chippendales toured Northern Europe in 1999 to crowds of women—*The Full Monty* (1997) writ large, even though some female spectators found the reversal of subject positions far from easy, rather like women who find it hard "to date a guy that is prettier and better maintained than me." For those who could face such things, straight male pole dancers were also available (Barham 1985; Burke 1999; Dyer 1992: 104; Harari 1993; Jenkins 1998: 92; Smith 2002; Rich 2006; Santer 2007).

Such changes are referenced in the commodity form. In the mid-1980s, Calvin Klein caused a sensation with the first scopic ad campaign using the sculpted male form to sell briefs across magazines and billboards, an emergent discourse associated with such photographers as Bruce Weber and Herb Ritts. The International Male catalog from Southern California made postcoital languor and precoital tumescence into market niches. Mesh V Bodywear is underwear modeled on the condom, a form of gentle armature that combines lightweight packaging with intense visibility. And by late 1995, Calvin Klein underwear advertisements featured a sexually aroused model (Crowe 2007; Miller 1998). Underwear for men has recently expanded to incorporate "action bikinis" and "athletic strings," some complete with condom pockets in the waistband and "sling support" to emphasize genitals. Worldwide sales of men's grooming products reached $7.3 billion in 2002, accounting for 15% of all beauty products sold, and increased by an annual average of 5.7% between 1997 and 2005. In 2002, *American Demographics* claimed "baby-boomer" men allocated $26,420 a year to "youth-enhancing products and services," and women just under $3,000 a year more, while both sexes devoted almost an hour a day to grooming (Euromonitor 2006; Weiss 2002; McCasland 2003). In 2004, US men spent $65 billion on fashion and grooming. That year, AC-Nielsen issued *What's Hot Around the Globe: Insights on Growth in Personal Care*. A study of fifty-six countries predicated on the existence of metrosexuality, it duly discovered that personal care's key sales growth comprised shower gels, deodorants, blades, and moisturizers—to men. Euromonitor predicted a 50% expansion in the male skin-care market between 2001 and 2006, and Datamonitor expected a 3.3% annual increase in sales to men through 2008. In 2005, L'Oréal, with its new Men's Expert line, saw a 49% growth in sales to men over the previous year. For the first time, men's antiperspirants outsell women's in the United States. Body sprays targeted at boys aged 10 and up form part of "age compression" via the sexualization of men across age groups. Gillette's TAG Body Spray for Men was promoted via an auction on eBay for teenage boys to buy a date with Carmen Electra, a married celebrity in her thirties, and was soon banned in several high schools because boys used the body spray instead of showering after phys-ed class. Hair-color sales to young males increased by 25% in the five years from 1998. In 2003, men's hair-care expenditure grew by more than 12% in the United States, to $727 million. "The Micro Touch" was released as the first "unwanted hair" application for men, organized around a metrosexual campaign; and a sample of college students disclosed that over 60% engaged in depilation to remove hair below the neck—an entirely new phenomenon (Trebay 2004; "ACNielsen" 2004; Lindsay 2005; Burbury 2003; Datamonitor 2004; Manning-Schaffel 2006; Beatty 2004; Neff 2005; Farran 2007; Euromonitor 2004; Postrel 2003: 29; Neff 2007; Fenley 2004; Boroughs et al. 2005).

Mid-town Manhattan now offers specialist ear-, hand-, and foot-waxing, with men comprising 40% of the clientele. Such sites provide pedicures and facials to the accompaniment of cable sports and Frank Sinatra, using manly euphemisms to describe procedures—coloring hair becomes "camouflage," and manicures are "hand detailing." Both Target and Saks Fifth Avenue opened men's cosmetics sections for the first time in the new century, aimed principally at straights, while Lancôme announced eight differences between men's and women's skins, necessitating new products. Meanwhile, apologists for Bush Minor's economic record pointed to officially undercounted new jobs in spas, nail salons, and massage parlors as signs of national economic health. Truly a digitally led recovery from recession. And men are now the fastest-growing part of the jewelry market, up to 10% of sales thanks to executive masculinity. In 2004, Garrad, Georg Jensen, and Cartier all launched comprehensive selections of male jewels (Stein 1999; Burstyn 1999: 21; Hall 1999; Lemon 1997; Weiss 2002; Postrel 2004; Flynn 2005).

The metrosexual's ecumenicism has encouraged white-oriented companies to target Latin@s and blacks for the first time. In Britain, a metrosexual even appears in diaper commercials—not to reflect the division of child-care labor but to appeal to women consumers. The United States sees 80% of grooms actively involved in planning weddings, as never before, and devoting vast sums to their own appearance thanks to advice from such services as groomsonline.com. Banana Republic, a chain dedicated to casual-wear clothing, recently found that its catalog contained items worn as business attire. It proceeded to establish partnerships with Credit Suisse,

Home Box Office, and First Boston, setting up ministores in these enter-prises to dispense free drinks and fashion advice. Even Microsoft, seem-ingly as impregnable to high style as a Roger Moore James Bond film, saw its campus populated by Prada as the century turned. Macho magazines in Britain, such as *Loaded,* were forced by audience targeting to supple-ment their hitherto-exclusive appeal to antifeminist, lager-swilling brutes by interpellating "the caring lad in cashmere" as well ("ideavillage's" 2004; Benady 2004; Caplan 2005; Dube 2007; Florida 2002; Robinson 2005).

The area of plastic, cosmetic, or aesthetic surgery is a particularly not-able part of this transformation. Records of Hindu facial surgery date from 600 B.C.; Roman gladiatorial wounds led to reconstructions; and rhinoplas-ties were undertaken in India from A.D. 1000. All such surgeries became more bearable and common with the appearance of antisepsis and anes-thesia during the 19th century. In the United States, cosmetic surgery was associated with modifying immigrant features, which were often articu-lated to nasal types. Debates over enhancement versus reconstruction saw plastic surgery marginalized within medicine, until the hand of the state made itself known: contemporary reconstructive surgery began as a means of treating male World War I veterans, who were motivated by the desire for economic autonomy. Following a return to disrepute and a debate over the right to self-invention, the cosmetic surgeon reemerged as a miracle worker in World War II, only to experience low esteem again with the peace, amid Papal condemnations of vanity. With the exception of military casualties, from that point to the 1960s, most US surgeons reported treating women and a few gay men, but they privately pathologized and ridiculed their patients. A binary was drawn between function and aesthetics, leading to a series of powerful debates from the 1920s that generally concluded with some level of agreement about a right to self-improvement. Certain men *were* undergoing procedures at this time to improve their marketability—a study of 50- to 60-year-old salesmen in 1961 disclosed that their incomes increased after face-lifts. And the gendered and sexualized nature of the cosmetic binary began to shift when the *New York Times* declared "Cos-metic Lib for Men" in 1977 (the year after Clinique introduced its first male skin-care product). Three years later, *Business Week* encouraged its readers to obtain "a new—and younger—face." The 1990s and since have seen the shop well and truly set up. *Clinics in Plastic Surgery* dedicated a special issue to men in 1991, and latter-day meetings of professional associations have been likened by the *Annals of Plastic Surgery* to "gender-bending," with more and more male clients seeking what is politely euphemized as "body contouring." Metrosexuality is welcomed as good business sense, as men "stream into the salons like lemmings falling over cliffs" to undergo a "wallet biopsy." The industry's $12 billion in annual revenue attracts surgeons who lack formal training in the area. Over the past five years, new entrants have departed obstetric wards, dermatological suites, and emergency rooms in search of less risky and more lucrative places to cut, avoiding costly insurance premiums and anticipating huge paydays in the process (Heyes 2007: 18; Crawley 2006: 53–54; Feldman 2004; Burton et al. 1995; Morain 2003; Kathy Davis 2003: 123; Holliday and Sanchez Taylor 2006: 186; Collison 2006; Salzman et al. 2005: 92; Singer 2006).

As noted in the Introduction to this book, Bob Dole parlayed a political career representing Kansas into lucrative endorsements for Visa and Viagra after a face-lift made him telegenic, while John Kerry is rumored to have a Botox habit, and US military recruiters highlight free or cheap elective plastic surgery for uniformed personnel and their families (with the policy alibi that this permits doctors to practice their art). The American Academy of Cosmetic Surgery figures indicate that more than six thousand five hundred men had face-lifts in 1996. In 1997, men accounted for a quarter of all such procedures, and the following year, straight couples were frequently scheduling surgery together (up 15% in a year). Between 1996 and 1998, male cosmetic surgery increased 34%, mostly because of liposuction, and 15% of plastic surgery in 2001 was performed on men (Rosen 2004; "Force" 2004; "Marketplace" 1999; Avni 2002). Data from the American Academy of Facial Plastic and Reconstructive Surgery (2002) disclose a 316% increase in hair transplants from 1999 to 2001. Youthfulness is a key motivation for 50% of women and 40% of men, and dating for 5% of women and 10% of men (Miller 2002).

The top five male surgical areas (breasts, hair, nose, stomach, and eyelids) were not selected two decades ago. In 2002, US men had more than 800,000 cosmetic procedures. Figures from the American Academy of Cosmetic Surgery (2003) and the American Society for Aesthetic Plastic Surgery (2002) are striking in the popularity of Botox and collagen procedures, chemical peels, and hair surgery to conceal signs of aging, and liposuction to reduce body weight, with similar rates for men and women (such numbers bizarrely tend to exclude circumcision and dental work [Holliday and Cairnie 2007: 58]). Over one million procedures were performed on men in 2003, and the American Society of Plastic Surgeons (2005b, 2006) saw a 44% surge in men seeking treatment in the five years to 2005 to 1.2 million, including climbs of 156% for "tummy tucks" and 233% for Botox injections, alongside dramatic expansion to incorporate Latin@s, African Americans, and Asians into the fold. China's cosmetic surgery numbers are being swelled by the appearance of the "urban pretty man." Estimates from Canada suggest that men composed 20% of clients in 2006, up from 5% in 2001, while the British Association of Aesthetic Plastic Surgeons experienced an 80% increase in male clients in 2005. That year brought a study from the American Society of Plastic Surgeons (2005a) that found that three-quarters of men favored surgery for themselves or others, and the year also saw the launch of the first magazine dedicated to patients, *New Beauty*. Cable television, which the society said had helped the shift to men, was offering the graphic drama *Nip/Tuck* and the reality show *Plastic Surgery: Before and After*, where participants had a chance to release themselves from their bodily biographies. When an independent commission of inquiry into what went wrong on September 11 reported four years after the attacks, evaluating the federal government's manifold failings before, during, and since, the bourgeois media subordinated coverage of these findings to trends in cosmetic surgery (Jameson 2006; Salzman et al. 2005: 95; Collison 2006; "As Another" 2007; "Bankers" 2006; Goldenberg 2005; Mitchell 2005; Engelberg 2005).

The new man is being governed as well as commodified. What the *New York Times* (Tien 1999) calls "the rising tide of male vanity" has real costs to conventional maleness. The middle-class US labor market now sees wage discrimination by beauty amongst men as well as women, and major corporations frequently require executives to tailor their body shapes to company *ethoi*. There is actually an income differential based on ugliness versus beauty that is more discriminatory for men than women: men who are deemed ugly lose 9% in salary, whereas ugly women lose 6%. Conversely, the beauty premium for men is 5% as opposed to 4% for women ("To Those That Have" 2007: 54). Fourteen percent of female patients versus 30% of male indicate that they wish to undergo cosmetic surgery for reasons connected to the workplace, a clear sign that men perceive age discrimination on the job. The American Society of Plastic Surgeons (2001) advises that male clients seek, *inter alia*, "a professional edge," and plasticsurgery.org (2007) warns men that "society places a high value on looking young and fit" via "a more balanced nose, a rejuvenated face, a trimmer waistline," which are worth it despite the lack of insurance to cover costs. Men even favor experimental "abdominal etching," which promises "a muscular, rippled appearance." Canadian cosmetic surgeons note a shift away from the desire for youthfulness as part of vanity: it is now more a matter of job protection. "Grooming" was deemed vital to business success by 89% of US men in 2003, and a 2004 ExecuNet (http://www.execunet.com) survey of senior corporate leeches aged between 40 and 50 saw 94% complaining of occupational discrimination by age. One-third of all graying male US workers in 1999 colored their hair to counter the effect of aging on their careers to avoid what is now known as the "silver ceiling." Studies by the hair-dye company Clairol reveal that men with gray hair are perceived as less successful, intelligent, and athletic than those without. Meanwhile, abetted by a newly deregulated ability to address consumers directly through television commercials, Propecia, a drug countering male hair loss, secured a 79% increase in visits by patients to doctors in search of prescriptions. Hair transplants were said to have grown 61% between 1993 and 1995. Similar trends are evident in the rise of tanning salons. In 1977, there were none; now there are over fifty thousand, with annual revenue in excess of $5 billion and men catching up to women amongst participants. Men's alibi is that indoor tanning is akin to muscle building. As the delightful authors of US marketing's major study of metrosexuality cheerfully avow in explaining why men must strive like this, "we're living in an era of infinite choice" (Hamermesh and Biddle 1994; Wells 1994; Freudenheim 1999; Rosen 2004; Salzman et al. 2005: 36, 60; Weiss 2002; Ahmed 2003; Herman 2006; Holliday and Cairnie 2007: 59; Vannini and McCright 2004: 310–11, 322–23).

While the burden of beauty remains firmly on women, a new trend is unmistakable: the surveillant gaze of sexual evaluation is being turned to men as never before. The gaze is simultaneously *internalized*, as a set of concerns, and *externalized*, as a set of interventions. South Korean figures from 2005 indicated that 86% of men aged 25 to 37 saw career advantages from looks, and 56% were dissatisfied with their appearance (Johne 2006). In 1997, 43% of US men up to their late 50s disclosed dissatisfaction with their appearance, compared to 34% in 1985 and 15% in 1972. *Playgirl* magazine's male centerfolds have undergone comprehensive transformations over the past quarter-century: the average model has lost 12 pounds of fat and gained 25 pounds of muscle. GI Joe dolls of the 1960s had biceps to a scale of 11.5 inches, an average dimension. In 1999, their biceps were at a scale of 26 inches, beyond that of any recorded bodybuilder. And when Barbie's boytoy Ken was re-released by Mattel in 2006, his musculature had increased as part of a makeover. Similar changes have happened to other dolls, such as *Star Wars* figures. These shifts signify a wider cultural shift. The psy-function now refers to "muscle dissatisfaction" among male TV viewers, while dietary supplements have migrated from the gym to the office in search of all-day amino acids. The new century has brought reports of a million men diagnosed with body dysmorphic disorder; psychiatrists have invented the "Adonis Complex" to account for vast increases in male eating and exercise disorders, with 25% of US eating problems reported by men—as disclosed by pharmacorps-funded research. The National Comorbidity Survey Replication disclosed that anorexia affected 0.9% of women and 0.3% of men, and bulimia 1.5% versus 0.5%, while Euromonitor reported that young men were using steroids in unprecedented numbers, coded as "Metrodrug." Not surprisingly, hypermasculinist citadels such as the Gold's Gym franchise were beavering away at their image at just this time to reach out and interpellate men hitherto intimidated by muscularity (Agliata and Tantleff-Dunn 2004; "Madeover Ken" 2006; Pope et al. 2000; Esposito 2006; Gellene 2007; Family & Friends Action Council 2007; Euromonitor 2006; Thomaselli 2007).

Clearly, we should not assume that progressive change is bundled with metrosexuality. Reifying all is not a good substitute for reifying some, while the $8 billion spent each year on cosmetics could put the children of the world through basic education across four generations. Schwarzenegger's shoes may just register an "upgrade" of service-sector capitalism. Significantly, the *Metrosexual Guide* ends with a description of "The Metrosexual Mind-Set: The Bottom Line," which is: "Your life is your own creation." Metrosexuals are neoliberal subjects governing themselves as new aesthetes generated from shifting relations of power and finance. They are "more responsible for creating their own individuality than ever before," in the words of Britain's Cosmetic Toiletry and Perfumery Association Director-General (Snyder 2006; Sardar and Davies 2002: 82; Flocker 2003: xi, xiii–xiv, 169; McRobbie 2002: 100; Flower 2004; McCarthy 2004).

In related developments, the "pink dollar" has become more and more significant. Gay media have long circulated information to businesses about the spending power of their putatively childless, middle-class readership. One magazine's slogan in advertising circles was "Gay Money, Big Market; Gay Market, Big Money"; another said that its readers "live as well as the Joneses, [but] we live a damn sight better." *Advertising Age* published occasional reports on gay marketing from the 1970s, and the *Advocate* pioneered market research in 1977 which disclosed that erotic/pornographic material needed to be marginalized, and production standards raised, in order to coax heteronormative companies to advertise. The exclusion of sexual material, and new investment in high style, attracted Seagram's and Simon & Schuster, *inter alia,* and advertising revenue doubled between 1990 and 1992. By 2006, the gay media received $276 million in advertising revenue, with almost two hundred *Fortune 500* companies amongst their customers. The mainstream media eventually took notice as well, and 1997 saw *Advertising Age's* front-cover headline emblazoned with "Big Advertisers Join Move to Embrace Gay Market." The *New York Times* made no references to queerness in its business pages throughout the 1970s, and male-oriented pieces appeared only occasionally in the 1980s. But news coverage tripled during 1992–93 and has remained significant, if inconsistent. During the 1990s, Hyundai began appointing gay-friendly staff to dealerships; IBM targeted gay-run small businesses; Subaru advertisements on buses and billboards had gay-advocacy bumper stickers and registration plates coded to appeal to queers; Polygram's classical-music division introduced a gay promotional budget; Miller beer supported Gay Games '94; Bud Light was a national sponsor to the 1999 San Francisco Folsom Street Fair, "the world's largest leather event"; and Dick Cheney's daughter Mary devised domestic-partner benefits for Coors, supposedly counteracting its antigay image of the past. Advertising expenditure in lesbian publications doubled in the period 1997–2001. On television, we have seen Ikea's famous US TV commercial showing two men furnishing their apartment together, Toyota's male car-buying couple, two men driving around in a Volkswagen searching for home furnishings, and a gay-themed Levi Strauss Dockers campaign, while 2003 Super Bowl commercials carried hidden gay themes that advertisers refused to encode openly. (Known as "gay window advertising" or "encrypted ads," these campaigns are designed to make queers feel special for being "in the know" while not offending simpleton straights.) The spring 1997 US network TV season saw twenty-two queer characters across the prime-time network schedule, and there were thirty in 2000—clear signs of niche targeting. Although gay activists claim that the network share deteriorated to 2% of characters (fifteen people) in 2006–7, cable became a mainstay of gay representation (thirty-five in drama in that year), especially on reality shows; and daytime soaps were also providential, albeit mostly featuring white men. In 2004, Viacom announced that MTV was developing a queer cable network. Investors were animated by $400 billion of consumer power, not cultural politics. Within three years, Logo was in over 27 million homes. In 2007, the Here! Network was on many cable systems and could also be watched via video-on-demand and through Internet TV providers. In the on-line domain, 1999 brought the first gay initial public offering, while gay and lesbian Web sites drew significant private investment. By 2005, the Web sites gay.com and planetout.com had established themselves as the biggest queer-affinity portals. On the one hand, they provided informational services desired by readers. On the other, they provided surveillance services desired by marketers. This combination attracted over 8 million registered visitors and such major advertisers as United Airlines, Citibank, Procter & Gamble, Chase, Miller Brewing, CBS, and Johnson & Johnson. Repeated market surveys sponsored by gay-friendly groups showed that queers were not more urban than rural and had consumer tastes across the board. Meanwhile, a five-year study of 3,000 professionals working for *Fortune 500* companies indicated that employees of gay managers were one-third more satisfied at work than other people (Alsop 1999a; Alsop 1999b; Fejes 2002; Rawlings 1993; Elliott 1998; Mecca 2002; Wilke 2003; Lacher 2007; Sender 2005: 126–28, 111; Ragusa 2005: 658, 655; O'Connor 1997; Bank 1999: B1; Hampp 2007; Mackie 2006; Jensen 2006; Urban 2006; Campbell 2005; "Study Reveals" 2006; Hampp 2007; "Gay/Lesbian Consumer" 2005; Carter and Elliott 2004; Friedman 2006). As Marx said, while a "commodity appears, at first sight, a very trivial thing, and easily understood . . . it is, in reality, a very queer thing" (1987: 76).

Television

EXTREME MAKEOVER APPLICATION
Deadline—Saturday, March 31, 2006
MAKING AN EXTREME VIDEO

Have Fun! If you are not having fun making the video, we are not having fun watching it.

Make sure whoever is filming you is someone you are comfortable with. Do not read from cards or over rehearse what you want to say. Just talk to us like a friend.

Making the video:

- Get creative and grab our attention immediately! Introduce yourself and tell us a bit about you. We get tons of applications, so try to stand out and think outside the box. Why do you deserve the *Extreme Makeover*? How will it change your life? Do you have any events coming up in the next few months that make this the perfect time?
- Go from head to toe explaining what you would like changed. You do not need to know the exact procedure, just tell us what you don't like about your current features.
- Get good close ups, about 30 seconds, of your face, profile and body. Also include close ups of any areas of concern that may be hard to see like teeth, complexion, scars etc. For your teeth, please get a good 10 seconds smiling from the front with teeth showing, bite closed. Then another 10 seconds in the same position from the side.
- Please watch the video after to make sure the lighting is good and we can accurately see your problem areas. The light should be shining on your face and not behind you where it may cause shadows. Also check for the sound quality.

—Application to appear on ABC's *Extreme Makeover*

They call themselves the Fab Five. They are: An interior designer, a fashion stylist, a chef, a beauty guru and someone we like to call the "concierge of cool"—who is responsible for all things hip, including music and pop culture. All five are talented, they're gay and they're determined to clue in the cluttered, clumsy straight men of the world. With help from family and friends, the Fab Five treat each new guy as a head-to-toe project. Soon, the straight man is educated on everything from hair products to Prada and Feng Shui to foreign films. At the end of every fashion-packed, fun-filled life-style makeover, a freshly scrubbed, newly enlightened guy emerges.

—http://www.bravotv.com/Queer_Eye/about

The application to appear on *Extreme Makeover* excerpted above performs dual tasks. At one level, it is what it says it is—a recruitment device. As such, it is unreliable and rapidly becoming outmoded. In its second, covert, role—surveillance—it is a neatly targeted way of securing data about viewers that can be sold to advertisers, achieved under the demotic sign of outreach and public participation via plastic surgery for the soldier who thinks his career is being held back by ugliness and for the fast-food manager who wants to advance his job prospects (Heyes 2007: 25). Which is where we meet *Extreme Makeover*'s cousin in surveillance, commodification, and governmentality—*Queer Eye for the Straight Guy* (QESG). It began in the northern summer of 2003 on the Bravo network[3] and quickly became a crucial metrosexual moment and the station's highest-ever rated hour, with 3.35 million viewers by the third episode. Parodies followed on *Saturday Night Live* and *MAD TV*, while Comedy Central offered *Straight Plan for the Gay Man* (Nutter 2004; Heller 2006: 3; Westerfelhaus and Lacroix 2006: 429). Simpson (2004) dubbed it *Metrosexuality: The Reality TV Show*, and the program avowed that it taught "the finer points of being a 'metrosexual'" (http://www.bravotv.com/Queer_Eye//Episodes/207/). In the winter of its first season, survey research proclaimed that more men went shopping with male friends the day after watching QESG episodes than at any other point in the week (Cohan 2007: 178).

What are its origins, beyond unfurling commodity interest in the queer dollar? QESG is part of the wider reality-television phenomenon, a strange hybrid of cost-cutting devices, game shows taken into the community, *cinéma vérité* conceits, scripts written in postproduction, and *ethoi* of Social Darwinism, surveillance, and gossip—bizarre blends of "tabloid journalism, documentary television, and popular entertainment." Makeover programs such as QESG take economically underprivileged people and offer them a style they cannot afford to sustain. QESG speaks to the responsibility of each person to master their drives and harness their energies to get better jobs, homes, looks, and families. It is significant that US reality TV has offered queer characters on over a dozen shows *and* that the entire genre is suffused with deregulatory *nostra* of individual responsibility, avarice, possessive individualism, hypercompetitiveness, and commodification, played out in the domestic sphere rather than the public world (Ouellette and Murray 2004: 8–9; Hill 2005: 15; Banet-Weiser and Portwood-Spacer 2006; Heller 2006; Bennett 2006: 408; Deery 2006: 161; Fraiman 2006). Bravo paired *QESG* with *Boy Meets Boy*, another gay reality show, on Tuesday evenings, thereby branding itself as an alternative to its corporate parent (Cohan 2007: 177). This allowed the network a certain chic quality "as the unofficial gay network" (DeJesus 2008: 46).

The genre derives from transformations in the political economy of TV, specifically deregulation. When veteran newsman Edward R. Murrow addressed the Radio-Television News Directors Association in 1958 (recreated in George Clooney's 2005 docudrama *Goodnight, and Good Luck*), he used the metaphor that television must "illuminate" and "inspire," or it would be "merely wires and light in a box." In a speech to the National Association of Broadcasters three years later, John F. Kennedy's Chair of the Federal Communications Commission (FCC), Newton Minow, called US TV a "vast wasteland" (Murrow 1958; Minow 1971). Murrow and Minow were urging broadcasters to show enlightened Cold War leadership, to prove that the United States was not the mindless consumer world that the Soviets claimed. The networks should live up to their legislative responsibilities and act in the public interest by informing and entertaining, going beyond what Minow later called "white suburbia's Dick-and-Jane world" (Minow 2001). The networks responded by doubling the time devoted to news each evening, and TV quickly became the dominant source of current affairs (Schudson and Tiofft 2005: 32). But twenty years later, Reagan's FCC head, Mark Fowler, celebrated reduction of the "box" to "transistors and tubes." He argued in an interview with *Reason* magazine that "television is just another appliance—it's a toaster with pictures" and hence in no need of regulation apart from ensuring its safety as an electrical appliance.[4]

Minow's and Fowler's expressions gave their vocalists instant and undimmed celebrity (Murrow already had such celebrity as the most-heralded audiovisual journalist in US history). Minow, named "top newsmaker" of 1961 in an Associated Press survey, was on TV and radio more than any other Kennedy official. The phrase "vast wasteland" has even— irony of ironies—provided raw material for the wasteland's parthenogenesis, as the answer to questions posed on numerous game shows, from

Jeopardy! to *Who Wants to Be a Millionaire?* The "toaster with pictures" is less celebrated but has been efficacious as a slogan for deregulation across successive administrations, and it remains in *Reason's* pantheon of libertarian quotations, alongside Reagan and others of his ilk. Where Minow stands for public culture's restraining (and ultimately conserving) function for capitalism, Fowler represents capitalism's brooding arrogance, its neoliberal lust to redefine use value via exchange value. Minow decries Fowler's vision, arguing that television "is not an ordinary business" because it has "public responsibilities" (Minow and Cate 2003: 408, 415). But Fowler's phrase has won the day, at least to this point. Minow's lives on as a recalcitrant moral irritant, not a policy slogan.

Fowler has had many fellow-travelers. Both the free-cable, free-video social movements of the 1960s and '70s, and the neoclassical, deregulatory intellectual movements of the 1970s and '80s, imagined a people's technology emerging from the wasteland of broadcast television, as portapak equipment, localism, and unrestrained markets provided alternatives to the numbing nationwide commercialism of the networks. The social-movement vision imagined a change occurring overnight; the technocratic vision imagined it in the "long run." One began with folksy culturalism, the other with technophilic futurism. Each claimed it in the name of diversity, and they even merged in the depoliticized "Californian ideology" of community media, much of which quickly embraced market forms. Neither formation engaged economic reality. But together they established the preconditions for unsettling a cozy, patriarchal, and quite competent television system that had combined, as TV should, what was good for you and what made you feel good, all on the one set of stations—that is, a comprehensive service. Such a service was promised by the enabling legislation that birthed and still governs the FCC, supposedly guaranteeing citizens that broadcasters serve "the public interest, convenience and necessity," a tradition that began when CBS set up a radio network in the 1920s founded on news rather than its rival NBC's predilection for entertainment (Mullen 2002; Barbrook and Cameron 1996; Scardino 2005).

In place of the universalism of the old networks, where sports, weather, news, life style, and drama programming had a comfortable and appropriate frottage, highly centralized but profoundly targeted consumer networks emerged in the 1990s that fetishized life style and consumption *tout court* over a blend of purchase and politics, of fun and foreign policy. Reality television, fixed upon by cultural critics who either mourn it as representative of a decline in journalistic standards or celebrate it as the sign of a newly feminized public sphere, should frankly be understood as a cost-cutting measure and an instance of niche marketing. The make-over varietal has a special focus on dramatic aesthetic transformations (Heyes 2007). The Kaiser Foundation's 2006 study of US reality TV (Christenson and Ivancin 2006) drew on encounters with television producers and health-care critics and professionals to get at the dynamics of how medicine and related topics are represented in the genre. It found that US reality TV, for all its populist alibis, constructs professional medical expertise as a kind of magic that is beyond the ken of ordinary people—and certainly beyond their engaged critique. Again and again, whether it's plastic surgeons or pediatricians, miraculous feats are achieved by heroic professionals who deliver ignorant and ugly people from the dross of the everyday, transcending what off-screen primary-care physicians have been able to do for them. For all the world reincarnated Ben Caseys, time after time these daring young doctors provide astonishing breakthroughs. The foundation's study could find nothing in US reality TV even remotely critical of this model of what "*they* can do." The representation of expertise deemed it ungovernable other than by its own caste. Such a landscape is not about powerful citizen-viewers; it's about deities in scrubs. The use of the commodity form to promise transcendence through the national health-care system, as embodied in patriarchal medicine, is sickening. And as with makeovers of houses and personal style, it offers a transcendence of the grubby working and lower-middle classes that viewers cannot afford to emulate. Helpless and ugly, patient bodies testify to the surgeons' skill (Heyes 2007: 19) as per fashion consultants confronting a lack of savoir-faire. Enter *Queer Eye*.

With excellent ratings, a soundtrack album that topped electronic-music sales charts, and revenue from many parts of the world via both export and format sales, *QESG* won an award from the Gay & Lesbian Alliance Against Defamation (GLAAD) and an Emmy for Outstanding Reality Program in 2004, and was variously heralded as a mainstream breakthrough text for queers, an exemplification of male vulnerability, the virtue of popular culture in an era of conservatism, *and* the epitome of Yanqui imperialism—the encapsulation of the "ambivalent text" in its allegedly carnivalesque instantiation of "commodity and difference" (Rogers 2003; Hart 2004; Fraiman 2006; Di Mattia 2007; Allatson 2006; Pullen 2007: 194, 207, 210). *Metrosource* places *QESG* in the pantheon of greatest moments of gay television: "it catapulted gay culture into the mainstream" (DeJesus 2008: 46). The American Film Institute nominated *Queer Eye* as its major cultural development for 2003, alongside copyright (Cohan 2007: 178). Some inevitably criticized it for stereotyping, including out Congressman

Barney Frank, while from the other side of politics, the Family Television Council thundered that it appealed to an "element in our culture already earning an advanced degree in Sin Acceptance." Media Research Center maven L. Brent Bozell III (as improbable as his name) called it "The Gay Supremacy Hour" and said, "I want to vomit." NBC, Bravo's network parent, first screened the show in 2003, drawing 6.7 million watchers despite some affiliates declining to screen the show until the middle of the night because of its queerness, leading to a write-in campaign orchestrated by GLAAD. Meanwhile, adherents of straightacting.com opposed the show because it didn't suit their preference for sport-loving, macho gay men, while neoconservatives were sly in their mix of endorsement and critique. Boston Red Sox baseballers who participated insisted they did so only to aid charity, even as they subjected themselves to floral footbaths, waxing, and other procedures. Taboos were under erasure, as per unwanted hair (Berila and Choudhuri 2005; Council quoted in Sender 2006: 132; Dossi 2005; Bozell 2003; "Tell" 2003; Rocchio and Rogers 2007; Clarkson 2005; Skinner 2003; Cometta 2005; Westerfelhaus and Lacroix 2006: 427; Allen 2006).

QESG embodied the ethos of reality TV: originating on cable, an underunionized sector of the industry, with small numbers of workers required for short periods, and production funds derived in part from the producer's credit-card award points (later turned into a marketing point by the card company). These flexible arrangements quickly led to a lawsuit on behalf of a queer star who was dispensed with after two episodes, while those left recognized that "we could be fired at any moment" ("David Collins" 2004; participants quoted in Giltz 2003). There was a furor when the Web site thesmokinggun.com disclosed that the Fab Five were receiving just $3,000 each per episode, with tiny raises and none of the typical perks of celebrity—they got mere fractions of the tens of thousands of dollars available to minor but unionized characters in broadcast drama. This contingent, flexible labor is textualized in the service-industry world of the genre, which creates "a parallel universe" for viewers (Lewis et al. 2005: 17).

QESG looked for its loser-male makeover targets in the suburban reaches of the tri-state area (New York, New Jersey, and Connecticut), men who needed to be transformed from ordinary guys into hipsters. Cosmopolitan queers descended on these hapless bridge-and-tunnel people, charged with increasing their marketability as husbands, fathers, and (more silently and saliently) employees. The program seemed to compromise its claims of "ideological edginess" in favor of turning "straight men into straight men with better shoes." Change was predicated on affluence (Allen 2006). The program's success can be understood in four ways. First, it represents the culmination of a surge of US television that offers a sanitary, light-skinned, middle-class queer urban world of fun, where gays and lesbians are to be laughed with, not at. Their difference is a new commodity of pleasure—safely different from, but compatible with, heteronormativity. Second, it is a sign that queerness is, indeed, a life style of practices that can be adopted, discarded, and redisposed promiscuously—in this case, disarticulated from its referent into metrosexuality. Third, it signifies the professionalization of queerness as a form of management consultancy for conventional masculinity, brought in to improve efficiency and effectiveness, like time-and-motion expertise, total quality management, or just-in-time techniques. And, finally, it indicates the spread of self-fashioning as a requirement of personal and professional achievement through the US middle-class labor force. Even the queer-language games of the show became systems of translation across cultures, while their camp ways showed the power of mainstream containment and a bias toward urban living that offended the self-regard of those who repeatedly laid noisy claim to being "the Heartland" (Weiss 2005; Lacroix and Westerfelhaus 2005; Rasmussen 2006: 812).

In Alexander Kluge's words, capitalism seeks "to designate the spectators themselves as entrepreneurs. The spectator must sit in the movie house or in front of the TV set like a commodity owner: like a miser grasping every detail and collecting surplus on everything" (1981–82: 210–11). And commodities were central to the secular transcendence of QESG. Viewers were gently led toward a makeover that would meld suburban heteronormativity with urban hipness. A virtual gay parachute corps solved a dilemma for capital: namely, that "white, heterosexual men have been hard to train as consumers" (Sender 2006: 133). QESG undertook "a full-scale humanitarian relief mission: Queers Without Borders" that reached "a virgin makeover-market niche in basic cable" (Chocano 2003). They did so in accord with US self-help literature for men, which focuses on augmenting capital, rather than the women's version, which seeks emotional resolutions to private-public dilemmas (McGee 2005). The QESG Web site offered the following: "FIND IT, GET IT, LOVE IT, USE IT. You've seen us work wonders for straight guys in need of some serious help. Get the same results at home with the same great products, services and suppliers that put the fairy dust in our Fab Five magic wands at 'QUEER EYE'S DESIGN FOR LIFE PRODUCT GUIDE' via www.bravotv.com/Queer_Eye_for_the_Straight_Guy/Shopping_Guide/." Sales were immense (Redden 2007: 150). No wonder Terry Sawyer worries that this implies the status of minstrelsy for queers, via their incarnation as "materialistic vamps" (2003). "Q[ueer]E[ye] isn't really about mutual understanding between homos and heteros. It's about mutual understanding between Bravo/NBC and Diesel . . . and Roberto Cavallia and Ralph Lauren and Via Spiga and Persol and Baskit Underwear," said *New York* magazine, while the *Village Voice* thundered that the "agenda is about tempting guys who have managed to get by without facials and instant tans to become consumers of same," distilling yet concealing "the essence of the infomercial: It meets a need you didn't know you had" (Dumenco 2003; Goldstein 2003). In that sense, a reactionary like Bozell is correct to call the program "almost a parody of product placement, a veritable plug-a-minute infomercial." The problem is that he also derides it for being "drenched in references to raw, perverted homosexual sex" (2003) (anxieties about commercialism encourage the oddest frottage).

The wholesale commodification of male subjectivity witnessed in *QESG* is actually about reasserting and resolidifying very conventional masculinity. The latter has long relied on women's work and queer work, or gay work at least, for its style: women and gay men have always contributed to straight men's looks and professionalism. The question is, has their contribution ever led to a feminization of the public sphere or to recognition of the legitimacy and centrality of queerness? *QESG* was the ultimate in the commodification and governmentalization of queerness as a set of techniques that could be applied and then cast aside. When that is done in the service of retaining conventional straight masculinity, one has to ask how progressive it actually is. And, of course, the program did not last forever, with a huge 2004 ratings slump prior to the inevitable detour of a failing program by focusing on weight issues as well as personal style in an attempt to reinvigorate itself in the fall of 2006, before being cashiered the following year, with Bravo asserting it had "really helped open the closet doors on gays and their presence on television and in popular culture" and claiming credit for featuring queer leads ("Bravo's 'Queer Eye'" 2006; Dossi 2005; Bravo quoted in Rocchio and Rogers 2007; Pullen 2007: 207).

Conclusion

There is a . . . long history of gays and lesbians serving as priestesses, holy fools, minstrels, and other religious-cultural functionaries in pagan, medieval Christian, African, Native American, and Asian cultures. Now their role has been translated: for the worshippers in the church of capitalism, they're the priests of good taste.
—Dan Friedman (2006)

[The metrosexual] was really more a creation of Madison Avenue than a real demographic.
—*Mediaweek* (Tony Case 2006)

In addition to this intrication with commodity fetishism, the trends I have outlined also produced a backlash. Attempts by queer marketers to emphasize the affluence of upper-class, white, male consumers distort average queer wealth and lead to arguments by the American Family Association and Supreme Court Justice Antonin Scalia that there is no need for public subvention of AIDS research and prevention or antidiscrimination protections for queers, despite evidence from the Census and the General Social Survey that same-sex, unmarried people have less income than their straight counterparts (Lenskyj 2005: 287; Ragusa 2005: 656; Guidotto 2006; Fejes 2002: 203–4).

And has there really been a grand change in the prevailing forms of masculinity? Richard Goldstein (2003a) suggests that various testosterone tendencies in popular culture, such as masculinist hip-hop and talk radio, were preconditions for the rapturous turn to the right since September 11, when hostile reactions to women have, in Molly Faulkner-Bond's words, "the cultural upper hand" (2006). *American Enterprise* magazine headlined its post–September 11 cover "Real Men, They're Back," and it has been argued that hypermasculinity became not just patriotic but "a G[rand]O[ld]P[arty] virtue." The *Boston Globe* hails a "menaissance" of "everyday men who wear work boots, change their own oil, get their hair cut at barbershops, and wouldn't have the faintest idea where to get a pedicure or mud mask" (Diaz 2006). When Harold Ford Jr.'s much-trumpeted 2006 campaign for a Senate seat in Tennessee failed, his loss was partly attributed to the winner's critique of him as "an attractive young man," while the *New York Observer* worried that "Obama has more feminine allure than Hillary" (quoted in "Fit to Serve" 2007; Doonan 2007). JWT (previously J. Walter Thompson) announced the 2005 invention of the "ubersexual," who smoked cigars and was tough at the same time as he was sophisticated. This was marked by some, such as Rush Limbaugh, as the defeat of feminism and the triumph of traditional masculinity. ABC News decreed the end of metrosexuality and the need for marketers to reassure men about their masculinity ("Metrosexual Is Out" 2006). So it comes as no surprise that the bourgeois media and the right fixated on John Edwards's haircut during the 2008 election campaign. They did so to illustrate "the effete mannerisms of those who claim to speak for the common man and woman" (Younge 2007).

Doubts were expressed about the "gender-wide" appeal of metrosexuality. *Campaign,* a British magazine covering advertising, accused the industry of focusing on "castrated dweebs." And new forms of dividing up male consumers adopted four categories: "patriarchs" (supposedly 37% of men), "power seekers" (23%), "metrosexuals" (24%), and "retrosexuals" (16%) (Jargon 2006). Much was made of Miller Brewing's 2006 "Men of the Square Table" advertising campaign. It featured "actor" Burt Reynolds, "wrestler" Triple H, and "footballer" Jerome Bettis forming a masculinist counterpublic sphere and an associated "Manlawpedia." Right-wing cultural critics gloried in this riposte to metrosexuality (Mullman 2007). Then there was the 2006 appearance of "fratire . . . a spate of testosterone-fuelled books about belligerence and debauchery, leglessness and legovers, which publishers hope will spawn the male equivalent of chick-lit" (Turner 2006) with such titles as *I Hope They Serve Beer in Hell* (a *New York Times*–certified bestseller), *The Alphabet of Manliness,* and *Real Men Don't Apologise.* Young men rarely buy books in the United States or Britain, so this development promised the prize of new markets (Harkin 2006). The *Scotsman,* which had earlier ranted at the narcissism of the metrosexual because he "likes what he sees reflected in the smoked glass of whatever fashionable bar he is in," decreed 2007 "The Year of the Retrosexual," a direct reaction to QESG's presumption that straight men were flawed, and the *Los Angeles Times* brayed that "*Deadwood* chic" was kicking "the metrosexual look out the saloon doors." The very marketers who had promoted metrosexuality in 2003 predicted its demise (Trew 2002; *Scotsman* 2006; Keeps 2007; Turner 2007). Terence Blacker, a columnist for the *Independent on Sunday,* derided metrosexuality not only as a marketing ploy but also as an ideological alibi for "vanity, self-obsession, stupidity, and a pointless, masturbatory, inward-looking obsession with sex" (2004).

The London *Times's* Andrew Billen (2006) confronted an unexpected dilemma:

What is the precise ratio between machismo and moisturiser that will get me laid?

Tomorrow, I unwisely wrote in these pages two and a bit years ago, belongs to us. The us I referenced were metrosexuals, sophisticated males who took trouble with their appearance, listened to women and suavely followed them to the table in the restaurant. We knew as much about arts, literature and cuisine as football and beer. We were, you know, just gay enough.

As for tomorrow, that, I suppose, must be now. But last week I feared I was wrong. Alarming publishing news from America made me wonder if metrosexuals had lost control of masculinity even before they had properly taken ownership. Condé Nast announced that it was closing *Cargo*, a male shopping magazine that, in the two years since its launch, had become the metrosexual source book. Its death followed those of *Sync*, which spoke to metrosexual man's inner gadget-nerd, and *Vitals*, which sought to bring "the concierge" experience to readers' lives.

His counterpart over at the *Observer Magazine*, Barbara Ellen (2007), argued:

> Just as men have evolved—to suit women, it seems—females have also evolved, to suit women, too. And this new breed of women are not going to take kindly to Metrosexual Man . . . gently insisting that they put down their whiskey tumbler, stop vomiting on the coffee table and get a good night's sleep. It may even come to pass that men begin daydreaming wistfully of a new breed of woman, who is sexy but house-trained, sensitive, and not forever ogling man-bits and so on.

In 2007, *Rolling Stone* magazine, primarily aimed at a youthful male audience, ran advertisements for Canadian Club that picture "YOUR DAD" as he was when young—going fishing, wearing Bee-Gees clothing, and sporting a perm—under the banner "YOUR DAD WAS NOT A METROSEXUAL." For Simpson, though, these trends confirmed the onward march of metrosex:

> The "menaisance" is mendacious. This isn't retrosexual at all, but hummer-sexual—a noisy, overblown, studied and frankly rather camp form of fake masculinity that likes to draw attention to itself and its allegedly old-fashioned "manliness," but tends—like driving an outsized military vehicle in the suburbs—to be a tad counterproductive . . . fetishized, "strapped-on," unsustainable, gas-guzzling masculinity. (2006c)

And the Miller Lite commercial? Sales plummeted by contrast to those of its rivals, and the campaign was ditched. After all, even NASCAR marketers were now promoting their "sport" metrosexually. Noted driver Jeff Gordon told KTLA *Morning News* that "you need to smell good" in an environment of "burning rubber and gasoline." He endorsed wine, watches, and body spray, and colleague Brian Vickers outed himself as metrosexual. Meanwhile, Mark Gauvreau Judge identified as "a conservative Metrosexual." Euromonitor continued to welcome the phenomenon, announcing that "the male shopping giant awakes." *Foreign Policy* magazine nominated the European Union "the world's first metrosexual superpower" because it "struts past the bumbling United States on the catwalk of global diplomacy." And epidemiologists proposed that men with "higher 'femininity' scores" lived longer and healthier lives (Harkin 2006; Ellison 2006; Donahue 2005; Kovacs 2005; Williams 2005; Jennine Lee 2005; Gladden 2005; Judge 2006; Khanna 2004; Euromonitor 2006; Globescan 2005; Hunt et al. 2007). Some of the hype surrounding metrosexuality may be overdrawn, but the numbers signal that the objectification and subjectification of men are on the move. Thanks to commodification and governmentalization, the male subject has been brought out into the bright light of narcissism and purchase in an epochal reordering of desire: "The Metrosexual isn't dead, he's just dead common" (Simpson 2006a).

Of course, national identity comes into play with masculinity in the United States. The period since 2001 in particular has staged this drama via regressive attitudes toward war, toward militarism, toward seeking an "other" who can be blamed for a whole mixture of things involving national security and the state of the economy. We are frequently told that, however unsubtle, there is a justifiable and beneficially unswerving nature to conservative and neoconservative masculinity that has given a certainty and purpose to the country that Clintonian metrosexuality did not, because it was more open, looser, less disciplined. At the same time, it is argued that the world economy would collapse if there were not a continued obsession with consumerism on the part of the citizens and residents of this country, so there's no doubt that the pro- and antimetrosexual forces within marketing and the bourgeois media confront contradictory complexities. Often the most important of these occurs not at the level of geopolitical rhetoric—"we've got to show that we're macho men"—but at the occupational level of advertising rhetoric: "we've got to invent a new neediness, a new nerdiness, a new style." Marketing cannot rest. It never just sits down and says, "Let's look at how old these people are, where they live, what their religion is and their race and gender." It can never be satisfied with empirical research. It has to invent (or uncover) new forms of subjectivity on a regular basis—faster than it would be possible for men to change. It has to make *itself* over.

Like most commodification and governmentalization, metrosexuality has numerous unintended consequences, coalescing with the new neoliberal world of TV to produce the phenomenon of QESG. In the words of the *New York Times*, QESG was a "postmodern television fairy tale" (Finn 2003). *Entertainment Weekly* dubbed it "a full-scale humanitarian relief mission: Queers Without Borders" (Chocano 2003). But its mission began with "that most suburban (and supremely straight) of vehicles, the family-sized SUV" (Lewis 2008: 67). And that grotesque mobile monument to marketing, a hideous scar of consumption, is as environmentally violent as any equivalent vehicle of capitalism. The show and its kind may not be training the populace at large to legitimize queerness (Friedman 2006). But nor are they responsible for the shambolic nature of US TV. For that we must examine three decades of ill-advised deregulation and the subsequent turn away from the idea of the media as a public trust and toward Wall Street share valuations as the one true measure of their success. At the same time, a country of ghost-fearing, god-bothering Yanquis and alien visitors has embraced a new form of superstition: neoliberal queerness, with a hypercommercial, tolerant worldview.

And the metrosexual's sculpted features, chiseled waistlines, well-appointed curves, dreamy eyes, administered hair, and casual threat that do not need traditional machismo to electrify? Like beauty and fitness of all kinds, the years will attenuate them. Age will weary them. But marketers will identify new names, new bodies, new Eros, new Euros. The makeover nation is always up for finding ways to remake itself anew.

CONCLUSION

Where race, creed, and class divide us, health offers the possibility of a common language.
  —David Healy (1997: 1)

[The] language of therapy . . . [is where] frauds, liars and cheats are always trying to escape. Thus President Clinton's spokesman claimed after his admission of his affair with Monica Lewinsky that he was "seeking closure." Like so many mendacious politicians, Clinton felt—as Lord Blair of Kut al-Amara will no doubt feel about his bloodbath in Iraq once he leaves No 10—the need to "move on."
  In the same way, our psycho-babble masters and mistresses—yes, there is a semantic problem there, too, isn't there?—announce after wars that it is a time for "healing."
  —Robert Fisk (2007)

THE EMINENT biologist Steven Rose suggests that "psychocivilised society" is a paradoxical blend of individuation and control, with consumerism pitted against sociality, and their relationship brokered by government (2006: 266). What would it mean to stand *for* sociality, to seek salvation in the secular world, the here and now—without divine intervention, the psy-function, or corporate commodities? Could we experience the self as working art, to be enjoyed through unpaid labor in a way that is not about deferred pleasure, is not tied to income, does not embroil us in commodity relations disguised as medicine, and does not catch young people in a net of adult obsessions? This would return us to Kant's call for self-knowledge as an autotelic drive rather than an instrument, as an end it itself rather than a means toward some endlessly deferred or recurring achievement (Manninen 2006). Such self-knowledge could produce a wisdom that transcended self-control through pharmacology, wage hikes through surgery, or job security through gel. It would be what Kant envisaged as *"man's emergence from his self-incurred immaturity,"* independent of religious, governmental, or commercial direction (1991: 54). It would elude what the *British Medical Journal* derides as "an unwinnable battle against death, pain, and sickness" waged at the price of adequate education, culture, food, and travel, in a world where the more you pay for health, the sicker you feel, and the "social construction of illness is being replaced by the corporate construction of disease" (Moynihan and Smith 2002: 859; Moynihan et al. 2002: 886).

We inhabit a world where flexibility is the mega-sign, and precariousness its flipside; where one person's calculated risk is another's burden of labor; where inequality is represented as a moral outcome. But not everyone succumbs to the faux rhetoric of empowerment that comes with the corporate or governmental makeover required of today's risky economic settings. Consider the developing discourse of casualized workers, of flexible labor renaming itself as the Precariat/précaires/precari@s/precari and going under the signs of "San Precario" and "Our Lady of the Precariat," who guard the spirit of the "flashing lights of life." The movement embodies a new style, a new identity, formed from young, female, foreign workers within the culture industries, services, and the knowledge sector, struggling for security against the impact of neoliberalism (Foti 2005). Since 2001, the Euromayday Network has organized Precariat parades in twenty European cities by "contortionists of flexibility . . . high-wire artists of mobility . . . jugglers of credit," along with apparitions by San Precario to protect his children against evil bosses ("Sign the Call!" 2006). In 2004, a group protested a new supermarket in Milan. In 2005, San Precario appeared in the form of a worker uniformed and supplicant on his knees, with a neon sign on his head. Participants note the instability of life today and hail a new class of sex workers, domestic servants, and creators at their Web site, http://maydaysur.org/. Their manifesto reads:

> Somos precarios y precarias, atípicos, temporales, móviles, flexibles
> Somos la gente que está en la cuerda floja, en equilibrio inestable
> Somos la gente deslocalizada y reconvertida. (quoted by Raunig 2004)
> [We are the precariat, atypical, temporary, mobile, flexible
> We are the people on the high wire, in unstable equilibrium
> We are the people displaced and made over.][1]

The Precariat suggests a complex connection between "eslóganes de los movimientos sociales, reapropiados por el neoliberalismo" (social-movement slogans reappropriated for neoliberalism). It recognizes that concepts like diversity, culture, and sustainability create spectacles, manage workers, and enable gentrification (Raunig 2004). Similarly, Espai en blanc "afirma que vivimos en la sociedad del conocimiento y en cambio no existen ideas" (affirms that we live in a society of knowledge and change where ideas don't exist) (http://sindominio.net/spip/espaienblanc/). Adbusters and culture jamming work in cognate ways (http://www.adbusters.org/home/.

When the Precariat and culture jammers declare a new "phenomenology of labor," born of a "world horizon of production" (Hardt and Negri 2000: 364), they are reoccupying and resignifying the space of corporate-driven divisions of labor. When bodies like the British Medical Association and the Mental Health Foundation look at the impact of privatizing public services and increased testing and other forms of surveillance on the young in the UK, and note subsequent increases in mental illness (especially ADHD), the psy-function is transcending its prescriptive fetishes and turning to an appropriate form of social etiology (James 2006). Britain's Centre for Economic Performance Mental Health Policy Group may use instrumentalism as its alibi, but the claim that cognitive-behavioral therapy can be more efficient than pharmacological intervention challenges decades of hegemony, setting the scene to broaden the psy-function beyond bottles and taboos (2006). And when the International Labor Organization's World Commission on the Social Dimension of Globalization favors "una globalización justa, integradora, gobernada democráticamente y que ofrezca oportunidades y beneficios tangibles a todo los países y a todas las personas" (a globalization that is just, integrated, democratically governed, and offering opportunities and tangible benefits to all nations and peoples), recognizing the necessity of "un enfoque centrado en las personas" (a focus centered on people) and trusting that "la revolución de las comunicaciones globales acentúa la conciencia de . . . disparidades" (2004: ix, xi) (the revolution in global communications augments consciousness of . . . inequality)—once more, this intervention occurs in the space of risk society, but challenges it, rejecting the fog of moral panics.

The distinguished *Guardian* columnist Gary Younge argues that the "notions of personal reinvention and economic meritocracy that lie at the heart of the American dream are far more powerful and endearing than the kind of class consciousness necessary to redress the imbalance between rich and poor" (2007). The data presented in the Introduction found the US population gambling on gods, gamboling with ghosts, accosting aliens, attracting angels, soliciting souls—and doing so under the seemingly welcome spell of a militaristic and neoliberal clerisy. But that is not the full picture. Beck notes that international issues tend to fuel nationalism: war, work, and immigration (2007). New forms and levels of inequality have arisen, in proportion to exposure to financial globalization and the international division of labor. Many people reject the nation's re-enchantment of its world: across the 1990s, the secular proportion of the US population doubled, to 14%, while the horrors meted out to people by Protestantism were whittling away at its numbers: it ceased to be the country's majority religious sect for the first time in 2005 (Portes and Rumbaut 2006: 308, 310). There continues to be public mistrust of corporate power. Seventy-seven percent of the US population believes that large companies wield too much power, 81% of the middle class realize that corporations operate in the interests of shareholders rather than employees, and 89% think businesses have a collective responsibility for workers and society. A 2006 poll disclosed that 80% consider executives overpaid. The National Election Study and the General Social Survey indicate that opinions on racial and sexual difference, schooling, and public prayer show significant harmonization over time, in a liberal direction (the main exception is abortion). Half the population recognizes the idiocy of involving Christian conservatives in policymaking, while ratings for televangelism are tiny and focused in a few Southern states. The preposterous reallocation of money by pharmacorps away from research and toward marketing has generated a backlash amongst both the medical profession and the public. And then there is environmental politics. The population tends to favor positions espoused by environmental groups over the policies of the Bush Minor administration, and prefers conservation to production as a focus of energy policy by 60% to 29%. A large majority supports policies consistent with the Kyoto Protocol international global-warming treaty on greenhouse-gas emissions, which Minor withdrew from. A majority opposes opening the Arctic National Wildlife Refuge in Alaska to oil exploration and rejects expanded use of nuclear energy. Three-quarters say that the government "should do whatever it takes" to conserve the environment. Over 80% of Yanquis favor reduction of greenhouse-gas emissions, and there is massive support for tax incentives to encourage corporate cleanliness, along with powerful endorsement amongst the youngest school pupils for protecting rainforests (Pew Research Center 2005: 17; DiMaggio 2003; Pew Forum on Religion & Public Life 2006; Wallechinsky 2006; Haste 2004: 420; Swatos 2007: 4964–65; Westcott 2005; "Billion" 2006: 69; Saad 2003; Pew Center for Global Climate Change 2002; Revkin 2003; Pew Forum on Religion & Public Life 2004b; "In the Money" 2007). We have seen that young people are far more cosmopolitan and more internationalist in their perspective than their elders. They recognize the need to transcend the barren anger of nationalism. Over two-thirds of nonsupervisory workers realize that their interests would be served by a more collaborative spirit, by working together in unions—and this is true of more than three-quarters of people aged under 30 (Lake Research Partners 2006). One in four people between 18 and 29 has no religious affiliation, compared with 16% of the total population (Pew Research Center 2006).

These are signs of hope, resources from within and outside the world of the makeover and the intellectual protectionism of US public life. They are signs that self-fashioning can go alongside progressive positions and even "raise questions about the legitimacy of both traditional social divisions *and* contemporary market values," as "'post-traditional' identity" becomes generalized (Sarah Berry 2000: 189). Our agenda as leftists can be set and refined in concert with such opposition to worker flexibility and psy-function script-scribbling. A focus on sites of refusal, where the objects of moral panic turn against the prelates of risk society, must inform debates about the great Yanqui makeover, recognizing the ill effects of a situation where "risk appears to have become a condition in itself rather than a possible preliminary to one" (McHoul and Rapley 2005a: 443).

This book began with the words of James Truslow Adams and his conviction that the "American Dream" characterized its history. Adams was writing during the Depression. He disparaged a focus on national income that did not consider its distribution in the face of "very marked injustice." Echoing the Edwardian Fabian Graham Wallas—and anticipating the Democratic President Lyndon Johnson—he called for the "Dream" to be made real through a "Great Society" that would elevate the population "not merely economically, but culturally." Adams lit on the Library of Congress as an institution that "exemplifies the dream," because it comes "straight from the heart of democracy"—a public entity that serves the population through freely available knowledge. He perorated by quoting an indigent migrant, Mary Antin, who wrote, perched on the steps of the Boston Public Library, that its treasures offered her a new "majestic past" and "shining future" (1941: 410–11, 413–14, 416–17). During the same period, Wallas's former student Walter Lippmann spoke of "a deep and intricate interdependence" that came with "living in a Great Society." It worked against militarism and other dehumanizing tendencies that emerged from "the incessant and indecisive struggle for domination and survival" (1943: 161, 376). Half a century later, Bruno Latour thinks that the interdependence generated by life in a risk society may have a similar effect in shifting us "from a time of succession to a time of co-existence," where historicity and commonality prevail (Latour with Kastrissianakis 2007).

I have sought to explain the implausibility of the American Dream, exposing its ideologues and urging those hailed by it to think again. My wager is that the imbalance can be addressed and that our best hope lies with the skeptical attitudes to religion and positive attitudes to internationalism and solidarity expressed by young people. They may embrace the makeover, but they do so in a knowing and critical way. We do not need more moral panics about popular culture, or additional investments in risk society. We do need to address the inequality brought on by the importation of manufactures, political action against unionism and progressive taxes, and "insider self-dealing" by corporate executives (Krugman 2007). The public attitudes of the early 21st century adumbrated above show that this vision of past and future lies beyond commodification and beyond the psy-function. It resides in a zone of material equality and public culture—an entirely different kind of makeover.

NOTES

Introduction

1. I owe these etymological insights to assistance from Peter Bliss of the University of California, Riverside Library System.

2. "Latin@" and "Chican@" are emergent ways of referring to people without resorting to two ugly forms: sexism and slashes.

3. Of Latin@ and Euro ancestry, Adams grew up in Brooklyn and spent time in Europe. He saw himself as immune to "sectional prejudices," conscious "only of being an American" and aware of "how different an American now is from the man or woman of any other nation" (1941: viii). His book contains grotesque racial distortions (Native Americans had "unstable . . . nervous systems" and "were of a markedly hysterical make-up" [7]) and is blind to the foundational role of enslaved African and all unpaid female labor in the country's emergence.

4. I place shudder quotes around "football," since the use of this word among 4% of the world's population to describe that rather delicate US sport (in which most players are unable to use their feet to manipulate the ball) is touching but laughable.

5. For more such instances, read *D[irect]T[o]C[onsumer] Perspectives,* the marketing magazine that looks to celebrity public relations as an alternative to manifest (honest) advertising.

6. Contemporary media references include Muhammad 2006; Wright and Rosenfeld 2003; Dewan 2000; Wilgoren 2002; A. Berry 2000; "New Guru" 2000; Lloyd 2002; Hendershott 2003; McLemee 2003; Shea 2003; Surowiecki 2004; Muschamp 2004; Barlow 2004; Ortiz 2005.

7. The extreme right has also adopted the term to describe criticisms of human rights abuses by the US military in Iraq (Krauthammer 2004).

Chapter 1

1. The eminent scholar Kurt Danziger was struck when he visited this benighted land by "the tremendous hold that disciplinary loyalties had on social psychologists in North America when compared to their counterparts in some other parts of the world. For us, it really wasn't that important" (Brock 1995).

2. It might be more appropriate to say that pharma *buys* culture rather than sidestepping it—corporations in this sector pay for 60% of compulsory continuing education in US medical schools (Carl Elliott 2004).

3. We should note that such flights of fancy were no stranger than many from our own time, of the type described in this and the next chapter.

4. Such rent-seeking conduct has always been part of the psy-function. Freud was a notable example of someone who sought to undermine more scholarly approaches (Hacking 1995: 44).

5. While youth culture is increasingly commodified, it can, of course, produce counterpublics (Giroux 2000: 13; Dolby 2003: 269).

Chapter 2

1. Ritalin is a registered trademark of Novartis Pharmaceuticals.

2. It would be wrong to assume that such conflicts of interest are unique to the United States, of course. The head of the Australian government's 2007 review of ADHD announced that he saw no ethical dilemmas in being paid by Novartis and Eli Lilly to sit on their advisory boards (Fife-Yeomans 2007)!

3. The DEA designation guarantees good data on levels of prescription, as the government sets an annual quota on the production of Schedule II substances in response to pharmaceutical-industry requests and the amount of sales by pharmacies (Diller 1998: 27).

Chapter 3

1. These pieces were published by Connell as a man. He subsequently transitioned to a woman; hence my mixed nomenclature.

2. I owe the wording and ideas here to Ann McClintock.

3. The title was changed to *Queer Eye* in its third season, when targeted makeovers expanded to include both queers and women.

4. Not surprisingly, Alfred Hitchcock said it earlier and said it better: "Television is like the American toaster, you push the button and the same thing pops up every time" (quoted in Wasko 2005: 10).

Conclusion

1. All translations are my own.

BIBLIOGRAPHY

Abayah, Antonio C. (2004, September 16). "Aimez-Vous Bush?" *Manila Standard.*

Abizadeh, Arash. (2002). "Does Liberal Democracy Presuppose a Cultural Nation? Four Arguments." *American Political Science Review* 96, no. 3: 495–509.

"About Active Citizenship." (2005). http://www/active-citizen.org.uk.

Abramowitz, Alan. (2001). "The Time for Change Model and the 2000 Election." *American Politics Research* 29, no. 3: 279–82.

Abu-Laban, Yasmeen. (2000). "Reconstructing an Inclusive Citizenship for a New Millennium: Globalization, Migration and Difference." *International Politics* 37, no. 4: 509–26.

Abu-Lughod, Lila. (1990). "Shifting Politics in Bedouin Love Poetry." *Language and the Politics of Emotion.* Ed. Catherine Lutz and Lila Abu-Lughod. Cambridge: Cambridge University Press. 24–45.

Accardo, Pasquale J. and Thomas A. Blondis. (2000a). "The Neurodevelopmental Assessment of the Child With ADHD." *Attention Deficits and Hyperactivity in Children and Adults: Diagnosis, Treatment, Management.* 2nd ed. Ed. P. J. Accardo, T. A. Blondis, B. Y. Whitman, and M. A. Stein. New York: Marcel Dekker. 141–61.

———. (2000b). "The Strauss Syndrome, Minimal Brain Dysfunction, and the Hyperactive Child: A Historical Introduction to Attention Deficit Hyperactivity Disorder." *Attention Deficits and Hyperactivity in Children and Adults: Diagnosis, Treatment, Management.* 2nd ed. Ed. P. J. Accardo, T. A. Blondis, B. Y. Whitman, and M. A. Stein. New York: Marcel Dekker. 1–11.

———. (2001). "What's All the Fuss About Ritalin?" *Journal of Pediatrics* 138, no. 1: 6–9.

"ACNielsen: 'Metrosexuals' Drive Growth in Personal Care Products." (2004, June 23). *Retail-Merchandiser.*

Acocella, Joan. (2003, August 18 and 25). "Little People." *The New Yorker:* 138–42.

Adams, James Truslow. (1941). *The Epic of America.* New York: Triangle Books.

"Adornment." (1860, October 27). *Vanity Fair:* 215.

Adorno, Theodor W. (1996). *The Culture Industry: Selected Essays on Mass Culture.* Trans. Gordon Finlayson, Nicholas Walker, Anson G. Rabinach, Wes Blomster, and Thomas

Y. Levin. Ed. J. M. Bernstein. London: Routledge.

"Adult ADHD Self-Report Scale (ASRS-v1.1) Symptom Checklist Instructions." (2004).

Agliata, Daniel and Stacey Tantleff-Dunn. (2004). "The Impact of Media Exposure on Males' Body Image." *Journal of Social and Clinical Psychology* 23, no. 1: 7–22.

Ahmed, Kamal. (2003, January 26). "Britons Swallow Cure-All Drugs." *Observer.*

Airey, Dawn. (2004). "RTS Huw Wheldon Memorial Lecture." Royal Television Society.

Aktan, Gunduz. (2004, May 15). "Denigration and Democratization." *Turkish Daily News.*

Albee, G. W. (1977). "The Protestant Ethic, Sex, and Psychotherapy." *American Psychologist* 32, no. 2: 150–61.

Albright, Jennifer. (2006). "Free Your Mind: The Right of Minors in New York to Choose Whether or Not to Be Treated With Psychotropic Drugs." *Albany Law Journal of Science & Technology* 16: 169–94.

Aldhous, Peter. (2006, April 29). "Do Drug Firm Links Sway Psychiatry?" *New Scientist:* 14.

Alexander, Jeffrey C. (2001). "Theorizing the "Modes of Incorporation": Assimilation, Hyphenation, and Multiculturalism as Varieties of Civil Participation." *Sociological Theory* 19, no. 3: 237–49.

Allan, Stuart. (2002). *Media, Risk and Science.* Buckingham: Open University Press.

Allatson, Paul. (2006). "Making Queer for the United States of Empire." *Australian Humanities Review* 28.

Allen, Brooke. (2005, February 21). "Our Godless Constitution." *The Nation:* 14–20.

Allen, David S. (2001). "The First Amendment and the Doctrine of Corporate Personhood: Collapsing the Press-Corporation Distinction." *Journalism: Theory, Practice and Criticism* 2, no. 3: 255–78.

Allen, Dennis W. (2006). "Making Over Masculinity: A Queer "I" for the Straight Guy." *Genders* 44.

Allen, Terry J. (2007 December). "Warning: Drug Ads Can Make You Sick." *In These Times.*

Alson, Ronald. (1999a, June 29). "But Brewers Employ In-Your-Mug Approach." *Wall Street Journal:* B1.

———. (1999b, June 29). "Cracking the Gay Market Code." *Wall Street Journal:* B1, B4.

Alterman, Eric. (2003). *What Liberal Media? The Truth About Bias and the News.* New York: Basic Books.

Álvarez, Gabriela. (2006, March 30–April 5). "Fino perfil de los metrosexuales." *Mundo Hispanico:* B4.

American Academy of Cosmetic Surgery. (2003). *Estimated Total Number of Patients Treated by All U. S.-Based American Academy of Cosmetic Surgery Members 2002.*

American Academy of Facial Plastic and Reconstructive Surgery. (2002). *2001 Membership Survey: Trends in Plastic Surgery.*

American Academy of Pediatric Dentistry. (2003, March 3). "Partnership to Promote Pediatric Dental Health."

American Dialect Society. (2004, January 13). "2003 Words of the Year."

American Medical Association. (2004, September 11). "Economic Impact of ADHD." *Medical News Today.*

American Political Science Association Task Force on Inequality and American Democracy. (2004). *American Democracy in an Age of Rising Inequality.*

American Society for Aesthetic Plastic Surgery. (2002). *Cosmetic Surgery National Data Bank 2002 Statistics.*

American Society of Plastic Surgeons. (2001, July 12). "Cosmetic Surgery for Men Tops 1 Million, Says American Society of Plastic Surgeons."

———. (2005a, January 24). "Most Men View Cosmetic Plastic Surgery Positively, New ASPS Survey Finds."

———. (2005b). *2005 Gender Quick Facts.*

———. (2006, March 16). "Dramatic Rise in Ethnic Plastic Surgery in 2005."

"The Americano Dream." (2005, July 16). *The Economist*: 8–9.

Amin, Samir. (1997). *Capitalism in the Age of Globalization.* London: Zed.

———. (2003). "World Poverty, Pauperization & Capital Accumulation." *Monthly Review* 55, no. 5: 1–9.

Andersen, Kenneth E. (2005). *Recovering the Civic Culture: The Imperative of Ethical Communication.* Boston: Pearson.

Anguita, Julio and Colectivo Prometeo. (2003). "Washington, Capital de Asiria." *Washington Contra el Mundo: Una Recopilación de Rebelión.org.* Ed. Pascual Serrano. Madrid: Foca. 43–48.

Annan, Kofi. (2003, November 21). Emma Lazarus Lecture on International Flows of Humanity.

Anwar, Yasmin. (2007, March 6). "Use of ADHD Medication Soars Worldwide." University of California Berkeley Press Release.

"APME Requests Pentagon Halt Harassment of Media in Iraq." (2003, November 12). *Associated Press.*

"Are You Living With Adult ADHD?" (2006, October 30). http://strattera.com/index.jsp.

Aristotle. (1963). "Politics." Trans. Benjamin Jowett. *Social and Political Philosophy: Readings from Plato to Gandhi.* Ed. John Somerville and Ronald E. Santoni. New York: Doubleday. 59–100.

Arnett, Peter. (2003, February 14). "You Are the Goebbels of Saddam's Regime." *Guardian.*

Aronowitz, Stanley. (2000). *The Knowledge Factory: Dismantling the Corporate University and Creating True Higher Learning.* Boston: Beacon Press.

Arthurs, Jane. (2004). *Television and Sexuality: Regulation and the Politics of Taste.* Birkenhead: Open University Press.

Asad, Talal. (2005). "Reflections on Laïcité & the Public Sphere." *Items and Issues* 5, no. 3: 1–11.

"As Another Mao-Era Taboo Collapses, New Wealth Buys a Fresh Face." (2007, March 9). *Japanofile.*

Association of Religion Data Archives. (2006). *Quick Stats.* http//:www.thearda.com/quickstats.

"Attention Deficit Hyperactivity Disorder (ADHD)." (2004). *India Parenting.*

Augustine. (1976). *Concerning the City of God Against the Pagans.* Trans. Henry Bettenson. Ed. David Knowles. Harmondsworth: Penguin.

Austria-del Rosario, Llewelyn Muriel. (2006, July 31). "Macho vs. Metro: Meet the Metrosexual." *American Chronicle.*

"An Avalanche of Unnecessary Vetting Set Off by Moral Panic." (2002, September 7). *Independent:* 18.

Avni, Sheerly. (2002, December 18). "The Unkindest Cut." http://www.salon.com.

Ayd, Frank. (1961). *Recognizing the Depressed Patient With Essentials of Management and Treatment.* New York: Grune & Stratton.

Bacevich, Andrew J. (2003). *American Empire: The Realities & Consequences of U.S. Diplomacy.* Cambridge: Harvard University Press.

Bachelor, D. C. (2004). "The Original Metrosexual Quiz." http://www.rooshv.com.

Back, Les, Michael Keith, Azra Khan, Kalbir Shukra, and John Solomos. (2002). "New Labour's White Heart: Politics, Multiculturalism and the Return of Assimilation."

Political Quarterly: 445–54.

"Back to the Beach?" (2005, January 8). *The Economist:* 54–55.

Bacon, David. (2004). "The Political Economy of Immigration Reform." *Multinational Monitor* 25, no. 11.

Banet-Weiser, Sarah and Laura Portwood-Spacer. (2006). "'I Just Want to be Me Again!': Beauty Pageants, Reality Television and Post-Feminism." *Feminist Theory* 7, no. 2: 255–72.

"Bangladesh: Metrosexual Is the Way to Go." (2006, August 14). http://www.fibre2fashion.com.

Bank, David. (1999, September 28). "On the Web, Gay Sites Start to Click." *Wall Street Journal:* B1, B6.

"Bankers Fuel Male Cosmetic Surgery Boom." (2006, September 23). *Independent:* 12.

Barboza, David. (2007, March 4). "The People's Republic of Sex Kittens and Metrosexuals." *New York Times:* 3.

Barbrook, Richard and Andy Cameron. (1996). "The Californian Ideology." *Science as Culture* 6: 44–72.

Barham, S. B. (1985). "The Phallus and the Man: An Analysis of Male Striptease." *Australian Ways: Anthropological Studies of an Industrialised Society.* Ed. Lenore Manderson. Sydney: Allen & Unwin: 51–65.

Barker, Martin. (1999). "Review." *Sociology* 33, no. 2: 224–27.

Barkley, Russell A. (1995). *Taking Charge of ADHD: The Complete, Authoritative Guide for Parents.* New York: Guilford.

Barkley, Russell A., Mareillen Fletcher, Lori Smallish, and Kenneth Fletcher. (2003). "Does the Treatment of Attention-Deficit/Hyperactivity Disorder With Stimulants Contribute to Drug Use/Abuse?" *Pediatrics* 111: 97–109.

"Barnes' Storming." (2005, March 12). *The Economist:* 57.

Barry, Eileen. (2002, May 14). "N.E. Is Leader in Rate of Ritalin Purchases." *Boston Globe:* A1.

"The Battle of the Books." (2007, December 2). *The Economist:* 80–82.

"Battle Stations." (2001, December 10). *The New Yorker.*

Baudelaire, Charles. (1972). *The Painter of Modern Life.* Trans. P. E. Charvet. New York: Viking.

Baudrillard, Jean. (1988). *Selected Writings.* Ed. Mark Poster. Stanford: Stanford University Press.

———. (1999). "Consumer Society." *Consumer Society in American History: A Reader.* Ed. Lawrence B. Glickman. Ithaca: Cornell University Press. 33–56.

Baylor Institute for Studies of Religion and Department of Sociology, Baylor University. (2006). *American Piety in the 21st Century: New Insights to the Depth and Complexity of Religion in the US.*

Beattie, Liza, Furzana Khan, and Greg Philo. (1999). "Race, Advertising and the Public Face of Television." *Message Received: Glasgow Media Group Research 1993–1998.* Ed. Greg Philo. Harlow: Longman. 149–70.

Beatty, Sally. (2004, October 29). "Cheap Fumes: Boys Have Their Reasons to Use Body Sprays." *Wall Street Journal:* A1, A10.

Beauvais, Caroline, Lindsey McKay, and Adam Seddon. (2001). *A Literature Review on Youth and Citizenship.* Ottawa: Canadian Policy Research Networks Inc.

Beck, Ulrich. (2007, July 13). "In the New, Anxious World, Leaders Must Learn to Think

Beyond Borders." *Guardian.*

Beck, Ulrich, Anthony Giddens, and Scott Lash. (1994). *Reflexive Modernization: Politics, Tradition and Aesthetics in the Modern Social Order.* Stanford: Stanford University Press.

Beck, Ulrich. (1999). *World Risk Society.* Cambridge: Polity Press.

———. (2001, November 5). "The Fight for a Cosmopolitan Future." *New Statesman.*

———. (2002). *Sobre el Terrorismo y la Guerra.* Trans. R. S. Cabó. Barcelona: Paidós.

"Behave, or Else." (2004, December 4). *The Economist:* 55.

Belkin, Lisa. (2004, July 18). "Office Messes." *New York Times Magazine.*

Bell, David and Jon Binnie. (2000). *The Sexual Citizen: Queer Politics and Beyond.* Cambridge: Polity Press.

Bellah, Robert N., Richard Madsen, William M. Sullivan, Ann Swidler, and Steven M. Tipton. (1992). *The Good Society.* New York: Alfred A. Knopf.

Benady, David. (2004, August 5). "Playing Fairer With Sex." *Marketing Week:* 26.

Benaim, Daniel, Visesh Kumar, and Priyanka Motaparthy. (2003, April 21). "TV's Conflicted Experts." *The Nation:* 6–7.

Bender, Eve. (2006). "Scare Tactics May Deter Blacks from ADHD Help." *Pyschiatric News* 41, no. 10: 16.

Bendrath, Ralf. (2003). "The American Cyber-Angst and the Real World—Any Link?" *Bombs and Bandwidth: The Emerging Relationship Between Information Technology and Security.* Ed. Robert Latham. New York: New Press. 49–73.

Benhabib, Seyla. (2002). *The Claims of Culture: Equality and Diversity in the Global Era.* Princeton: Princeton University Press.

Bennett, Jeffrey A. (2006). "In Defense of Gaydar: Reality Television and the Politics of the Glance." *Critical Studies in Media Communication* 23, no. 5: 408–25.

Bennett, William J. (1992). *The Devaluing of America: The Fight for Our Culture and Our Children.* New York: Touchstone.

Berila, Beth and Devika Dibya Choudhuri. (2005). "Metrosexuality the Middle Class Way: Exploring Race, Class, and Gender in *Queer Eye for the Straight Guy.*" *Genders* 42.

Berkowitz, Bill. (2003, August 28). "Wounded, Weary and Disappeared." http://tompaine.com.

Berman, S. M., S. Strauss, and N. Verhage. (2000). "Treating Mental Illness in Students: A New Strategy." *Chronicle of Higher Education:* B9.

Bernstein, Jared. (2006). *All Together Now: Common Sense for a Fair Economy.* San Francisco: Berrett-Koehler.

Bernstein, Richard. (2003). "The Fetish of Difference." *The Fractious Nation? Unity and Division in American Life.* Ed. Jonathan Rieder. Assoc. Ed. Stephen Steinlight. Berkeley: University of California Press. 57–66.

Berry, A. (2000). "Leadership in a New Millennium: The Challenge of the 'Risk Society.'" *Leadership and Development Journal* 21: 5–12.

Berry, Sarah. (2000). *Screen Style: Fashion and Femininity in 1930s Hollywood.* Minneapolis: University of Minnesota Press.

Beyers, W. B. (2002). "Culture, Services and Regional Development." *Service Industries Journal* 22, no. 1: 4–34.

"Beyond the Pill." (2007, October 27). *The Economist:* 76.

"Big Business." (2003, September 27). *The Economist:* 64, 67.

Billen, Andrew. (2006, April 6). "Metrosexual, RIP?"

"Billion Dollar Pills." (2007, January 27). *The Economist:* 69–71.

Bitterwaitress.com. "Media Information." (2004, June 16). http://bitterwaitress.com.

Birke, Lynda. (1990, August 18). "Selling Science to the Public." *New Scientist:* 32–36.

Black Youth Project. (2007 February). *The Attitudes and Behavior of Young Black Americans: Research Summary.* Center for the Study of Race, Politics, and Culture, University of Chicago.

Blacker, Terence. (2004, January 7). "Time for Metrosexual Men to Return to the Closet." *Independent on Sunday.*

Blech, Jörg. (2006). *Inventing Disease and Pushing Pills: Pharmaceutical Companies and the Medicalisation of Normal Life.* Trans. Gisela Wallor Hajjar. London: Routledge.

Bloemraad, Irene. (2006). *Becoming a Citizen: Incorporating Immigrants and Refugees in the United States.* Berkeley: University of California Press.

Bloom, S. G. (2000, May 23). "Sex-Free Bliss?" http://www.salon.com.

Blumer, Herbert and Philip M. Hauser. (1933). *Movies, Delinquency and Crime.* New York: Macmillan.

Blumer, Herbert. (1933). *Movies and Conduct.* New York: Macmillan.

Boehlert, Eric. (2002, August 26). "Too Hot to Handle." http://alternet.org.

Bonk, Thomas. (2007, November 14). "PGA's Drug Plan Includes One-Year Ban for First Violation." *Los Angeles Times.*

Bordo, Susan. (1999). *The Male Body: A New Look at Men in Public and in Private.* New York: Farrar, Strauss and Giroux.

Borger, Julian. (2004, June 22). "Democrat Shrink Takes Unflattering Look Into Depths of Bush." *Guardian.*

Borna, Shaheen and James M. Stearns. (2002). "The Ethics and Efficacy of Selling National Citizenship." *Journal of Business Ethics* 37, no. 2: 193–207.

Boscagli, Maurizia. (1992–93). "A Moving Story: Masculine Tears and the Humanity of Televized Emotions." *Discourse* 15, no. 2: 64–79.

Bosse, Eric and Greg Palast. (2003, March 17). "Anybody Using This First Amendment?" http://alternet.org.

Bowman, James. (1993, November 13). "Letters From Washington." *Times Literary Supplement:* 18.

———. (1999, February 12). "Letter From Washington." *Times Literary Supplement:* 15.

Boyle, David. (2003, October 6). "The Syndrome That Became an Epidemic." *New Statesman.*

Bozell, L. Brent. (2003, July 18). "'Queer Eye' for the Straight Girl." http://www.media research.org.

"Bravo's 'Queer Eye' Taking on Weight Issues as Well as Style Problems." (2006, August 21). *Reality TV World.*

Brazao, Dale and Patricia Orwen. (2001a, September 9). "Adult Addiction to Ritalin on the Rise, Say Experts." *Toronto Star.*

———. (2001b, September 9). "A Cautionary Tale, a Bird and a Little Blue Pill." *Toronto Star.*

"Breaking Records." (2005, February 12). *The Economist:* 12–13.

Breggin, P. R. (1994). *Toxic Psychiatry: Why Therapy, Empathy, and Love Must Replace the Drugs, Electroshock, and Biochemical Theories of the "New Psychiatry."* New York: St. Martin's Press.

———. (1998). *Talking Back to Ritalin: What Doctors Aren't Telling You About Stimulants for Children*. Monroe: Common Courage Press.

Breithaupt, Holger and Katrin Weigmann. (2004). "Manipulating Your Mind." *European Molecular Biology Organization* 5, no. 3: 230–32.

Brewer, Paul R., Sean Aday, and Kimberly Gross. (2005). "Do Americans Trust Other Nations? A Panel Study." *Social Science Quarterly* 86, no. 1: 36–51.

Brewis, Alexandra, Karen L. Schmidt, and Mary Meyer. (2000). "ADHD-Type Behavior and Harmful Dysfunction in Childhood: A Cross-Cultural Model." *American Anthropologist* 102, no. 4: 823–28.

———. (2002). "On the Biocultural Study of Children's Hyperactive and Inattentive Behavior." *American Anthropologist* 104, no. 1: 287–89.

Briggs, Asa and Peter Burke. (2003). *A Social History of the Media: From Gutenberg to the Internet*. Cambridge: Polity.

Brimelow, Peter. (1996). *Alien Nation: Common Sense About America's Immigration Disaster*. New York: HarperPerennial.

Brint, Steven. (2001). "Professionals and the 'Knowledge Economy': Rethinking the Theory of Postindustrial Society." *Current Sociology* 49, no. 4: 101–32.

"'British' Is Already Inclusive and Elastic." (2000, October 12). *Independent*: 3.

Broadberry, Stephen and Sayantan Ghosal. (2002). "From the Counting House to the Modern Office: Explaining Anglo-American Productivity Differences in Services, 1870–1999." *Journal of Economic History* 62, no. 4: 967–98.

Brock, Adrian. (1995). "An Interview With Kurt Danziger." *Cheiron Newsletter* 13: 4–9.

Brooke, James (2000, August 6). "Peppery Plea for Tolerance From a Chef in Montreal." *New York Times*: K9.

Brooks, Renana. (2003, June 30). "A Nation of Victims." *The Nation*: 20–22.

Brown, Chris. (2000). "Cultural Diversity and International Political Theory." *Review of International Studies* 26, no. 2: 199–213.

Brown, Chuck. (2006, September 30). "Metrosexuality a Genuine Threat to Modern Man." *Guelph Mercury*: E3.

Brown, Michael E. and Šumit Ganguly. (2003). "Introduction." *Fighting Words: Language Policy and Ethnic Relations in Asia*. Ed. Michael E. Brown and Šumit Ganguly. Cambridge: MIT Press. 1–17.

Brown, Ronald T., Robert W. Amler, Wendy S. Freeman, James M. Perrin, Martin T. Stein, Heidi M. Feldman, Karen Pierce, Mark L. Wolraich, and the Committee on Quality Improvement, Subcommittee on Attention-Deficit/Hyperactivity Disorder. (2005). "American Academy of Pediatrics Technical Report: Treatment of Attention-Deficit/ Hyperactivity Disorder: Overview of the Evidence." *Pediatrics* 115, no. 6: e749–57.

Brownell, M., D. T. Mayer, and D. Chateau. (2006). "The Incidence of Methylphenidate Use by Canadian Children: What Is the Impact of Socioeconomic Status and Urban or Rural Residence?" *Canadian Journal of Psychiatry* 51, no. 13: 847–54.

Buchanan, Roferick B. (2003). "Legislative Warriors: American Psychiatrists, Psychologists, and Competing Claims Over Psychotherapy in the 1950s." *Journal of History of the Behavioral Sciences* 39, no. 3: 225–49.

Burawoy, Michael, Joseph A. Blum, Sheba George, Zsuzsa Gille, Teresa Gowan, Lynne Haney, Maren Klawiter, Steven H. Lopez, Seán Ó Riain, and Millie Thayer. (2000). *Global Ethnography: Forces, Connections, and Imaginations in a Postmodern World*. Berkeley: University of California Press.

Burbury, Rochelle. (2003, June 23). "Men Spending More on Grooming." *Australian Finan-*

cial Review.

Burchell, David. (2002). "What to Do With the Civic Body?" *Continuum* 16, no. 1: 67–79.

Burke, Edmund. (1994). "The Restraints on Men Are Among Their Rights." *Citizenship*. Ed. Paul Barry Clarke. London: Pluto Press. 121–23.

Burke, Rose Marie. (1999, April 8). "Chippendales Let It All Hang Out in Europe." *Wall Street Journal:* A16.

Burroughs, Michael, Guy Cafri, and J. Kevin Thompson. (2005). "Male Body Depilation: Prevalence and Associated Features of Body Hair Removal." *Sex Roles* 52, nos. 9–10: 637–44.

Burstyn, Varda. (1999). *The Rites of Men: Manhood, Politics, and the Culture of Sport.* Toronto: University of Toronto Press.

Burton, Scott, Richard G. Netemeyer, and Donald R. Lichtenstein. (1995). "Gender Differences for Appearance-Related Attitudes and Behaviors: Implications for Consumer Welfare." *Journal of Public Policy & Marketing* 14, no. 1.

Bush, George W. (2001). "Address to a Joint Session of Congress and the American People." *Harvard Journal of Law and Public Policy* 25, no. 2: xiii–xx.

———. (2005, January 21). "Second Inaugural Address." *Washington Post.*

Bushell, Andrew and Brent Cunningham. (2003 March/April). "Being There." *Columbia Journalism Review.*

Business for Social Responsibility. (2004). http://bsr.org.

Buss, Doris and Didi Herman. (2003). *Globalizing Family Values: The Christian Right in International Politics.* Minneapolis: University of Minnesota Press.

Butsch, Richard. (2000). *The Making of American Audiences: From Stage to Television, 1750–1990.* Cambridge: Cambridge University Press.

Butterfield, A. (2003, February 3). "Monuments and Memories." *New Republic.*

Buxton, Rodney A. (2004). "Sexual Orientation and Television." *Museum of Broadcast Communications Encyclopedia of Television.* 2nd ed. Ed. Horace Newcomb. New York: Fitzroy Dearborn. 2066–72.

"Buy Blue's Mission." (2004, December 16). http://www.buyblue.org.

Caldararao, Niccolo. (2002). "Comment on Brewis et al." *American Anthropologist* 104, no. 1: 282–83.

Campbell, John Edward. (2005). "Outing PlanetOut: Surveillance, Gay Marketing and Internet Affinity Portals." *New Media & Society* 7, no. 5: 663–83.

"A Campus Forum on Multiculturalism." (1990, December 9). *New York Times:* 5.

Cancian, Francesca M. (1986). "The Feminization of Love." *Signs* 11, no. 4: 692–709.

Canguilhem, Georges. (1994). *A Vital Rationalist: Selected Writings of Georges Canguilhem.* Trans. Arthur Goldhammer. Ed. François Delaporte. New York: Zone Books.

Cantwell, D. P. (1999). "Attention Deficit Disorder: A Review of the Past Ten Years." *Understanding, Diagnosing, and Treating AD/HD in Children and Adolescents: An Integrative Approach Reiss-Davis Child Study Center, Volume Three.* Ed. A. Incorvaia, B. S. Mark-Goldstein, and L. Tessmer. Northvale: Jason Aronson. 3–23.

Capella, P. and S. Boseley. (1999, February 24). "UN Agency on the Offensive Against the Abuse of 'Lifestyle' Drugs." *Guardian.*

Caplan, Jeremy. (2005, October 3). "Metrosexual Matrimony: When Modern Men Prepare to Wed, Many Wax, Tan and Help Plan. Here Come the 'Groomzillas.'" *Time:* 67.

Carey, Benedict. (2006a, June 6). "Use of Antipsychotics by the Young Rose Fivefold." *New York Times.*

———. (2006b, December 22). "Parenting as Therapy for Child's Mental Disorders." *New York Times.*

Carey, William B. and Lawrence H. Diller. (2001). "Concerns About Ritalin." *Journal of Pediatrics* 139, no. 2: 338–39.

Carlyle, Thomas. (1837). *The French Revolution: A History.* London: Chapman & Hall.

———. (1999). *Sartor Resartus.* Oxford: Oxford University Press.

Carr, David. (2003, March 25). "Reporting Reflects Anxiety." *New York Times.*

Carreño, José. (2001). "El día en que los estadunidenses desperataron de un sueño." *11 de septiembre de 2001.* Ed. Frida Modak. Buenos Aires: Grupo Editorial Lumen. 20–23.

Carter, Bill and Stuart Elliott. (2004, May 26). "MTV to Start First Network Aimed at Gays." *New York Times:* C1, C6.

Case, Tony. (2006, September 4). "Editors Turn Cold Shoulder to the Metrosexual." *Mediaweek.*

Casper, Monica J. and Lynn M. Morgan. (2004 December). *Anthropology News:* 17–18.

Casqueiro, Javier. (2003, August 24). "La Ola 'Metrosexual' Irrumpe en la Televisión de Estados Unidos." *El País:* 26.

Cass, Dennis. (2007 March/April). "Brain Teasers." *Mother Jones:* 79–81.

Castles, Stephen and Alastair Davidson. (2000). *Citizenship and Migration: Globalization and the Politics of Belonging.* Basingstoke: Macmillan.

Castles, Stephen and Mark J. Miller. (2003). *The Age of Migration.* 3rd ed. New York: Guilford Press.

Center for American Progress and Foreign Policy. (2007, February 13). "The Terrorism Index."

Center for Information & Research on Civic Learning & Engagement. (2004, November 3). *Youth Turnout Up Sharply in 2004.*

Centre for Economic Performance, Mental Health Policy Group. (2006). *The Depression Report: A New Deal for Depression and Anxiety Disorders.*

"Centrifugal Forces." (2005, July 16). *The Economist:* 4–7.

"The Challenge of Slums." (2003, October 1). *UN-HABITAT.*

Chan, Carol. (2006, September 9). "City's Metrosexual Juggernaut Gains Steam." *South China Morning Post:* 7.

Charters, W. W. (1933). *Motion Pictures and Youth: A Summary.* New York: Macmillan.

Chase-Dunn, Christopher and Terry Boswell. (2004). "Global Democracy: A World-Systems Perspective." *Proto Sociology: An International Journal of Interdisciplinary Research* 20: 15–29.

Chatterjee, Partha. (1993). *The Nation and Its Fragments: Colonial and Postcolonial Histories.* Princeton: Princeton University Press.

Chatterjee, Pratap. (2004, August 4). "Information Warriors." http://corpwatch.org.

Chaudhry, Lakshmi. (2004, October 29). "The Wimp Factor." http://alternet.org.

Chen, Michelle. (2007, February 9). "Drugmakers Hurry Sales, Delay Safety Studies." *New Standard.*

Chester, Jeff. (2002). "Strict Scrutiny: Why Journalists Should Be Concerned About New Federal Industry Media Deregulation Proposals." *Harvard International Journal of Press/Politics* 7, no. 2: 105–15.

———. (2003, April 1). "Time Is Now to Fight for Future of TV." http://alternet.org.

Chesterton, G. K. (1932). "A Defence of Detective Stories." *Essays of To-Day: An Anthology.* Ed. F. H. Pritchard. London: George G. Harrap. 226–29.

Chicago Council on Foreign Relations/Program on International Policy Attitudes. (2005, March 1). "Large Bipartisan Majority of Americans Favors Referring Darfur War Crime Cases to International Criminal Court."

Children & Adults With Attention Deficit Disorders. (2005). *CHADD Annual Report 2004–2005.*

———. (2006). "CHADD's Income and Expenditures (2005–2006)."

Children's Defense Fund. (2004, July 13). *The State of America's Children 2004: A Continuing Portrait of Inequality Fifty Years After* Brown v. Board of Education.

The Children's Society. (2006). *Good Childhood? A Question for Our Times: A National Inquiry Launch Report.* London.

"Children's Television: Too Much of a Good Thing?" (2004, December 18). *The Economist:* 97–98.

"Chile-Indigenas: Relator de la ONU se reunira con indigenas chilenos." (2003, July 18). *Spanish Newswire Services.*

Chocano, Carina. (2003, July 15). "Queer Eye for the Straight Guy." *Entertainment Weekly.*

———. (2003, August 8). "Queer Eye for the Straight Guy." *Entertainment Weekly.*

Christakis, Dimitri A., Frederick J. Zimmerman, David L. DiGiuseppe, and Carolyn A. McCarty. (2004). "Early Television Exposure and Subsequent Attentional Problems in Children." *Pediatrics* 113: 708–13.

Christenson, Peter and Maria Ivancin. (2006 October). *The "Reality" of Health: Reality Television and the Public Health.* Henry J. Kaiser Foundation.

Citizens Commission on Human Rights. (2003). "New Press Releases." http://www.cchr. org.

Citizenship Foundation. (2004). *Individuals Engaging in Society.*

Clark, A. (2000a, November 18). "The Man Who Sold America Calmer Kids." *Guardian.*

———. (2000b, December 12). "Shire in 5.9bn Merger." *Guardian.*

Clark, Jessica and Bob McChesney. (2001, September 24). "Nattering Networks: How Mass Media Fails Democracy." *LiP.*

Clarke, Adele E., Laura Mamo, Jennifer R. Fishman, Janet K. Shim, and Jennifer Ruth Fosket. (2003). "Biomedicalization: Technoscientific Transformations of Health, Illness, and U.S. Biomedicine." *American Sociological Review* 68, no. 2: 161–94.

Clarkson, Jay. (2005). "Contesting Masculinity's Makeover: *Queer Eye,* Consumer Masculinity, and 'Straight-Acting' Gays." *Journal of Communication Inquiry* 29, no. 3: 235–55.

Clarren, Rebecca. (2005, March 14). "Dirty Politics, Foul Air." *The Nation:* 6–8.

Claussen, Dane S. (2004). *Anti-Intellectualism in American Media: Magazines & Higher Education.* New York: Peter Lang.

Clinton, Bill. (2002, September 10). "The Path to Peace." http://www.salon.com.

Clinton, William J. (1997). "Second Inaugural Address January 20, 1997." *Presidential Studies Quarterly* 27, no. 1: 110.

Cohan, Steven. (2007). "Queer Eye for the Straight Guise: Camp, Postfeminism, and the Fab Five's Makeovers of Masculinity." *Interrogating Postfeminism: Gender and the Politics of Popular Culture.* Ed. Yvonne Tasker and Diane Negra. Durham: Duke University Press. 176–200.

Cohen, Jeffrey E. (1999). "The Polls: Favorability Ratings of Presidents." *Presidential Studies Quarterly* 29, no. 3: 690.

———. (2004). "If the News Is So Bad, Why Are Presidential Polls So High? Presidents, the News Media, and the Mass Public in an Era of New Media." *Presidential Studies Quarterly* 34, no. 3: 493–516.

Cohen, P. (1999). *Rethinking the Youth Question: Education, Labor, and Cultural Studies*. Durham: Duke University Press.

Cohen, Robin. (1991). *Contested Domains: Debates in International Labor Studies*. London: Zed.

———. (1997). *Global Diasporas: An Introduction*. Seattle: University of Washington Press.

———. (2003). "Crossing the Line." *Index on Censorship* 32, no. 2: 60–69.

Cohen, Stanley. (1973). *Folk Devils & Moral Panics: The Creation of the Mods and Rockers*. St. Albans: Paladin.

Cohen, Stephen S. and J. Bradford DeLong. (2005 January/February). "Shaken and Stirred." *Atlantic Monthly:* 112–17.

Coleman, Wil. (1990). "Doing Masculinity/Doing Theory." *Men, Masculinities and Social Theory*. Ed. Jeff Hearn and David Morgan. London: Unwin Hyman. 186–99.

Collison, Robert. (2006, September 30). "Men and the Pursuit of Youthfulness." *National Post:* FW4.

Coltrane, Scott. (2001). "Marketing the Marriage 'Solution': Misplaced Simplicity in the Politics of Fatherhood: 2001 Presidential Address to the Pacific Sociological Association." *Sociological Perspectives* 44, no. 4: 387–418.

Cometta, Louise K. (2005, March 21). "Red Sox Get 'Queer Eye' Makeover." http://espn. go.com.

Compton, James. (2004). "News as Spectacle: The Political Economy and Aesthetics of 24/7 News." *Democratic Communiqué* 19: 49–74.

The Conference Board. (2002). *European Research Working Group on Corporate Citizenship*.

"Congressional Report Uncovers Chemical Security Risks Throughout the Country." (2005). *OMB Watcher* 6, no. 14.

Connell, R. W. (1987). *Gender and Power: Society, the Person, and Sexual Politics*. Cambridge: Polity Press.

———. (1992). "A Very Straight Gay: Masculinity, Homosexual Experience, and the Dynamics of Gender." *American Sociological Review* 57, no. 6: 735–51.

———. (1995). *Masculinities*. Berkeley: University of California Press.

———. (1998). "Masculinities and Globalization." *Men and Masculinities* 1, no. 1: 3–23.

———. (2001). *The Men and the Boys*. Berkeley: University of California Press.

Conrad, Peter. (1975). "The Discovery of Hyperkinesis: Notes on the Medicalization of Deviant Behavior." *Social Problems* 23, no. 1: 12–21.

Conrad, Peter and Deborah Potter. (2000). "From Hyperactive Children to ADHD Adults: Observations on the Expansion of Medical Categories." *Social Problems* 47, no. 4: 559–82.

Cook, Daniel Thomas. (2002). "Introduction: Interrogating Symbolic Childhood." *Symbolic Childhood*. Ed. Daniel Thomas Cook. New York: Peter Lang. 1–14.

———. (2007). "Children's Consumer Culture." *Encyclopedia of Sociology*. Ed. George Ritzer. Malden: Blackwell.

Cook, Daniel Thomas and Susan B. Kaiser. (2004). "Betwixt and Be Tween." *Journal of Consumer Culture* 4, no. 2: 203–27.

Cook, Margaret. (2004, November 15). "Who Can Cure the Pharmaceuticals?" *New Statesman*.

Cooksey, Elizabeth and Phil Brown. (1998). "Spinning on Its Axes: *DSM* and the Social Construction of Psychiatric Diagnosis." *International Journal of Health Services* 28, no. 3: 525–54.

Coutin, Susan Bibler. (2003). "Cultural Logics of Belonging and Movement: Transnationalism, Naturalization, and U.S. Immigration Politics." *American Ethnologist* 30, no. 4: 508–26.

"Covered for Climate Change." (2004 November/December). *Foreign Policy:* 18.

Cowan, Jane K., Marie-Bénédicte Dembour, and Richard A. Wilson. (2001). "Introduction." *Culture and Rights: Anthropological Perspectives.* Ed. Jane K. Cowan, Marie-Bénédicte Dembour, and Richard A. Wilson. Cambridge: Cambridge University Press. 1–26.

Cowap, Simon. (2004). "The Trouble With CBT." *Australian Family Physician* 33, no. 7: 555.

Cox, Emily R., Brenda R. Motheral, Rochelle R. Henderson, and Doug Mager. (2003). "Geographic Variation in the Prevalence of Stimulant Medication Use Among Children 5 to 14 Years Old: Results From a Commercially Insured U.S. Sample." *Pediatrics* 111: 237–43.

"CPL to Test Pro Gamers for Drug Use in 2007." http://www.gamepro.com.

Crawley, Melissa. (2006). "Making Over the New Adam." *The Great American Makeover: Television, History, Nation.* Ed. Dana Heller. New York: Palgrave Macmillan. 51–64.

Critcher, Chas. (2003). *Moral Panics and the Media.* Buckingham: Open University Press.

Crook, Clive. (2005, January 22). "The Good Company." *The Economist:* 3–4, Survey.

Crowe, Jerry. (2007, May 7). "Hintnaus' Fame Was Never Fleeting, But It Was Brief." *Los Angeles Times:* D2.

Curtis, P. (2002, January 22). "Creative Accounting." *Guardian.*

D'Entremont, Jim. (2003). "Clear and Present Danger." *Index on Censorship* 32, no. 3: 124–28.

Dale, Edgar. (1933). *The Content of Motion Pictures.* New York: Macmillan.

Daly, Rich. (2006). "Hawaii Psychiatrists Try to Derail Psychologist Prescribing Bill." *Psychiatry News* 41, no. 7: 4.

Damon, William. (2004). "What Is Positive Youth Development?" *Annals of the American Academy of Political and Social Science* 591: 13–24.

Daniels, A. M. (1998). "Review." *British Medical Journal* 7: 1327.

Danziger, Kurt. (1998). *Constructing the Subject: Historical Origins of Psychological Research.* Cambridge: Cambridge University Press.

Das, Veena. (2002). *Critical Events: An Anthropological Perspective on Contemporary India,* New Delhi: Oxford University Press.

Datamonitor.com (2004). *Changing Personal Care Behaviors and Occasions.* DMCM1020. http://www.datamonitor.com.

"Dave Collins, Creator of 'Queer Eye for the Straight Guy,' to Star in New Ad Campaign for Open." (2004, February 23). https://home.americanexpress.com/home.

Davis, Ann, Joseph Pereira, and William M. Bulkeley. (2002, August 15). "Security Concerns Bring New Focus on Body Language." *Wall Street Journal:* A1, A6.

Davis, Erik. (2000, September 1). "Take the Red Pill." http://www.alternet.org.

Davis, Kathy. (2002). "'A Dubious Equality': Men, Women and Cosmetic Surgery." *Body & Society* 8, no. 1: 49–65.

———. (2003). *Dubious Equalities and Embodied Differences: Cultural Studies on Cosmetic Surgery.* Lanham: Rowman & Littlefield.

Day, Gary. (2002). "A Brief History of How Culture and Commerce Were Really Made for Each Other." *Critical Quarterly* 44, no. 3: 37–44.

De Albuquerque, Afonso. (2003, April 16). "Brazil." http://www.opendemocracy.net.

Dean, Hartley. (2001). "Green Citizenship." *Social Policy & Administration* 35, no. 5: 490–505.

DeNavas-Walt, Carmen, Bernadette D. Proctor, and Cheryl Hill Lee. (2006). *Income, Poverty, and Health Insurance Coverage in the United States: 2005.* U.S. Census Bureau Current Population Reports P60–231. Washington: US Government Printing Office.

de Pedro, Jesús Prieto. (1991). "Concepto y Otros Aspectos del Patrimonio Cultural en la Constitución." *Estudios sobre la Constitución Española: Homenaje al Profesor Eduardo Garcia de Enterria.* Madrid: Editorial Civitas, S. A. 1551–72.

de Spinoza, Benedict. (1955). *On the Improvement of Understanding. The Ethics. Correspondence.* Trans. R. H. M. Elwes. New York: Dover Publications.

Debord, Guy. (1995). *The Society of the Spectacle.* Trans. Donald Nicolson-Smith. New York: Zone.

Deepti. (2005, October 22). "Watch Your Man." *Tribune.*

Deery, June. (2006). "Interior Design: Commodifying Self and Place in *Extreme Makeover, Extreme Makeover: Home Edition,* and *The Swan.*" *The Great American Makeover: Television, History, Nation.* Ed. Dana Heller. New York: Palgrave Macmillan. 159–73.

DeFao, Janine. (2006, September 11). "TV Channel for Babies? Pediatricians Say Turn It Off." *San Francisco Chronicle.*

"Defining MetroSexuality." (2003 September/October/November). *Metrosource:* 16–17.

DeGrandpre, Richard. (1999). *Ritalin Nation: Rapid-Fire Culture and the Transformation of Human Consciousness.* New York: W. W. Norton.

———. (2006). *The Cult of Pharmacology: How America Became the World's Most Troubled Drug Culture.* Durham: Duke University Press.

DeJesus, Erin. (2008 February/March). "The Gayest Moments in TV History." *Metrosource:* 42–47.

DerDerian, James. (2002). "The War of Networks." *Theory & Event* 5, no. 4.

Descartes, René. (1977). *Philosophical Writings.* Trans. and Ed. Elizabeth Anscombe and Peter Thomas Geach. Sunbury-on-Thames: Nelson University Paperbacks/Open University.

Dettre, Maureen. (2001, June 18). "NSW: Concern Over Rising No. Kids in Care on Ritalin: Inquiry." *AAP General News.*

Dewan, Shaila K. (2004, October 14). "Do Horror Films Filter the Horrors of History?" *New York Times:* B9.

Diaz, Johnny. (2006, June 20). "Tough Love." *Boston Globe:* E1.

Diego, José Díaz. (2006). "La i-lógica de los géneros: Metrosexuales, masculinidad y apoderamientos." *AIBR: Revista de Antropología Iberoamericana* 1, no. 1: 157–67.

DiIulio, John J. Jr. (2003). "The Moral Compassion of True Conservatism." *The Fractious Nation? Unity and Division in American Life.* Ed. Jonathan Rieder. Assoc. Ed. Stephen Steinlight. Berkeley: University of California Press. 217–24.

Dilday, K. A. (2003, May 1). "Lost in Translation: The Narrowing of the American Mind." http://www.opendemocracy.net.

Diller, Lawrence H. (1998). *Running on Ritalin: A Physician Reflects on Children, Society, and Performance in a Pill.* New York: Bantam.

———. (2000, September 25). "Just Say Yes to Ritalin." http://www.salon.com.

———. (2001). "Adderall and the FDA." *Journal of the American Academy of Child & Adolescent Psychiatry* 40, no. 7: 737.

DiMaggio, Paul. (1994). "Culture and Economy." *The Handbook of Economic Sociology.* Ed. Neil J. Smelser and Richard Swedberg. Princeton: Princeton University Press. 27–57.

———. (2003). "The Myth of Culture War: The Disparity Between Private Opinion and Public Politics." *The Fractious Nation? Unity and Division in American Life.* Ed. Jonathan Rieder. Assoc. Ed. Stephen Steinlight. Berkeley: University of California Press. 79–97.

Di Mattia, Joanna L. (2007). "The Gentle Art of Manscaping: Lessons in Hetero-Masculinity from the Queer Eye Guys." *Makeover Television: Realities Remodelled.* Ed. Dana Heller. London: I. B. Tauris. 133–49.

Dionne, E. J. Jr. (2003). "Shaking Off the Past: Third Ways, Fourth Ways, and the Urgency of Politics." *The Fractious Nation? Unity and Division in American Life.* Ed. Jonathan Rieder. Assoc. Ed. Stephen Steinlight. Berkeley: University of California Press. 225–47.

"Doctors, Lawyers Debate Ritalin." (2001, June 19). *United Press International.*

Dolby, Nadine. (2003). "Popular Culture and Democratic Practice." *Harvard Educational Review* 73, no. 3: 258–84.

Dolny, Michael. (2003 July/August). "Spectrum Narrows Further in 2002: Progressive, Domestic Think Tanks See Drop." *EXTRA! Update.*

———. (2005, May/June). "Right, Center Think Tanks Still Most Quoted." *EXTRA!*: 28–29.

Domke, David, Mark D. Watts, Dhavan V. Shah, and David P. Fan. (1999). "The Politics of Conservative Elites and the 'Liberal Media' Argument." *Journal of Communication* 49, no. 1: 35–58.

Donahue, Wendy. (2005, October 30). "Begone, Girlie Man. Hello, Confident Ubersexual." *Chicago Tribune.*

Donzelot, Jacques. (1979). *The Policing of Families.* New York: Pantheon.

———. (1991). "The Mobilization of Society." *The Foucault Effect.* Ed. Graham Burchell, Colin Gordon, and Peter Miller. London: Harvester Wheatsheaf.

Doonan, Simon. (2007, January 8). "Transmanhattan! Guys, Gals Whirl in Big Gender Blender." *New York Observer.*

Dossi, Joel. (2005, January 3). "The Rise and Fall of *Queer Eye for the Straight Guy.*" http://alternet.org.

Double Indemnity. (1944). Dir. Billy Wilder. Paramount Pictures.

Douglas, Susan J. (2004, July 1). "We Are What We Watch." *In These Times.*

Dowd, Maureen. (2003, July 6). "Ritalin for America." *New York Times.*

Downing, John and Charles Husband. (2005). *Representing "Race": Racisms, Ethnicities and Media.* London: Sage.

"Drug Withdrawal Shocks Shire." (2005, February 15). http://pmlive.com.

Drutman, Lee and Charlie Cray. (2005, March 14). "The People's Business: Controlling Corporations and Restoring Democracy." *In These Times:* 16–19, 28.

Dube, Rebecca. (2007, April 26). "Run, Here Comes Godzilla." *Globe and Mail:* L3.

Dumenco, Simon. (2003, August 11). "The Buysexual Agenda." *New York Magazine.*

Durham, Deborah. (2004). "Disappearing Youth: Youth as a Social Shifter in Botswana." *American Ethnologist* 31, no. 4: 589–605.

Dyer, Richard. (1992). *Only Entertainment.* New York: Routledge.

Dylan, Bob. (2004). *Chronicles: Volume One.* New York: Simon & Schuster.

Eberstadt, Mary. (1999). "Why Ritalin Rules." *Policy Review* 94: 24–40.

Eccleston, Roy. (2006, July 8). "Inquiry Into Ritalin for Preschoolers." *Australian*.

Ehrenreich, Barbara. (1990). *Fear of Falling: The Inner Life of the Middle Class*. New York: HarperPerennial.

"Electronics, Unleaded." (2005, March 12). *The Economist*: 6–7.

Elias, Marilyn. (2007, May 3). "Mentally Ill Die 25 Years Earlier, on Average." *USA Today*.

Ellen, Barbara. (2007, April 29). "Facials, Manicures, Emotional Outbursts." *Observer Magazine*: 6.

Elliott, Carl. (2003a June) "American Bioscience Meets the American Dream." *American Prospect*: 39.

———. (2003b). *Better Than Well: American Medicine Meets the American Dream*. New York: W. W. Norton.

———. (2004). "Pharma Goes to the Laundry: Public Relations and the Business of Medical Education." *Hastings Centre Report* 34, no. 5: 18–24.

Elliott, Emory. (2001). "Foreword." *The Puritan Origins of American Sex*. Ed. Tracy Fessenden, Nicholas F. Radel, and Magdalena J. Zaborowska. New York: Routledge. ix–xii.

Elliott, Stuart. (1998, October 19). "Levi Strauss Begins a Far-Reaching Marketing Campaign to Reach Gay Men and Lesbians." *New York Times*: C11.

Ellison, Sarah. (2006, March 28). "Condé Nast to Fold Men's Shopping Magazine *Cargo*." *Wall Street Journal*: B7.

El Nasser, Haya and Lorrie Grant. (2005b, June 9.) "Immigration Causes Age, Race Split." *USA Today*: 1A.

Elsaesser, Thomas. (1999). "The Dandy in Hitchcock." *Alfred Hitchcock: Centenary Essays*. Ed. Richard Allen and S. Ishii-Gonzalès. London: British Film Institute. 3–13.

Elster, Jon. (2003). "The Market and the Forum: Three Varieties of Political Theory." *Philosophy and Democracy: An Anthology*. Ed. Thomas Christiano. Oxford: Oxford University Press. 138–58.

"The End?" (1999, February 13). *The Economist*: 17–18.

Engelberg, Keren. (2005, January 21). "Making the Cut." *Jewish Journal*.

"English Test for Immigrants." (2002, February 10). *Economic Times New Delhi*: 13.

Ennew, Judith. (2002). "Future Generations and Global Standards: Children's Rights at the Start of the Millennium." *Exotic No More: Anthropology on the Front Lines*. Ed. Jeremy MacClancy. Chicago: University of Chicago Press. 338–50.

Erskine, Chris. (2006, July 20). "The Post-Metrosexual Man." *Los Angeles Times*.

Esposito, Christine. (2006). "Making Health Manly." *Nutraceuticals World* 9, no. 6: 40.

Euromonitor. (2004, June 18). *Men's Hair Care: Virile Growth*." http://www.euromonitor.com.

———. (2006, November 8). *Metrosexuality—The Male Shopping Giant Awakes*. http://www.euromonitor.com.

European Union Consultative Platform on Mental Health. (2006). *Improving the Mental Health of the Population: Towards a Strategy on Mental Health for the European Union*.

"Ever Higher Society, Ever Harder to Ascend." (2005, January 1). *The Economist*: 22–24.

Eviatar, Daphne. (2003, July 7). "The Press and Private Lynch." *The Nation*: 18–20.

"Excerpts From Discussion of Resolution on Censure." (1998, December 13). *New York Times*: 47.

"Executive Summary: The President's New Freedom Initiative for People With Disabilities: The 2004 Progress Report." (2005).

"Faith in the System." (2004 September/October). *Mother Jones:* 26–27.

Falk, Pasi. (1994). *The Consuming Body.* London: Sage.

Fallon, Kathleen M. (2003). "Transforming Women's Citizenship Rights Within an Emerging Democratic State: The Case of Ghana." *Gender & Society* 17, no. 4: 525–43.

Family & Friends Action Council. (2007, January 30). *"National Household Survey:* Eating Disorders Often Untreated, Often Impair Lives."

Farhi, Paul. (2003, April 6). "Everybody Wins." *American Journalism Review.*

Farran, Laia. (2007 January). "Boys Will Be Girls." *Velocity.*

Farrell, Elizabeth F. (2003, September 26). "Paying Attention to Students Who Can't." *Chronicle of Higher Education:* A50–A51.

Fass, Allison. (2002, April 4). "Advertising." *New York Times:* C5.

Faulkner-Bond, Molly. (2006, December 2). "Independent Women Can Choose to 'Date Down.'" *Sirens.*

Feldman, Allen. (2005). "On the Actuarial Gaze: From 9/11 to Abu Ghraib." *Cultural Studies* 19, no. 2: 203–26.

"FDA Directs ADHD Drug Manufacturers to Notify Patients About Cardiovascular Adverse Events and Psychiatric Adverse Events." (2007, February 21). U.S. Food and Drug Administration.

Fejes, Fred. (2002). "Advertising and the Political Economy of Lesbian/Gay Identity." *Sex & Money: Feminism and Political Economy in the Media.* Ed. Eileen R. Meehan and Ellen Riordan. Minneapolis: University of Minnesota Press. 196–208.

Feldman, Eric. (2004). "Before & After." *American Heritage* 55, no. 1.

Fenley, Garth. (2004, August 1). "Image-Conscious Metrosexuals Are Changing the Way Men Shop." *Display & Design Ideas.*

Ferguson, Iain and Caspar Henderson. (2003, March 12). "Corporate Timeline." http://www.opendemocracy.net.

Fernández-Armesto, Felipe. (2002). "Too Rich, Too Thin?" *Demos Collection* 18: 19–24.

Fessenden, Tracy, Nicholas F. Radel, and Magdalena J. Zaborowska. (2001). "Introduction: The Puritan Origins of American Sex." *The Puritan Origins of American Sex.* Ed. Tracy Fessenden, Nicholas F. Radel, and Magdalena J. Zaborowska. New York: Routledge. 1–20.

Fierlbeck, K. (1996). "The Ambivalent Potential of Cultural Identity." *Canadian Journal of Political Science/Revue canadienne de science politique* 29, no. 1: 3–22.

Fife-Yeoman, Janet. (2007, April 30). "Attention Divided?" *Daily Telegraph:* 9.

Fine, Ben and Ellen Leopold. (1993). *The World of Consumption.* London: Routledge.

Finn, Robin. (2003, November 21). "The Queer Brain Behind 'Queer Eye.'" *New York Times.*

Fisk, Robert. (2007, January 13). "This Jargon Disease Is Choking Language." *Independent.*

"Fit to Serve." (2007, January 20). *The Economist:* 71.

Fitzpatrick, Mike. (2003). "Doctoring the Risk Society." *The Lancet* 362: 1772.

Flanders, Laura. (2001, November 9). "Media Criticism in Mono." *WorkingForChange.*

Flint, Andrew R. and Joy Porter. (2005). "Jimmy Carter: The Re-Emergence of Faith-Based Politics and the Abortion Rights Issue." *Presidential Studies Quarterly* 35, no. 1: 28–51.

Flocker, Michael. (2003). *The Metrosexual Guide to Style: A Handbook for the Modern Man.* Cambridge, MA: Da Capo Press.

Florida, Richard. (2002). *The Rise of the Creative Class: And How It's Transforming Work, Leisure, Community and Everyday Life.* New York: Basic Books.

Flower, Chris. (2004). "Foreword." *The Self-Esteem Society.* Helen McCarthy. London: Demos. 5.

Flynn, Emily Vencat. (2005, October 31). "Diamonds Are for Men." *Newsweek:* 36.

Fogel, A. (1993). "The Prose of Populations and the Magic of Demography." *Western Humanities Review* 47, no. 4: 312–37.

"Force Enlargement." (2004, July 31). *The Economist:* 30.

"Forging a Nation." (2004, October 23). *The Economist:* 44.

Forman, Henry James. (1933). *Our Movie Made Children.* New York: Macmillan.

"Foro Cultural: Ministra Espanola dice que la cultura es pilar para el desarollo." (2004, June 30). *Spanish Newswire Services.*

Foster, John Bellamy. (2002). "The Rediscovery of Imperialism." *Monthly Review* 54, no. 6: 1–16.

Foti, Alex. (2005). "MAYDAY MAYDAY: Euro Flex Workers, Time to Get a Move on!" http://republicart.net.

Foucault, Michel. (1972). *The Archaeology of Knowledge.* Trans. A. M. Sheridan Smith. London: Tavistock.

———. (1973). *The Order of Things: An Archaeology of the Human Sciences.* New York: Vintage Books.

———. (1978). "Politics and the Study of Discourse." Trans. A. M. Nazzaro. Rev. Colin Gordon. *Ideology and Consciousness* 3: 7–26.

———. (1979a). *Discipline and Punish: The Birth of the Prison.* Trans. Alan Sheridan. New York: Vintage Books.

———. (1979b). "Power and Form: Notes." Trans. W. Suchting. *Michel Foucault: Power, Truth, Strategy.* Ed. Meaghan Morris and Paul Patton. Sydney: Feral Publications. 59–66.

———. (1979c). "Truth and Power." Trans. Paul Patton and Meaghan Morris. *Michel Foucault: Power, Truth, Strategy.* Ed. Meaghan Morris and Paul Patton. Sydney: Feral Publications. 29–48.

———. (1982). "The Subject and Power." Trans. L. Sawyer. *Critical Inquiry* 8, no. 4: 777–95.

———. (1984). *The History of Sexuality: An Introduction.* Trans. Robert Hurley. Harmondsworth: Penguin.

———. (1986). *The Use of Pleasure: The History of Sexuality Volume Two.* Trans. Robert Hurley. London: Penguin Books.

———. (1987). *Mental Illness and Psychology.* Trans. Alan Sheridan. Berkeley: University of California Press.

———. (1988). *The Care of the Self: The History of Sexuality Volume Three.* Trans. Robert Hurley. New York: Vintage.

———. (1989a). "The Concern for Truth." Trans. John Johnston. *Foucault Live: (Interviews, 1966–84).* Ed. Sylvère Lotringer. New York: Semiotext(e) Foreign Agents Series. 293–308.

———. (1989b). "The End of the Monarchy of Sex." Trans. D. M. Marchi. *Foucault Live: (Interviews, 1966–84).* Ed. Sylvère Lotringer. New York: Semiotext(e) Foreign Agents Series. 137–55.

———. (1989c). "How Much Does It Cost for Reason to Tell the Truth." Trans. M. Foret and M. Martius. *Foucault Live: (Interviews, 1966–84).* Ed. Sylvère Lotringer. New York: Semiotext(e) Foreign Agents Series. 234–56.

————. (1989d). "The Masked Philosopher." Trans. John Johnston. *Foucault Live: (Interviews, 1966–84)*. Ed. Sylvère Lotringer. New York: Semiotext(e) Foreign Agents Series. 193–202.

————. (1989e). "What Calls for Punishment?" Trans. John Johnston. *Foucault Live: (Interviews, 1966–84)*. Ed. Sylvère Lotringer. New York: Semiotext(e) Foreign Agents Series. 279–92.

————. (1991a). "Governmentality." Trans. Pasquale Pasquino. *The Foucault Effect: Studies in Governmentality*. Ed. Graham Burchell, Colin Gordon, and Peter Miller. London: Harvester Wheatsheaf. 87–104.

————. (1991b). *Remarks on Marx: Conversations With Duccio Trombadorii*. Trans. J. R. Goldstein and J. Cascaito. New York: Semiotext(e).

————. (1994). "Problematics: Excerpts From Conversations." *Crash: Nostalgia for the Absence of Cyberspace*. Ed. R. Reynolds and T. Zummer. New York: Thread Waxing Space. 121–27.

————. (1997). *Ethics: Subjectivity and Truth: The Essential Works of Foucault 1954–1984 Volume One*. Trans. Robert Hurley et al. Ed. Paul Rabinow. New York: Free Press.

————. (2000). *Power: Essential Works of Foucault 1954–1984 Volume Three*. Ed. J. D. Faubion. New York: New Press.

————. (2001). *Fearless Speech*. Ed. Joseph Pearson. Los Angeles: Semiotext(e).

————. (2003a). *"Society Must Be Defended": Lectures at the Collège de France 1975–1976*. Trans. David Macey. Ed. Mauro Bertani and Alessandro Fontana. New York: Picador.

————. (2003b). *Abnormal: Lectures at the Collège de France 1974–1975*. Trans. Graham Buchell. Ed. Valerio Marchetti and Antonella Salomoni. New York: Picador.

————. (2006). *Psychiatric Power: Lectures at the Collège de France, 1973–74*. Trans. Graham Burchell. Ed. Jacques Lagrange. Basingstoke: Palgrave Macmillan.

Foucault, Michel and Richard Sennett. (1982). "Sexuality and Solitude." *Humanities in Review* 1: 3–21.

Foundation for Child Development. (2004). *Index of Child Well-Being (CWI), 1975–2002, With Projections for 2003*.

Fox, C. (1989, January 21). "Decade of the 'New Man' Is Here." *Australian Financial Review*: 46.

Fox, Susannah. (2004). *Prescription Drugs Online*. Washington, DC: Pew Internet & American Life Project.

Fraiman, Susan. (2006). "Shelter Writing: Desperate Housekeeping from *Crusoe* to *Queer Eye*." *New Literary History* 37: 341–59.

Francis, David. (2007, November 13). "U.S. Falls to No. 15 in Average Worker Income." *Christian Science Monitor*.

Francis, David R. (2005, March 14). "As Corporate Taxes Shrink, Who Pays?" *Christian Science Monitor*.

Frank, Thomas. (2000). *One Market Under God: Extreme Capitalism, Market Populism, and the End of Economic Democracy*. New York: Anchor Books/Random House.

Fraser, Kathryn. (2007). "'Now I Am Ready to Tell How Bodies Are Changed Into Different Bodies . . .'—Ovid, *The Metamorphoses*." *Makeover Television: Realities Remodelled*. Ed. Dana Heller. London: I. B. Tauris. 177–92.

Freedom from Religion Foundation. (2004, December 20). "Health & Human Services Suspends Funds to Faith-Based Mentoring Group Being Sued by Watchdog Foundation."

Freeman, Richard. (2004 June). "Fighting Turnout Burnout." *American Prospect:* A16.

Freudenheim, Milt. (1999, September 6). "Employers Focus on Weight as a Workplace Health Issue." *New York Times:* A15.

Friedman, Dan. (2006). "Straight Eye for the Consumer Guy." http://zeek.net.

From Cause to Cure: Mental Health and Nervous System Conditions—A Special Advertising Supplement. (2002, October 27). *New York Times Magazine.*

Fugh-Berman, Adriane. (2005). "The Corporate Coauthor." *Journal of General Internal Medicine* 20: 546–48.

Fukuyama, Francis. (2002, May 13). "Sorry, But Your Soul Just Died." *Guardian:* Features 2.

The Full Monty. (1997). Dir. Peter Cattaneo. Redwave Films.

Furedi, Frank. (2005, September 26). "The Market in Fear." *Spiked.*

Gabaccia, Donna R. (2006, November 1). "Today's Immigration Policy Debates: Do We Need a Little History?" *Migration Information Source.*

Gallup Polls. (2002–3). http:www.gallup.com.

Galston, William A. (2002). "Participación ciudadana en los Estados Unidos: Un análisis empírico." *Deonstruyendo la Ciudadanía: Avances y Retos en el Desarrollo de la Cultura Democrática en México.* Mexico: Secretaría de Gobernación/Secretaria de Educación Publica/Instituto Federal Electoral. 279–93.

Gamson, Joshua. (1994). *Claims to Fame: Celebrity in Contemporary America.* Berkeley: University of California Press.

García Canclini, Néstor. (1995). *Hybrid Cultures: Strategies for Entering and Leaving Modernity.* Trans. Christopher L. Chiappari and Silvia L. López. Minneapolis: University of Minnesota Press.

———. (1999). *Imaginarios Urbanos.* 2nd ed. Buenos Aires: Eudeba.

———. (2001a). *Citizens and Consumers.* Trans. George Yúdice. Minneapolis: University of Minnesota Press.

———. (2001b). "Pensar en Medio de la Tormenta." *Imaginarios de Nación: Pensar en Medio de la Tormenta.* Ed. Jesús Martin-Barbero. Bogotá: Ministerio de Cultura. 11–15.

———. (2002). *Latinoamericanos Buscando Lugar en este Siglo.* Buenos Aires: Paidós.

———. (2004). *Differentes, Desiguales y Desconectados: Mapas de la Interculturalidad.* Barcelona: Editorial Gedisa.

Garfinkel, Harold. (1992). *Studies in Ethnomethodology.* Cambridge: Polity Press.

Garfinkle, Norton. (2006). *The American Dream vs. the Gospel of Wealth: The Fight for a Productive Middle-Class Economy.* New Haven: Yale University Press.

"Garrett of 'Newsday' Rips Tribune Co. 'Greed' in Exit Memo." (2005, March 1). *Editor & Publisher.*

Gates, Kelly, Marie Leger, and Dan McGee. (2002). "Public Health Messages Pharmaceutical Advertising: Drug-Dealing Direct to Consumer." *Television Studies.* Ed. Toby Miller. Assoc. Ed. Andrew Lockett. London: British Film Institute. 84–87.

Gaus, Mischa. (2007 February). "Interrogations Behind Barbed Wire." *In These Times:* 26–29.

"Gay/Lesbian Consumer Online Study Adds More Than 175 New Brands." (2005, November 1). Scarborough Research.

Gellene, Denise. (2007, February 1). "Men Found to Be Anorexic, Bulimic Also." *Los Angeles Times:* A12.

———. (2007, November 13). "Hyperactive Children Catch Up With Peers, Study Finds." *Los Angeles Times.*

"Generation Rx: National Study Reveals New Category of Substance Abuse Emerging." (2005, April 21). Partnership for a Drug-Free America.

"The Gentleman's Bailout." (2008, April 7). *The Nation*: 3–4.

Getis, Victoria. (1998). "Experts and Juvenile Delinquency, 1900–1935." *Generations of Youth: Youth Cultures and History in Twentieth-Century America*. Ed. Joe Austin and Michael Nevin Willard. New York: New York University Press. 21–35.

Gettelman, Elizabeth. (2004 November/December). "The K(a-ching!) Street Congressman." *Mother Jones*: 24.

"Ghostwriting: The Basics." (2003 April). *Canadian Broadcasting News*.

Gibson, William. (2003). *Pattern Recognition*. New York: G. P. Putnam's Sons.

Giddens, Anthony and Will Hutton. (2000a). "Preface." *Global Capitalism*. Ed. Will Hutton and Anthony Giddens. New York: New Press. vii–xi.

———. (2000b). "In Conversation." *Global Capitalism*. Ed. Will Hutton and Anthony Giddens. New York: New Press. 1–51.

Gilbert, J. (1986). *America's Reaction to the Juvenile Delinquent in the 1950s*. New York: Oxford University Press.

Gillam, Tony. (2004). "Voices." *Mental Health Practice* 8, no. 1: 37.

Gillespie, Nick. (2003 April). "Moral Panic Buttons." *Reason*: 4.

Gillham, Jane and Karen Reivich. (2004). "Cultivating Optimism in Childhood and Adolescence." *Annals of the American Academy of Political and Social Science* 591: 146–63.

Gilligan, Carol. (1997, February 16). "A Therapist Examines the Hidden Problem of Male Depression." *New York Times Book Review*: 24.

Giltz, Michael. (2003, September 2). "Queer Eye Confidential." *LookSmart*.

Ginther, Claire. (1996). "Is There a Ritalin Media Frenzy?" *Psychiatric Times* 13, no. 2.

"Girls Get Extra School Help While Boys Get Ritalin." (2003, August 29). *USA Today*: 8A.

Giroux, Henry A. (2000). *Stealing Innocence: Youth, Corporate Power, and the Politics of Culture*. New York: St. Martin's Press.

Gladden, Rebecca. (2005, February 14). "Jeff Gordon: NASCAR's Reigning Metrosexual." *Insider Racing News*.

Glassner, Barry. (1999). *The Culture of Fear: Why Americans Are Afraid of the Wrong Things*. New York: Basic Books.

Glickman, Lawrence B. (1999). "Introduction: Born to Shop? Consumer History and American History." *Consumer Society in American History: A Reader*. Ed. Lawrence B. Glickman. Ithaca: Cornell University Press. 1–14.

"Global Finance: Time for a Redesign?" (1999, January 30). *The Economist*: Survey Global Finance, 4–8.

Global March Against Child Labour. (2004). http://globalmarch.org.

"Global Poll Slams Bush Leadership." (2005, January 18). http://news.bbc.co.uk.

GlobeScan. (2003, June 4). "World Public Opinion Says World Not Going in Right Direction."

GlobeScan/Program on International Policy Attitudes. (2005). "In 20 of 23 Countries Polled Citizens Want Europe to Be More Influential Than US."

Goldenberg, Suzanne. (2005, January 17). "Nip and Tuck Gets Its Own Magazine." *Guardian*.

Goldstein, Richard. (2003a, March 24). "Neo-Macho Man: Pop Culture and Post-9/11 Politics." *The Nation*: 16–19.

———. (2003b, March 26–April 1). "The Shock and Awe Show." *Village Voice*.

———. (2003c, July 23–29). "What Queer Eye?" *Village Voice.*

Goldstein, Sam. (2006). "The Marketing of ADHD." *Annals of the American Psychotherapy Association* 9, no. 2: 32–34.

"The God Slot." (2006, September 16). *The Economist:* 38.

Gomes, Lee. (2002, December 9). "Boomtown: Globalization Is Now a Two-Way Street—Good News for the U.S." *Wall Street Journal:* B1.

"The Good Company." (2005, January 22). *The Economist:* 11.

Goode, Erica. (2000, July 18). "Once Again, Prozac Takes Center Stage, in Furor." *New York Times:* F1–F2.

———. (2003, January 14). "Study Finds Jump in Children Taking Psychiatric Drugs." *New York Times:* A21.

Goode, Erich. (2000). "No Need to Panic? A Bumper Crop of Books on Moral Panics." *Sociological Forum* 15, no. 3: 543–52.

Goodman, Bill and Reid Steadman. (2002). "Services: Business Demand Rivals Consumer Demand in Driving Job Growth." *Monthly Labor Review* 125, no. 4: 3–16.

Goodnight, and Good Luck. (2005). Dir. George Clooney. Warner Independent Pictures.

Gottlieb, Scott. (2000, July 23). "Cashing in on the Real and Imaginary Health Anxieties of Americans Is a Lucrative Business." *Los Angeles Times.*

Graham, Jordanne. (2004a, August). "Bush Wants to Be Your Shrink." *Intervention Magazine.*

———. (2004b, November 28). "Big Brother in Your Medicine Cabinet." *Intervention Magazine.*

Gramsci, Antonio. (1971). *Selections From the Prison Notebooks.* Trans. Quentin Hoare and Geoffrey Nowell-Smith. New York: International Publishers.

Grantham, Bill. (1998). "America the Menace: France's Feud With Hollywood." *World Policy Journal* 15, no. 2: 58–66.

Greenberg, Gary. (2005 January/February). "Placebo Panacea." *Mother Jones:* 20.

Greene, Ronald Walter. (1999). *Malthusian Worlds: U.S. Leadership and the Governing of the Population Crisis.* Boulder: Westview Press.

Greenhouse, Linda. (2003, March 19). "Libertarians Join Liberals in Opposing Sodomy Laws." *New York Times.*

Greenhouse, Steven and David Leonhardt. (2006, August 28). "Real Wages Fail to Match a Rise in Productivity." *New York Times:* A1, A13.

Greenslade, Roy. (2003, February 17). "Their Master's Voice." *Guardian.*

Greider, William. (2005, February 28). "The New Colossus." *The Nation:* 13–18.

Grieve, Tim. (2003, March 25). "'Shut Your Mouth.'" http://www.salon.com.

Griffin, Christine. (1993). *Representations of Youth: The Study of Youth and Adolescence in Britain and America.* Cambridge: Polity Press.

Grossberg, Lawrence. (1994). "The Political Status of Youth and Youth Culture." *Adolescents and Their Music: If It's Too Loud, You're Too Old.* Ed. J. S. Epstein. New York: Garland. 25–46.

———. (2005). *Caught in the Crossfire: Kids, Politics, and America's Future.* Boulder: Paradigm Publishers.

Guidotto, Nadia. (2005). "Cashing in on Queers: From Liberation to Commodification." *Canadian Online Journal of Queer Studies in Education* 2, no. 1.

Gunther, Marc. (2001, October 15). "How One Advertising Agency Is Scrambling to Find Words and Images for the Moment." *Fortune.*

Habermas, Jürgen. (2003). *The Future of Human Nature*. Trans. William Rehg, Max Pensky, and Helen Besiter. Cambridge: Polity Press.

Hacker, Jacob S. (2006). *The Great Risk Shift: The Assault on American Jobs, Families, Health Care, and Retirement and How You Can Fight Back*. New York: Oxford University Press.

Hacking, Ian. (1995). *Rewriting the Soul: Multiple Personality and the Sciences of Memory*. Princeton: Princeton University Press.

Haisken, Elizabeth. (2000). "Virtual Virility, or, Does Medicine Make the Man?" *Men & Masculinities* 2, no. 4: 388–409.

Halasz, George, Gil Anaf, Peter Ellingsen, Anne Manne, and Frances Thomson Salo. (2002). *Cries Unheard: A New Look at Attention Hyperactivity Deficit Disorder*. Altona: Common Ground.

Hale, N. (1995). *The Rise and Crisis of Psychoanalysis in the United States: Freud and the Americans, 1917–1985*. New York: Oxford University Press.

Haley, Kathy. (2003, November 24). "Five Star TV." *Multichannel News*: 3A.

Hall, C. (2000, May 8). "Pediatricians' Group Issues Guide for ADD Diagnosis." *San Francisco Chronicle*: A1.

Hall, Kevin G. (2006, November 3). "The Rich Are Getting Much Richer, Much Faster Than Everyone Else." *McClatchy Newspapers*.

Hall, Stephen S. (1999, August 22). "The Bully in the Mirror." *New York Times Magazine*: 30–35, 58–65.

Hamermesh, S. D. and J. E. Biddle. (1994). "Beauty and the Labor Market." *American Economic Review* 84, no. 5: 1174–94.

Hampp, Andrew. (2007, August 6). "An Ad in Which Boy Gets Girls . . . or Boy." *Advertising Age*.

Hannah, Matthew G. (2001). "Sampling and the Politics of Representation in US Census 2000." *Environment and Planning D: Society and Space* 19, no. 5: 515–34.

Hansen, Susan, Alec McHoul, and Mark Rapley With Hayley Miller and Toby Miller. (2003). *Beyond Help: A Consumer's Guide to Psychology*. Ross-on-Wye: PCCS Books.

Harari, Fiona. (1993, June 15). "The New Face of Beauty." *Australian*: 15.

Hardt, Michael and Antonio Negri. (2000). *Empire*. Cambridge: Harvard University Press.

Hari, Johann. (2007, March 15). "Change Our Schools, Not Our Children." *Independent*: 42.

Harkin, James. (2006, September 16). "The Return of the Real Man." *Financial Times*: 22.

Harré, Rom. (2004). "Staking Our Claim for Qualitative Psychology as Science." *Qualitative Research in Psychology* 1: 3–14.

Harris, Gardiner. (2005, March 25). "Citizens' Group Wants Hyperactivity Drug Taken Off the Market." *New York Times*.

———. (2006, August 22). "F.D.A. Strenghtens Warnings on Stimulants." *New York Times*.

Harris, Gardiner, Benedict Carey, and Janet Roberts. (2007, May 10). "Industry's Role in Children's Antipsychotics." *New York Times*.

Harris, Patrick. (2006, June 8). "Wake Up: The American Dream Is Over." *Observer*.

Hart, Kylo-Patrick R. (2004). "We're Here, We're Queer—And We're Better Than You: The Representational Superiority of Gay Men to Heterosexuals on *Queer Eye for the Straight Guy*." *Journal of Men's Studies* 12.

Hartford Institute for Religion Research. (2007). *Fast Facts*.

Hartley, John. (1998). "'When Your Child Grows Up Too Fast': Juvenation and the Boundaries of the Social in the News Media." *Continuum: Journal of Media & Cultural Studies* 12, no. 1: 9–30.

———. (2003). *A Short History of Cultural Studies*. London: Sage.

Harwood, Valerie. (2006). *Diagnosing "Disorderly" Children: A Critique of Behaviour Disorder Discourses*. Abingdon: Routledge.

Hassell, Greg. (2001, September 25). "Altruistic Ads Try to Unite Americans." *Houston Chronicle*.

Haste, Helen. (2004). "Constructing the Citizen." *Political Psychology* 25, no. 3: 413–39.

Hastings, Michael. (2003, February 26). "Billboard Ban." *Newsweek*.

Haug, W. F. (1986). *Critique of Commodity Aesthetics: Appearance, Sexuality and Advertising in Capitalist Society*. Trans. Robert Bock. Cambridge: Polity Press.

Hausman, Ken. (2002). "Last of Ritalin-Based Lawsuits Against APA Comes to a Close." *Psychiatric News* 37, no. 7: 1.

Healy, David. (1997). *The Antidepressant Era*. Cambridge: Harvard University Press.

———. (2002). *The Creation of Psychopharmacology*. Cambridge: Harvard University Press.

Healy, David and Michael E. Thase, ed. Mary Cannon, Kwame McKenzie, and Andrew Sims. (2003). "Is Academic Psychiatry for Sale?" *British Journal of Psychiatry* 182: 388–90.

Healy, Jane M. (2004). "Early Television Exposure and Subsequent Attention Problems in Children." *Pediatrics* 113: 917–18.

Healy, Melissa. (2004, May 24). "Losing Focus." *Los Angeles Times*.

———. (2006, December 18). "Many of the 'ADD Generation' Say No to Meds." *Los Angeles Times*.

———. (2007, November 5). "Are We Too Quick to Medicate Children?" *Los Angeles Times*.

Hearn, Kelly. (2004, November 29). "Here, Kiddie, Kiddie." http://alternet.org.

———. (2005, March 28). "Miracle Malpractice." http://www.alternet.org.

Heavey, Susan. (2006, April 7). "U.S. FDA Approves First Skin Patch for ADHD." *Reuters*.

Hedges, Chris. (2007, January 19). "The Radical Christian Right Is Built on Suburban Despair." http://alternet.org.

Hegel, Georg Wilhelm Friedrich. (1988). *Lectures on the Philosophy of History: Introduction: Reason in History*. Trans. H. B. Nisbet and Duncan Forbes. Cambridge: Cambridge University Press.

Heins, Marjorie. (2002). *Not in Front of the Children: "Indecency," Censorship, and the Innocence of Youth*. New York: Hill and Wang.

Held, David, Anthony McGrew, David Goldblatt, and Jonathan Perraton. (1999). *Global Transformations: Politics, Economics and Culture*. Stanford: Stanford University Press.

Heller, Dana. (2006). "Before: 'Things Just Keep Getting Better . . .'" *The Great American Makeover: Television, History, Nation*. Ed. Dana Heller. New York: Palgrave Macmillan. 1–7.

Henwood, Doug. (2006). "LBO at 20." *Left Business Observer* 114: 1–7.

Hepstintall, E. and E. Taylor. (1996). "Sex Differences and Their Significance." *Hyperactivity Disorders of Childhood*. Ed. S. Sandberg. Cambridge: Cambridge University Press. 329–49.

Herman, Burt. (2006, April 16). "S. Korea Sees Boom in Male Plastic Surgery." http://www.sfgate.com.

Herman, Ellen. (1996). *The Romance of American Psychology: Political Culture in the Age of Experts*. Berkeley: University of California Press.

——. (1998). "Project Camelot and the Career of Cold-War Psychology." *Universities and Empire: Money and Politics in the Social Sciences During the Cold War*. Ed. Christopher Simpson. New York: New Press. 97–133.

——. (2001). "How Children Turn Out and How Psychology Turns Them Out." *History of Psychology* 4, no. 3: 297–316.

Hewlett, Theresa, Susan Hansen, and Mark Rapley. (2005). "'Like Bees to a Honey Pot': ADHD as Rhetoric." *Journal of Critical Psychology, Counselling, and Psychotherapy* 5, no. 2: 94–103.

Heyes, Cressida J. (2007). "Cosmetic Surgery and the Televisual Makeover: A Foucauldian Feminist Reading." *Feminist Media Studies* 7, no. 1: 17–32.

Hibbert, Katharine. (2007, November 8). "Ways to Make You Think Better." *Guardian*.

Hickey, Neil. (2004 May/June). "TV: Hype Takes a Hit." *Columbia Journalism Review*: 6.

Hier, Sean P. (2003). "Risk and Panic in Late Modernity: Implications of the Converging Sites of Social Anxiety." *British Journal of Sociology* 54, no. 1: 3–20.

Hightower, Jim. (2000, March 24). "Babies on Drugs." http://alternet.org.

Hill, Annette. (2005). *Reality TV: Audiences and Popular Factual Television*. London: Routledge.

Himmelstein, Jerome L. and Mayer Zald. (1984). "American Conservatism and Government Funding of the Social Sciences and Arts." *Sociological Inquiry* 54, no. 2: 171–87.

Hindess, Barry. (1993). "Marxism." *A Companion to Contemporary Political Philosophy*. Ed. Robert E. Goodin and Philip Pettit. Oxford: Blackwell. 312–32.

Hinshaw, S. P. (2000). "Introduction." *Attention Deficits and Hyperactivity in Children and Adults: Diagnosis, Treatment, Management*. 2nd ed. Ed. P. J. Accardo, T. A. Blondis, B. Y. Whitman, and M. A. Stein. New York: Marcel Dekker. xiii–xvii.

Hinsliff, G. (2000, September 3). "Sedative Drug Ban for Under-5s." *Guardian*.

"Hispanic and Asian Populations Expand." (2000, August 30). *New York Times*: A16.

Hispanic Fact Pack. (2005). *Advertising Age* with Association of Hispanic Advertising Agencies.

Hobbes, Thomas. (2002). *On the Citizen*. Trans. and Ed. Richard Tuck and Michael Silverthorne. Cambridge: Cambridge University Press.

Hochschild, Arlie Russell. (1994). "The Commercial Spirit of Intimate Life and the Abduction of Feminism: Signs From Women's Advice Books." *Theory, Culture & Society* 11, no. 2: 1–24.

Hoey, John, Caralee E. Kaplan, Tom Lemslie, Kenneth M. Flegel, K. S. Joseph, Anita Palepu, and Anne Marie Todkill. (1999). "Science, Sex, and Semantics: The Firing of George Lundberg." *Canadian Medical Association Journal/Journal de la association médical canadienne* 160, no. 4: 507–8.

Hoffman, Heinrich. (1999). *Struwwelpeter: Fearful Stories & Vile Pictures to Instruct Good Little Folks*. New York: Feral House.

Hogle, Linda F. (2005). "Enhancement Technologies and the Body." *Annual Review of Anthropology* 34: 695–716.

Holbrook, Thomas M. (2001). "(Mis)reading the Political Tea Leaves." *American Politics Research* 29, no. 3: 297–301.

Holden, John, Lydia Howland, and Daniel Stedman Jones. (2002). "Closing the Loop." *Demos Collection* 18: 5–15.

Holliday, Ruth and Allie Cairnie. (2007). "Man Made Plastic: Investigating Men's Consumption of Aesthetic Surgery." *Journal of Consumer Culture* 7, no. 1: 57–78.

Holliday, Ruth and Jacqueline Sanchez Taylor. (2006). "Aesthetic Surgery as False Beauty." *Feminist Theory* 7, no. 2: 179–95.

Honeyman, Katrina and Andrew Godley. (2003). "Introduction: Doing Business With Fashion." *Textile History* 34, no. 2: 101–6.

Honig, Bonnie. (1998). "Immigrant America? How Foreignness 'Solves' Democracy's Problems." *Social Text* 56: 1–27.

Hontz, Jenny. (1999, March 8–14). "Media Blows Off Standards: Media Takes Up Bawdy-Building." *Variety*: 58.

Horn, D. (1995). "'This Norm Which Is Not One: Reading the Female Body in Lobroso's Anthropology." *Deviant Bodies*. Ed. Jennifer Terry and Jacqueline Urla. Bloomington: Indiana University Press. 109–28.

Horton, Richard. (2005). "Threats to Human Survival: A WIRE to Warn the World." *Lancet* 365, no. 9455.

Horton, Sarah. (2004). "Different Subjects: The Health Care System's Participation in the Differential Construction of the Cultural Citizenship of Cuban Refugees and Mexican Immigrants." *Medical Anthropology Quarterly* 18, no. 4: 472–89.

House Appropriations Committee—Minority. (2003) http://www.house.gov/appropriations_democrats/caughtonfilm.htm.

House Education & the Workforce Committee. (2003, March 12). "Bill Introduced to Protect Parents From Being Forced to Medicate Students Before School."

House of Representatives 5005. (2002). Homeland Security Act of 2002.

House of Representatives, Subcommittee on Early Childhood, Youth and Families, Committee on Education and the Workforce. (2000, May 16). *Ritalin Use Among Youth: Examining the Issues and Concerns.*

The HSM Group. (2004). "Productivity Impact Model: Calculating the Impact of Depression in the Workplace and the Benefits of Treatment." http://depressioncalculator.com/Welcome.asp.

Human Rights Watch. (2003). *Ill-Equipped: U.S. Prisons and Offenders With Mental Illness.* New York.

———. (2006, September 6). "U.S.: Number of Mentally Ill in Prisons Quadrupled."

Hume, David. (1955). *An Inquiry Concerning Human Understanding With a Supplement: An Abstract of a Treatise of Human Nature.* Indianapolis: Bobbs-Merrill.

Hunt, Kate, Heather Lewars, Carol Emslie, and G. David Batty. (2007). "Decreased Risk of Death From Coronary Heart Disease Amongst Men With Higher 'Femininity' Scores: A General Population Cohort Study." *International Journal of Epidemiology.*

Hutton, Will. (2003a, January 5). "Crunch Time for Uncle Sam." *Observer.*

———. (2003b). *A Declaration of Interdependence: Why America Should Join the World.* New York: W. W. Norton.

Hyman, S. (2000, May 16). "Statement for the Record on Methylphenidate (Ritalin) for Children With ADHD." http://waisgate.hhs.gov/cgibin/waisgate?

"ideavillage's As Seen on TV Line Is an Alternative for Men and Women." (2004, June 1). *Retail-Merchandiser.*

Iglesias, Enrique V. (2000). "Prólogo." *Capital Social y Cultura: Claves Estratégicas para el Desarollo.* Ed. Bernardo Kliksberg and Luciano Tomassini. Washington: Banco Interamericano de Desarrollo/Fundación Felipe Herrera, Universidad de Maryland/Fondo de Cultura Económica. 7–9.

"In God's Name." (2007, November 3). *The Economist*: 3–5.

International Business Leaders Forum. (2004). Corporate Social Responsibility Forum. http://iblf.org.

"International Consensus Statement on ADHD." (2002). *Clinical Child and Family Psychology Review* 5, no. 2: 89–111.

"In the Money." (2007, January 20). *The Economist:* Special Report.

Irizarry, Lisa. (2007, March 5). "Clothes Make the Man." *Staten Island Advance:* 25.

Ivins, Molly. (2005, February 17). "Screw the Children." http://alternet.org.

Jack, Andrew. (2006, March 26). "Blaming the Big Drug Makers." *Los Angeles Times:* C2.

Jacobson, Ken. (2002). "ADHD in Cross-Cultural Perspective: Some Empirical Results." *American Anthropologist* 104, no. 1: 283–86.

Jakobsen, Janet R. and Ann Pellegrini. (2003). *Love the Sin: Sexual Regulation and the Limits of Religious Tolerance.* New York: New York University Press.

James, Beccy. (2006 July). "Mental Health: Much More Than a 'State of Mind.'" *Socialist Review.*

Jameson, Fredric. (1991). *Postmodernism, or, the Cultural Logic of Late Capitalism.* London: Verso.

Jameson, Marnell. (2006, October 16). "How to Keep What You've Got." *Los Angeles Times:* F7.

Jaramillo, Deborah L. (2006). "Pills Gone Wild: Medium Specificity and the Regulation of Prescription Drug Advertising on Television." *Television & New Media* 7, no. 3: 261–81.

Jarboe, Michelle. (2006, August 29). "Black Market for ADD Drugs." http://youthradio.org.

Jargon, Julie. (2006, October 16). "She Knows Her Men." *Crain's Chicago Business:* 3.

Jauffred, Martha. (2006, November 30). "De *Dandis* a Metrosexuales." *El Economista:* 8.

Jeffrey, Craig and Linda McDowell. (2004). "Youth in a Comparative Perspective: Global Change, Local Lives." *Youth & Society* 36, no. 2: 131–42.

Jeffries, Stuart. (2006, February 11). "Risky Business." *Guardian.*

Jencks, Christopher. (2004 June). "Our Unequal Democracy." *American Prospect:* A2–A4.

Jenkins, Emily. (1998). *Tongue First: Adventures in Physical Culture.* New York: Henry Holt.

Jenkins, Philip. (1999). *Synthetic Panics: The Symbolic Politics of Designer Drugs.* New York: New York University Press.

Jensen, Michael. (2006, December 19). "The Year in Queer TV: Eleven Highs and Lows from 2006." http://www.afterelton.com.

Jensen, Richard. (1996). "The Culture Wars, 1965–1995: A Historian's Map." *Journal of Social History* 29: 17–38.

Jerome, Jerome K. (2000). *Three Men in a Boat.* New York: Penguin Classics. Originally published 1938.

Johne, Marjo. (2006, August 9). "Boomers Put a New Face on Their Careers." *Globe and Mail:* C1.

Johnson, Bradley. (2005, May 2). "How U.S. Consumers Spend their Time." *AdAge.*

Johnson, Carol. (2002). "Heteronormative Citizenship and the Politics of Passing." *Sexualities* 5, no. 3: 317–36.

Johnson, James. (2000). "Why Respect Culture?" *American Journal of Political Science* 44, no. 3: 405–18.

Johnson, Peter. (2003, February 24). "Media Question Authority Over War Protests." *USA Today.*

Jones, Jeffrey P. (2001). "Forums for Citizenship in Popular Culture." *Politics, Discourse and American Society: New Agendas.* Ed. R. P. Hart and B. H. Sparrow. Boulder: Rowman & Littlefield. 193–210.

Jones, K. (1999). *Taming the Troublesome Child: American Families, Child Guidance, and the Limits of Psychiatric Authority.* Cambridge: Harvard University Press.

"Juan Valdez Affronte Starbucks." (2004 February). *L'Actualité:* 17.

Jud, Staller and Stephen V. Faraone. (2006). "Attention-Deficit Hyperactivity Disorder in Girls: Epidemiology and Management." *CNS Drugs* 20, no. 2: 107–23.

Judge, Mark Gauvreau. (2006, January 4). "Right-Wingtips." *American Spectator.*

Kaiser Family Foundation. (2000 August). "Teen Sexual Activity."

Kakutani, Michiko. (1999, January 12). "The Modern Political Novel as a Mirror of the Bizarre." *New York Times:* E1, E10.

Kalins, Dorothy. (2004, August 23). "A Master of the Art of Living." *Newsweek:* 71.

Kallick, David Dyssegaard. (2002). *Progressive Think Tanks: What Exists, What's Missing?* Report for the Program on Governance and Public Policy. Open Society Institute.

Kalyanpur, Maya. (1997, November 22). "Signs of Greying Childhood." *Times of India.*

Kant, Immanuel. (1991). *Political Writings.* 2nd ed. Trans. H. B. Nisbet. Ed. Hans Reiss. Cambridge: Cambridge University Press.

Kaplan, Esther. (2004, November 1). "Follow the Money." *The Nation:* 20–23.

Kapur, Jyotsna. (2005). *Coining for Capital: Movies, Marketing, and the Transformation of Childhood.* New Brunswick: Rutgers University Press.

Karr, Timothy. (2005, April 12). "Is Cheap Broadband Un-American?" *Media Citizen.*

Kass, Leon R. (2003, January 16–17). "Beyond Therapy: Biotechnology and the Pursuit of Human Improvement." Discussion Paper for the President's Council on Bioethics.

Kaufmann, Eric. (2006). "Breeding for God." *Prospect Magazine:* 128.

Keeler, Dan. (2002 May). "Spread the Love and Make It Pay." *Global Finance:* 20–25.

Keeps, David A. (2007, March 18). "The Outlaw Rides Again." *Los Angeles Times:* P4.

Keeter, Scott, Cliff Zukin, Molly Andolina, and Krista Jenkins. (2002). *The Civic and Political Health of the Nation: A Generational Portrait.* Center for Information & Research on Civic Learning & Engagement.

Keillor, Garrison. (2004, August 26). "We're Not in Lake Wobegon Anymore." *In These Times.*

Kellner, Douglas. (2003). *From 9/11 to Terror War: The Dangers of the Bush Legacy.* Lanham: Rowman & Littlefield.

Kent, L. (2004). "Recent Advances in the Genetics of Attention Deficit Hyperactivity Disorder." *Current Psychiatry Reports* 6, no. 2: 143–48.

Kerr, Anne. (2003). "Genetics and Citizenship." *Society* 40, no. 6: 44–50.

Kessen, William. (1979). "The American Child and Other Cultural Inventions." *American Psychologist* 34, no. 10: 815–20.

Kettebekov, Sanshzar and Rajeev Sharma. (2001). "Toward Natural Gesture/Speech Control of a Large Display." *Lecture Notes in Computer Science:* 2254.

Khanna, Parag. (2004 July/August). "The Metrosexual Superpower." *Foreign Policy.*

"Kids & Cash." (2004 November/December). *Mother Jones:* 28–29.

"Kids' Role in Securing USA." (2004, August 10). *USA Today.*

Kimmel, Michael S. (1992). "Reading Men: Men, Masculinity, and Publishing." *Contemporary Sociology* 21, no. 2: 162–71.

———. (1997). *Manhood in America: A Cultural History.* New York: Free Press.

Kirsch, Irving, Brett J. Deacon, Tania B. Huedo-Medina, Alan Scoboria, Thomas J. Moore, and Blair T. Johnson. (2008). "Initial Severity and Antidepressant Benefits: A Meta-Analysis of Data Submitted to the Food and Drug Administration." *PLOS Medicine* 5, no. 2.

Kitch, Carolyn. (2003). "Generational Identity and Memory in American Newsmagazines." *Journalism: Theory, Practice and Criticism* 4, no. 2: 185–202.

Kline, Stephen. (1993). *Out of the Garden: Toys, TV, and Children's Culture in the Age of Marketing*. London: Verso.

Kluge, Alexander. (1981–82). "On Film and the Public Sphere." Trans. Thomas Y. Levin and Miriam B. Hansen. *New German Critique*: 24–25.

Kolec, Ethan A. (2006). "Recreational Prescription Drug Use Among College Students." *NASPA Journal* 43, no. 1.

Kors, Joshua. (2007, April 9). "How Specialist Town Lost His Benefits." *The Nation*: 11–18.

Kory, Deborah. (2007, June 27). "How Psychologists Aid Torture." http://alternet.org.

Kotkin, Joel and David Friedman. (2006, December 3). "Rebuilding the Middle Class." *Los Angeles Times*: M6.

Kovac, Carl. (2001, September 1). "Drug Company Breaks 30 Year Agreement on Patient Advertising." *British Medical Journal* 323: 470.

Kovacs, Joe. (2005, October 11). "Rush Limbaugh Wonders: Am I an 'Ubersexual'?" *WorldNetDaily*.

Kramer, Peter D. (2003). "Foreword." *Better Than Well: American Medicine Meets the American Dream*, by Carl Elliott. New York: W. W. Norton. ix–xiii.

Krauskopf, Lewis. (2001, August 23). "Reformulated Version of Ritalin Nears Approval." *The Record*: B1.

Krauthammer, Charles. (2004, May 14). "The Abu Ghraib Panic." *Washington Post*.

Krikorian, Mark. (2004, June 22). "Post-Americans." *National Review Online*. http://www.nationalreview.com.

Krugman, Paul. (2007, March 9). "How to Save the Middle Class From Extinction." http://alternet.org.

Kuczynski, Alex. (1998, December 7). "The First Lady Strikes a Pose for the Media Elite." *New York Times*: C1, C8.

Kurlantzick, Joshua. (2004, November/December). "Outfront." *Mother Jones*: 15–17.

Kutchins, Herb and Stuart A. Kirk. (1997). *Making Us Crazy: DSM: The Psychiatric Bible and the Creation of Mental Disorders*. New York: Free Press.

Lacey, H. (1996, October 27). "Drug Him When He Teases." *Independent*: 12.

Lachter, Irene. (2007, April 13). "Gay Characters Increase in Complexity, If Not Frequency." *Hollywood Reporter*.

Lacroix, Celeste and Robert Westerfelhaus. (2005). "From the Closet to the Loft: Liminal License and Socio-Sexual Separation in *Queer Eye for the Straight Guy*." *Qualitative Research Reports in Communication* 6, no. 1: 11–19.

Lake, Celinda and Daniel Gotoff. (2006). *The Role of the Economy in the 2006 Elections: A Post-Election Recap*. Washington: Lake Research Partners.

Lake Research Partners. (2006). *The American Dream Survey 2006*.

Lakoff, Andrew. (2000). "Adaptive Will: The Evolution of Attention Deficit Disorder." *Journal of the History of the Behavioral Sciences* 36, no. 2: 149–69.

Langman, Lauren. (2002). "Suppose They Gave a Culture War and No One Came." *American Behavioral Scientist* 46, no. 4: 501–34.

Lasch, Christopher. (1978). *The Culture of Narcissism: American Life in an Age of Diminishing Expectations*. New York: Norton.

Latour, Bruno. (1993). *We Have Never Been Modern*. Trans. Catherine Porter. Cambridge: Harvard University Press.

Latour, Bruno, With Konstantin Kastrissianakis. (2007, March 22). "We Are All Reactionaries Today." "Re-Public: Re-Imagining Democracy—English Version." http://www.re-public.gr.

Lawrence, D. H. (1953). *Studies in Classic American Literature*. Garden City: Doubleday.

Lawrence, Geoffrey and Lynda Herbert-Cheshire. (2003 August). "Regional Restructuring, Neoliberalism, Individualisation and Community: The Recent Australian Experience." Paper presented to the European Society for Rural Sociology Congress, Sligo.

Layman, Geoffrey C. (1999). "'Culture Wars' in the American Party System: Religious and Cultural Change Among Partisan Activists Since 1972." *American Politics Quarterly* 27, no. 1: 89–121.

Layton, M. J. and L. Washburn. (2000, October 1). "'Hyperactive' Kids: Victims of a Plot?—Lawsuit Alleges Scheme to Sell Ritalin." *Record*: 1.

Le Bon, Gustave. (1899). *Psychologie des Foules*. Paris: Alcan.

Leadbeater, Charles. (2004). *Personalisation Through Participation: A New Script for Public Services*. London: Demos.

Lechner, Norbert. (2003). "¿Como Reconstruimos un Nosotros?" *Metapolítica* 29: 52–65.

Lee, Jennifer. (2005, April 10). "The Man Date." *New York Times*.

Lee, Jennine. (2005, January 31). "NASCAR Goes Metrosexual." *Time*: 18.

Lee, Linda. (2003, October). "Out of Order." *Vogue*: 316–21.

Leguineche, Manu. (2002). "Cuidado con lo que dice, cuidado con lo que pregunta." *La Télévisión en Tiempos de Guerra*. Ed. Paco Lobatón. Barcelona: Editorial Gedisa. 13–21.

Leibowitz, D. (2000, August 8). "Parents Prosecuted for Taking Son Off Ritalin." *Arizona Republic*.

Leinwand, Donna. (2007, March 13). "Misuse of Pharmaceuticals Linked to More ER Visits." *USA Today*: 2A.

Leland, John. (2001, July 29). "Big Pharma Ogles Yasgur's Farm." *New York Times*: WK3.

Lemish, Dafna. (2007). *Children and Television: A Global Perspective*. Malden: Blackwell.

Lemon, B. (1997, July 22). "Male Beauty." *Advocate* 738: 30–32.

Lenskyj, Helen Jefferson. (2005). "Gay Games or Gay Olympics? Corporate Sponsorship Issues." *Global Sport Sponsorship*. Ed. John Amis and T. Bettina Cornwell. Oxford: Berg.

Lenzer, Jeanne. (2006, October 30). "Study Break." *New Republic*: 13.

Lenzer, Jeanne and Ron Paul. (2006, March 3). "El 'Big Pharma' caza escolares en EEUU." Trans. Ernesto Carmona. http://www.rebelion.org.

Leo, Jonathan. (2002). "American Preschoolers on Ritalin." *Society* 39, no. 2: 52–60.

Leonard, Andrew. (2007, November 30). "How Much Is That Earthquake in the Window?" http://www.salon.com.

Lerner, S. (2000, April 11). "The Shrink Brigade." *Village Voice*: 32.

Let There Be Light. (1946). Dir. John Huston. US Army Pictorial Services.

Levine, Robert A. (2007). "Ethnographic Studies of Childhood: A Historical Overview." *American Anthropologist* 109, no. 2: 247–60.

Levitt, Peggy. (2001). "Transnational Migration: Taking Stock and Future Directions."

Global Networks 1, no. 3: 195–216.

Lewis, Bradley. (2006). *Moving Beyond Prozac, DSM, & the New Psychiatry: The Birth of Postpsychiatry.* Ann Arbor: University of Michigan Press.

Lewis, Jon. (1992). *The Road to Romance & Ruin: Teen Films and Youth Culture.* New York: Routledge.

Lewis, Justin. (2001). *Constructing Public Opinion: How Political Elites Do What They Like and Why We Seem to Go Along With It.* New York: Columbia University Press.

Lewis, Justin, Sanna Inthorn, and Karin Wahl-Jorgensen. (2005). *Citizens or Consumers? What the Media Tell Us About Political Participation.* Maidenhead: Open University Press.

Lewis, Michael. (2007, August 26). "In Nature's Casino." *New York Times Magazine.*

Lewis, Tania. (2008). *Smart Living: Lifestyle Media and Popular Expertise.* New York: Peter Lang.

Lewontin, R. C. (1997). "The Cold War and the Transformation of the Academy." *The Cold War and the University: Toward an Intellectual History of the Postwar Years.* Ed. Noam Chomsky. New York: New Press. 1–34.

Lexington. (2004, August 7). "It's a Man's World." *The Economist*: 28.

Liebel, Manfred. (2004). *A Will of Their Own: Cross-Cultural Perspectives on Working Children.* Trans. Colin Boone and Jess Rotherburger. London: Zed.

Liljeström, Rita. (1983). "The Public Child, the Commercial Child, and Our Child." *The Child and Other Cultural Inventions.* Ed. Frank S. Kessel and Alexander W. Siegel. New York: Praeger. 124–52.

Lindsay, Greg. (2005, June 13). "Did Marketing Kill the Great American Alpha Male?" *Advertising Age*: 1.

Lippmann, Walter. (1943). *The Good Society.* New York: Grosset & Dunlap.

"Living Dangerously." (2004, January 24). *The Economist.*

Livingstone, K. (1997). "Ritalin: Miracle Drug or Cop-Out?" *Public Interest*: 127.

Lloyd, John. (2002, January 12). "Wanted." *Financial Times*: FT1, Weekend.

Lobe, Jim. (2003a, January 4). "All the World's a TV Screen." *Asia Times.*

Lock, T. M. and D. B. Bender. (2000). *Attention Deficits and Hyperactivity in Children and Adults: Diagnosis, Treatment, Management.* 2nd ed. Ed. P. J. Accardo, T. A. Blondis, B. Y. Whitman, and M. A. Stein. New York: Marcel Dekker. 29–56.

Locke, John. (1990). *Two Treatises of Government.* London: J. M. Dent & Sons.

Loring, Marti and Brian Powell. (1988). "Gender, Race, and *DSM-III*: A Study of Psychiatric Diagnostic Behavior." *Journal of Health and Social Behavior* 29, no. 1: 1–22.

Lovato, Roberto. (2004, June 28). "Fear of a Brown Planet." *The Nation*: 17–21.

Love, Maryann Cusimano. (2003). "Global Media and Foreign Policy." *Media Power, Media Politics.* Ed. Mark J. Rozell. Lanham: Rowman & Littlefield. 235–64.

Lowry, Brian. (2003, February 26). "Will the TV Factory Shape a New War?" *Calendar Live.*

Luhrmann, Tanya M. (2004). "Metakinesis: How God Becomes Intimate in Contemporary U.S. Christianity." *American Anthropologist* 106, no. 3: 518–28.

Luk, S. L. (1996). "Cross-Cultural Aspects." *Hyperactivity Disorders of Childhood.* Ed. S. Sandberg. Cambridge: Cambridge University Press. 350–81.

Lukacs, John. (2002 January). "The Fifties: Another View." *Harper's Magazine*: 64–70.

Lunbeck, E. (1994). *The Psychiatric Persuasion: Knowledge, Gender, and Power in Modern America.* Princeton: Princeton University Press.

Lynch, Alexander. (2005, March 14). "The Media Lobby." http://alternet.org.

MacArthur, John. (2003, June 6). "All the News That's Fudged to Print." *Globe & Mail.*

Mackie, Drew. (2006, December 7). "The State of Gay TV Today." http://www.afterelton. com.

"Madeover Ken Hopes to Win Back Barbie." (2006, February 10). http://www.cnn.com.

Madrick, Jeff. (2007, February 5). "Goodbye, Horatio Alger." *The Nation:* 2024.

Maira, Luis. (2002). "El Amarre Institucional del General Pinochet y las Restricciones de la Transición Chilena." *Globalización, Identidad y Democracia: México y América Latina.* Ed. Julio Labastida Martín del Campo and Antonio Camou. Mexico: Siglo Veintiuno Editores. 82–110.

Maira, Sunaina and Elisabeth Soep. (2004). "United Status of Adolescence? Reconsidering US Youth Culture Studies." *Young: Nordic Journal of Youth Research* 12, no. 3: 245–69.

Maitland, Alison. (2002, September 11). "How to Become Good in All Areas." *Financial Times:* 10.

"Make It Cheaper, and Cheaper." (2003, December 13). *The Economist:* 6–8.

"Make It Convenient." (2003, December 13). *The Economist:* 10–11.

Malacrida, Claudia. (2002). "Alternative Therapies and Attention Deficit Disorder: Discourses of Maternal Responsibility and Risk." *Gender & Society* 16, no. 3: 366–85.

———. (2003). *Cold Comfort: Mothers, Professionals, and Attention Deficit Disorder.* Toronto: University of Toronto Press.

Malcom, Janet. (1998, October 5). "Talk of the Town." *The New Yorker:* 32.

Males, Mike A. (1996). *The Scapegoat Generation: America's War on Adolescents.* Monroe: Common Courage Press.

———. (2004 January/February). "With Friends Like These." *EXTRA!:* 15–16.

Males, Mike. (2006a, September 17). "It's a Crime How We Misjudge the Young." *Los Angeles Times:* M6.

———. (2006b, September/October). "More Dangerous Than Anyone Thought." *EXTRA!:* 29–30.

Malkki, Liisa and Emily Martin. (2003). "Children and the Gendered Politics of Globalization: In Remembrance of Sharon Stephens." *American Ethnologist* 30, no. 2: 216–24.

Manes, Billy. (2003, August 27). "Straight Eye for the Queer Guy." http://metrotimes.com.

Maney, Kevin. (2003, July 24). "IBM Makes Play for 'Next-Generation Pixar.'" *USA Today.*

Manguel, Alberto. (1996). *A History of Reading.* New York: Viking.

Mann, Michael. (2003). *Incoherent Empire.* London: Verso.

Manne, Anne. (2003 April/May). "Cries Unheard." *Arena Magazine:* 47–56.

Manninen, B. A. (2006). "Medicating the Mind: A Kantian Analysis of Overprescribing Psychoactive Drugs." *Journal of Medical Ethics* 32: 100–105.

Manning-Schaffel, Vivian. (2006, May 24). "Metrosexuals: A Well-Groomed Market?" *Business Week.*

Marinoff, L. (2000, July 16). "Más Platón y Menos Prozac." *El País:* 14–15.

"Marketplace." (1999, June 3). National Public Radio.

Markillie, Paul. (2005, April 2). "Crowned at Last." *The Economist:* 3–6.

Marsa, Linda. (2005 January/February). "Sleep for Sale." *Mother Jones:* 20.

Marshall, E. (2000, August 4). "Epidemiology: Duke Study Faults Overuse of Stimulants for Children." *Science.*

Marshall, Eliot. (1988). "Nobel Economist Robert Solow." *Dialogue* 82: 8–9.

Marshall, P. David. (1997). *Celebrity and Power: Fame in Contemporary Culture.* Minneapolis: University of Minnesota Press.

Martin, Christopher R. (2004). *Framed! Labor and the Corporate Media*. Ithaca: ILR Press/ Cornell University Press.

Martin, Emily. (2006). "Pharmaceutical Virtue." *Culture, Medicine and Psychiatry* 30: 157–74.

Martin, Randy. (2002). *Financialization of Daily Life*. Philadelphia: Temple University Press.

Martín-Barbero, Jesús. (2000). "Nuevos mapas culturales de la integración y el desarrollo." *Capital Social y Cultura: Claves Estratégicas para el Desarollo*. Ed. Bernardo Kliksberg and Luciano Tomassini. Washington: Banco Interamericano de Desarollo/Fundación Felipe Herrera, Universidad de Maryland/Fondo de Cultura Económica. 335–58.

———. (2001a). "Introducción." *Imaginarios de Nación: Pensar en Medio de la Tormenta*. Ed. Jesús Martin-Barbero. Bogotá: Ministerio de Cultura. 7–10.

———. (2001b). "Colombia: Ausencia de Relato y Desubicaciones de lo Nacional." *Imaginarios de Nación: Pensar en Medio de la Tormenta*. Ed. Jesús Martin-Barbero. Bogotá: Ministerio de Cultura. 17–28.

———. (2003). "Proyectos de Modernidad en América Latina." *Metapolítica* 29: 35–51.

Martín-Baró, Ignacio. (1996). *Writings for a Liberation Theology*. Trans. Adrianne Aron, Phillip Berryman, Cindy Forster, Anne Wallace, Tod Sloan, and Jean Carroll. Ed. Adrianne Aron and Shawn Corne. Cambridge: Harvard University Press.

Martinez, Dawn Belkin. (2005). "Mental Health Care After Capitalism." *Radical Psychology*.

Marx, Karl. (1987). *Capital: A Critique of Political Economy. Volume 1: The Process of Capitalist Production*. Trans. Samuel Moore and Edward Aveling. Ed. Frederick Engels. New York: International Publishers.

———. (1994). "Human Emancipation." *Citizenship*. Ed. Paul Barry Clarke. London: Pluto Press. 137–40.

Marx, Karl and Frederick Engels. (1995). *The German Ideology: Part One*. Ed. C. J. Arthur. New York: International Publishers.

Maryniak, Irena. (2003). "The New Slave Trade." *Index on Censorship* 32, no. 3: 87.

Maslin, Janet. (2000, June 29). "Exploring a Dark Side of Depression Remedies." *New York Times*: E11.

Mason, R. (1999, May 19). "The Gift of Clarification." *Jerusalem Post*.

Massing, Michael. (2001, October 15). "Press Watch." *The Nation*.

Massey, Douglas S. (2003). "The United States in the World Community: The Limits of National Sovereignty." *The Fractious Nation? Unity and Division in American Life*. Ed. Jonathan Rieder. Assoc. Ed. Stephen Steinlight. Berkeley: University of California Press. 143–54.

Mathieson, Thomas. (1997). "The Viewer Society: Michel Foucault's 'Panopticon' Revisited." *Theoretical Criminology* 1, no. 2: 215–34.

Mattelart, Armand. (2003). *The Information Society*. Trans. Susan G. Taponier and James A. Cohen. London: Sage Publications.

Matthews, Virginia. (2003, February 25). "Trust in Community Schemes." *Independent*.

Maxwell, Richard. (2002, December 20). "Citizens, You Are What You Buy." *Times Higher Education Supplement*.

May, Mark A. and Frank K. Shuttleworth. (1933). *The Social Conduct and Attitudes of Movie Fans*. New York: Macmillan.

Mazzarella, Sharon R. (2003). "Constructing Youth: Media, Youth, and the Politics of Representation." *A Companion to Media Studies*. Ed. Angharad N. Valdivia. Malden: Blackwell. 227–46.

McBurnett, K., L. J. Pfiffner, and Y. L. Ottolini. (2000). "Types of ADHD in *DSM-IV*." *Attention Deficits and Hyperactivity in Children and Adults: Diagnosis, Treatment, Management*. 2nd ed. Ed. J. Accardo, T .A. Blondis, B. Y. Whitman, and M. A. Stein. New York: Marcel Dekker. 229–40.

McCallum, David. (1993). "Problem Children and Familial Relations." *Child and Citizen: Genealogies of Schooling and Subjectivity*. Ed. Denise Meredyth and Deborah Tyler. Brisbane: Institute for Cultural Policy Studies. 129–52.

McCarthy, Helen. (2004). *The Self-Esteem Society*. London: Demos.

McCasland, Mitch. (2003, July 22). "Marketing to Peacocks." http://www.marketingprofs. com.

McChesney, Robert W. (2003). "The Problem of Journalism: A Political/Economic Contribution to an Explanation of the Crisis in Contemporary US Journalism." *Journalism Studies* 4, no. 3: 299–329.

McChesney, Robert W. and John Bellamy Foster. (2003). "The Commercial Tidal Wave." *Monthly Review* 54, no. 10: 1–16.

McDonald, William. (2001, April 9). "Ifs, ands or buts of Drugs for Restless U.S. Children." *New York Times:* E8.

McGee, Micki. (2005). *Self-Help, Inc.: Makeover Culture in American Life*. New York: Oxford University Press.

McHoul, Alec and Mark Rapley. (2001). "Ghost: Do not Forget; This Visitation / Is but to Whet Thy Almost Blunted Purpose: Culture, Psychology and 'Being Human.'" *Culture & Psychology* 7, no. 4: 433–51.

———. (2005a). "A Case of Attention-Deficit/Hyperactivity Disorder Diagnosis: Sir Karl and Francis B. Slug It Out on the Consulting Room Floor." *Discourse & Society* 16, no. 3: 419–49.

———. (2005b). "Re-Presenting Culture and the Self." *Theory & Psychology* 15, no. 4: 431–47.

McHugh, Kathleen Anne. (1999). *American Domesticity: From How-To Manual to Hollywood Melodrama*. New York: Oxford University Press.

McLemee, Scott. (2003, August 31). "Murder in Black and White." *Newsday:* D29.

McRobbie, Angela. (2002). "From Holloway to Hollywood: Happiness at Work in the New Cultural Economy." *Cultural Economy: Cultural Analysis and Commercial Life*. Ed. Paul du Gay and Michael Pryke. London: Sage. 97–114.

Mecca, Tommi Avicolli. (2002, June 7). "Gay Shame." http://alternet.org.

Meek, Nigel. (1998). "'Society' Does Not Exist (And If It Did It Shouldn't)." *Political Notes:* 144.

Mencken, H. L. (1956). *The Essential Mencken*. Ed. Alistair Cooke. New York: Vintage.

Messinger, E. C. (1978). "Violence to the Brain." *Semiotexte* 3, no. 2: 66–71.

Messner, Michael A. (1997). *Politics of Masculinities: Men in Movements*. Thousand Oaks: Sage.

Metrosexual. (2006). Dir. Yongyoot Thongkongtoon. Golden Village Entertainment.

"Metrosexual Is Out, Macho Is In." (2006, June 19). *ABC News*.

"Metrosexual Man Ruled the Iron Age." (2006, August 2). *Australian:* 12.

"'Metrosexual' Tops List of Banned Words." (2003, December 31). *CBC Arts*.

"Metrosexuals: The Future of Men?" (2003, June 22). *Euro RSCG Worldwide*.

Meyer, J., J. Boli, G. M. Thomas, and F. O. Ramirez. (1997). "World Society and the Nation-State." *American Journal of Sociology* 103, no. 1: 144–81.

Micheletti, Michele. (2003). *Political Virtue and Shopping: Individuals, Consumerism, and Collective Action.* New York: Palgrave Macmillan.

Michels, Robert. (1915). *Political Parties: A Sociological Study of the Oligarchical Tendencies of Modern Democracy.* Trans. Eden and Cedar Paul. London: Jarrold & Sons.

Mickenberg, Julia L. (2006). "American Studies and Childhood Studies: Lessons from Consumer Culture." *American Quarterly* 58, no. 4: 1217–27.

Midgley, Carol. (2003, February 21). "Kiddie Coke: A New Peril in the Playground." *Times:* 2, 4.

Miliband, David. (2004). "Foreword." *Personalisation Through Participation: A New Script for Public Services,* by Charles Leadbeater. London: Demos. 11–14.

Mill, John Stuart. (1974). *On Liberty.* Harmondsworth: Penguin.

Miller, Martin. (2002, October 21). "Instant Brawn." *Los Angeles Times:* 1.

Miller, Peter and Ted O'Leary. (2002). "Rethinking the Factory: Caterpillar Inc." *Cultural Values* 6, nos. 1–2: 91–117.

Miller, Toby. (1993). *The Well-Tempered Self: Citizenship, Culture, and the Postmodern Subject.* Baltimore: The Johns Hopkins University Press.

———. (1998). *Technologies of Truth: Cultural Citizenship and the Popular Media.* Minneapolis: University of Minnesota Press.

———. (2001). *SportSex.* Philadelphia: Temple University Press.

———. (2003). *Spyscreen: Espionage on Film & TV from the 1930s to the 1960s.* New York: Oxford University Press.

Miller, Toby, Geoffrey Lawrence, Jim McKay, and David Rowe. (2001). *Globalization and Sport: Playing the World.* London: Sage.

Miller, Toby, Nitin Govil, John McMurria, Richard Maxwell, and Ting Wang. (2005). *Global Hollywood 2.* London: British Film Institute.

Millman, Dan. (1979). *The Warrior Athlete: Body, Mind and Spirit: Self-Transformation Through Total Training.* Walpole: Stillpoint.

"Un Millón y Medio de Mexicanos Padecen del Transtorno por Hiperactividad." (2004, January 14). *Excélsior:* 4.

Minow, Martha. (2002). "About Women, About Culture: About Them, About Us." *Engaging Cultural Differences: The Multicultural Challenge in Liberal Democracies.* Ed. Richard A. Schweder, Martha Minow, and Hazel Rose Markus. New York: Russell Sage Foundation. 252–67.

———. (2003). "Fragments or Ties? The Defense of Difference." *The Fractious Nation? Unity and Division in American Life.* Ed. Jonathan Rieder. Assoc. Ed. Stephen Steinlight. Berkeley: University of California Press. 67–78.

Minow, Newton. (1971). "The Broadcasters Are Public Trustees." *Radio & Television: Readings in the Mass Media.* Ed. Allen Kirschener and Linda Kirschener. New York: Odyssey Press. 207–17.

Minow, Newton N. (2001, May 9). "Television, More Vast Than Ever, Turns Toxic." *USA Today:* 15A.

Minow, Newton N. and Fred H. Cate. (2003). "Revisiting the Vast Wasteland." *Federal Communications Law Journal* 55.

Mitchell, Alice Miller. (1929). *Children and the Movies.* Chicago: University of Chicago Press.

Mitchell, Greg. (2005, December 6). "Media Fell Short in Covering 9/11 'Report Card.'" *Editor & Publisher*.

Mitchell, Katharyne. (2003). "Educating the National Citizen in Neoliberal Times: From the Multicultural Self to the Strategic Cosmopolitan." *Transactions of the Institute of British Geographers* 28, no. 4: 387–403.

Modak, Frida. (2001). "Introducción: La gran interrogante." *11 de septiembre de 2001.* Ed. Frida Modak. Buenos Aires: Grupo Editorial Lumen. 3–4.

Moffatt, Barton and Carl Elliott. (2007). "Ghost Marketing: Pharmaceutical Companies and Ghostwritten Journal Articles." *Perspectives in Biology and Medicine* 50, no. 1: 18–31.

Monbiot, George. (2003). *The Age of Consent: A Manifesto for a New World Order.* London: Flamingo.

Montero, Douglas. (2002, September 27). "Ritalin Pusher Changes His Tune on Schools." *New York Post*: 19.

Montgomery, Heather. (2001). "Imposing Rights? A Case Study of Child Prostitution in Thailand." *Culture and Rights: Anthropological Perspectives.* Ed. Jane K. Cowan, Marie-Bénédicte Dembour, and Richard A. Wilson. Cambridge: Cambridge University Press. 80–101.

Mooney, Chris. (2004 November/December). "Blinded by Science." *Columbia Journalism Review.*

Moore, Robert and Douglas Gillette. (1992). *The King Within: Accessing the King in the Male Psyche.* New York: Avon.

Morain, William D. (2003). "The Gender Genie." *Annals of Plastic Surgery* 52, no. 1: 109–10.

"More Generous Than Thou." (2005, January 8). *The Economist*: 26–27.

Mosca, Gaetano. (1939). *The Ruling Class.* Trans. Hannah D. Kahn. Ed. Arthur Livingston. New York: McGraw-Hill.

Mosco, Vincent. (2004). *The Digital Sublime: Myth, Power, and Cyberspace.* Cambridge: MIT Press.

Moses, Lucia. (2003, March 25). "What's in a Deadline?" *Editor & Publisher.*

Mosisa, Abraham T. (2002 May). "The Role of Foreign-Born Workers in the U.S. Economy." *Monthly Labor Review*: 3–14.

Motley, Clay. (2006). "Making Over Body and Soul: *In His Steps* and the Roots of Evangelical Popular Culture." *The Great American Makeover: Television, History, Nation.* Ed. Dana Heller. New York: Palgrave Macmillan. 85–103.

Mouffe, Chantal, ed. (1992). *Dimensions of Radical Democracy: Pluralism, Citizenship, Community.* London: Verso.

Mouffe, Chantal. (1993). *The Return of the Political.* London: Verso.

Moynihan, Ray. (2004). "The Intangible Magic of Celebrity Marketing." *PLoS Medicine* 1, no. 2: 102–4.

Moynihan, Ray and Richard Smith. (2002). "Too Much Medicine?" *British Medical Journal* 324: 859–60.

Moynihan, Ray, Iona Heath, and David Henry. (2002). "Selling Sickness: The Pharmaceutical Industry and Disease Mongering." *British Medical Journal* 324: 886–90.

Muhammad, Amjid. (2006, September 5). "An Election Looms, So Howard Incites Moral Panic." *The Age.*

Mukhia, Harbans. (2002, January 19). "Liberal Democracy and Its Slippages." *Economic and Political Weekly.*

Mullen, Megan. (2002). "The Fall and Rise of Cable Narrowcasting." *Convergence* 8, no. 1: 62–83.

Mullman, Jeremy. (2007, January 22). "Miller Repeals 'Man Law.'" *Advertising Age.*

Murdock, Graham. (1997). "The Re-Enchantment of the World: Religion and the Transformations of Modernity." *Rethinking Media, Religion, and Culture.* Ed. S. M. Hoover and K. Lundby. London: Sage Publications. 85–101.

Murlowe, John. (1997, October 16). "Public Schools: Pushing Drugs?" *Investor's Business Daily:* 1–2.

Murrow, Edward R. (1958, October 15). Speech to the Radio-Television News Directors Association, Chicago.

Muschamp, Herbert. (2004, August 29). "The New Arcadia." *New York Times:* 224.

Musto, D. (1995, March 31). "No Cure But Care." *Times Literary Supplement:* 6.

Nairn, Tom. (2003, January 9, 16, and 23; February 4 and 20). "Democracy & Power: American Power & the World." http://www.opendemocracy.net.

National Institute of Mental Health. (2006). *Attention Deficit Hyperactivity Disorder.* Bethesda: National Institute of Mental Health.

National Institute on Drug Abuse. (2006). *NIDA InfoFacts: Methylphenidate (Ritalin).*

"A Nation Apart." (2003, November 8). *The Economist:* 3–4.

Neff, Jack. (2005, May 3). "Gillette Offers Teenage Boys Date With Carmen Electra." *AdAge.*

———. (2007, April 28). "Body Slam: RGX Ridicules More Sophomoric Sprays." *Advertising Age.*

"New Guidelines for Attention Deficit Disorder." (2001, October 1). *New York Times:* A18.

"New Guru Guide: Ulrich Beck." (2000 June). *Management Today:* 50.

Newport, Frank and Joseph Carroll. (2003, March 6). "Support for Bush Significantly Higher Among More Religious Americans." *Gallup Poll Analyses.*

"News." (2003, March 25). http://motherjones.com.

Nichols, Kendra. (2004, December 17). "The Other Performance-Enhancing Drugs." *Chronicle of Higher Education:* A41–A42.

Nightingale, Paul and Paul Martin. (2004). "The Myth of the Biotech Revolution." *TRENDS in Biotechnology* 22, no. 11: 564–69.

Nisbet, Erik C. and James Shanahan. (2004 December). *MSRG Special Report: Restrictions on Civil Liberties, Views of Islam, & Muslim Americans.* Media & Society Research Group, Cornell University.

Nixon, Sean. (1996). *Hard Looks: Masculinities, Spectatorship and Contemporary Consumption.* New York: St. Martin's Press.

———. (2003). *Advertising Cultures: Gender, Commerce, Creativity.* London: Sage.

"No Desire to Argue." (2004 April). *EXTRA!Update:* 2.

"Nutraceuticals for Children: An Extraordinary Market Opportunity." (2003 April). *Business and Industry:* 34.

Nutter, Chris. (2004). "Circling the Square." *Gay & Lesbian Review Worldwide* 11, no. 6: 19–22.

O'Brien, Glenn. (1990a). "Interview." *Interview* 20, no. 5: 127.

———. (1990b). "Meanwhile, Back at the Rancho." *Interview* 20, no. 4: 151.

O'Connor, J. J. (1997, April 30). "Coming Out Party: The Closet Opens, Finally." *New York Times:* C18.

O'Connor, Rebecca K. (2005). "Introduction." *Is There Life After Death?* Ed. Rebecca K.

O'Connor. Detroit: Greenhaven Press. 8–10.

O'Malley, Pat. (2001). "Discontinuity, Government and Risk: A Response to Rigakos and Hadden." *Theoretical Criminology* 5, no. 1: 85–92.

O'Meara, Kelly Patricia. (2003, September 1). "In ADHD Studies, Pictures May Lie." *The Nation*: 38.

Oak, Eileen. (2004). "What's in a Name? ADHD and Social Role Valorization Theory: Its Relevance for Developing Emancipatory Practice." *International Journal of Disability, Community & Rehabilitation* 3, no. 1.

Observatoire de la Finance and the United Nations Institute for Training and Research. (2003). *Economic and Financial Globalization: What the Numbers Say.* New York: United Nations.

Ocampo, José Antonio. (2005). "Globalization, Development and Democracy." *Items and Issues* 5, no. 3: 11–20.

"O Come All Ye Faithful." (2007, November 3). *The Economist*: 6–11.

"The Odd Couple: Biotechnology and the Media." (2003). *AgBiotech in the News* 2, no. 11.

Office of the United States Trade Representative. (2001). *The President's 2000 Annual Report on the Trade Agreements Program.* Washington, DC.

Oliver, M. (2000, October 31). "Ritalin—Wonder Drug or 'Monster' Creator." *Guardian.*

One Flew over the Cuckoo's Nest. (1976). Dir. Milos Forman. Fantasy Films.

"Open Up." (2008, January 5). *The Economist*: 3–5.

Orange County. (2002). Dir. Jack Kasdan. MTV Films.

Organización Internacional del Trabajo. (2004). *Por una globalización justa: Informe de la Comisión Mundial sobre la Dimensión Social de la Globalización.* Geneva: OIT.

Organisation for Economic Co-Operation and Development. (2004). *Biotechnology for Sustainable Growth and Development.*

Orr, D. (2000, November 1). "Do We Need to Drug Our Children?" *Independent.*

Ortiz, Jon. (2005, January 29). "Fans Hold Court on Skullcaps, NBA's Culture Clash." *Sacramento Bee*: A1.

Orwell, George. (1982). *The Lion and the Unicorn: Socialism and the English Genius.* Harmondsworth: Penguin.

Ouellette, Laurie and Susan Murray. (2004). "Introduction." *Reality TV: Remaking Television Culture.* Ed. Susan Murray and Laurie Ouellette. New York: New York University Press.

"Out of the Shadows, Into the World." (2004, June 19). *The Economist*: 26–28.

"The Oval Office Collection." (1998, December 27). *New York Times*: S9 P1.

Ozarin, Lucy O. and Gary McMillan. (2003). *The American Psychiatric Association: Historical Highlights.* Arlington, VA: American Psychiatric Association.

Pace, Enzo. (2007). "Fundamentalism." *Blackwell Encyclopedia of Sociology.* Ed. George Ritzer. Malden: Blackwell. 1813–16.

Paley, Maggie. (1999). *The Book of the Penis.* New York: Grove Press.

Palmer, Michael, Oliver Boyd-Barrett, and Terhi Rantanen. (1998). "Global Financial News." *The Globalisation of News.* Ed. Oliver Boyd-Barrett and Terhi Rantanen. London: Sage Publications. 61–78.

Parents Television Council. (2005). http://www.parentstv.org.

Pareto, Vilfredo. (1976). *Sociological Writings.* Trans. Derick Mirfin. Ed. S. E. Finer. Oxford: Basil Blackwell.

Park, David W. (2004). "The Couch and the Clinic: The Cultural Authority of Popular Psychiatry and Psychoanalysis." *Cultural Studies* 18, no. 1: 109–33.

Park, Nansook. (2004a). "Character Strengths and Positive Youth Development." *Annals of the American Academy of Political and Social Science* 591: 40–54.

———. (2004b). "The Role of Subjective Well-Being in Positive Youth Development." *Annals of the American Academy of Political and Social Science* 591: 25–39.

The Passion of the Christ. (2004). Dir. Mel Gibson. Icon Productions.

Peck, Janice. (1993). *The Gods of Televangelism: The Crisis of Meaning and the Appeal of Religious Television.* Cresskill: Hampton Press.

Perring, Christian. (1997). "Medicating Children: The Case of Ritalin." *Bioethics* 11, nos. 3–4: 228–40.

"Personal Care Products Aspire to Pamper Men." (2004 May). *BrandPackaging.*

"Perspectives." (2004, July 5). *Newsweek:* 21.

Petersen, Melody. (2002, November 22). "Madison Ave. Plays Growing Role in Drug Research." *New York Times.*

———. (2008, January 27). "Pharma's Queasy Feeling." *Los Angeles Times:* M1–2, M10–11.

Peterson, Christopher. (2004a). "Positive Social Science." *Annals of the American Academy of Political and Social Science* 591: 186–201.

———. (2004b). "Preface." *Annals of the American Academy of Political and Social Science* 591: 6–12.

Petridis, Alexis. (2006, November 25). "I Smell a Rat in Men's Fragrance." *Guardian.*

Petrina, Stephen. (2006). "The Medicalization of Education: A Historiographic Analysis." *History of Education Quarterly* 46, no. 4: 503–31.

Pew Center for Global Climate Change. (2002). *Pew Center Analysis of President Bush's February 14th Climate Change Plan.*

Pew Forum on Religion & Public Life. (2004a). *The American Religious Landscape and Politics, 2004.*

———. (2004b). *Religion and the Environment: Polls Show Strong Backing for Environmental Protection Across Religious Groups.*

———. (2006a). *Many Americans Uneasy With Mix of Religion and Politics.*

———. (2006b). *Spirit and Power: A 10-Country Survey of Pentecostals.*

Pew Hispanic Center. (2006). *From 200 Million to 300 Million: The Numbers Behind Population Growth.*

———. (2008). *Statistical Portrait of the Foreign-Born Population in the United States, 2006.*

Pew Internet & American Life Project. (2003). *Consumption of Information Goods and Services in the United States.*

———. (2004). *Faith Online.*

Pew Research Center for the People & the Press. (2002a). *What the World Thinks in 2002: How Global Publics View: Their Lives, Their Countries, America.*

———. (2002b). *Among Wealthy Nations . . . U.S. Stands Alone in Its Embrace of Religion.*

———. (2003a). *Polls in Close Agreement on Public Views of War.*

———. (2003b). *Different Faiths, Different Messages.*

———. (2003c). *Views of a Changing World June 2003.*

———. (2003d). *Strong Opposition to Media Cross-Ownership Emerges: Public Wants Neutrality and Pro-American Point of View.*

———. (2003e). *Broad Opposition to Genetically Modified Foods—Modest Transatlantic Gap.*

———. (2003f). *The 2004 Political Landscape: Evenly Divided and Increasingly Polarized.*

———. (2004a). *A Global Generation Gap: Adapting to a New World.*

———. (2004b). *Mistrust of America in Europe Ever Higher, Muslim Anger Persists.*

———. (2004c). *Religion and the Presidential Vote.*

———. (2004d). *Trouble Behind, Trouble Ahead? A Year of Contention at Home and Abroad.* 2003 Year-End Report.

———. (2005a). *Global Opinion: The Spread of Anti-Americanism.*

———. (2005b). *The Internet and Campaign 2004.*

Pew Research Center. (2005). *Trends 2005.*

———. (2006). "The U.S. Religious Landscape Survey Reveals a Fluid and Diverse Pattern of Faith."

———. Pew Research Center. (2008). *U.S. Population Projections: 2005–2050.*

Phalen, K. F. (2000, September 12). "Treatment of Choice." *Washington Post.*

Phillips, Christine B. (2006). "Medicine Goes to School: Teachers as Sickness Brokers for ADHD." *PLoS Medicine* 3, no. 4: 433–35.

Phillips, Kevin. (2006). *American Theocracy: The Peril and Politics of Radical Religion, Oil, and Borrowed Money in the 21st Century.* New York: Viking.

Piccalo, Gina. (2004, August 22). "The Pitch That You Won't See Coming." *Los Angeles Times:* E1, E26.

Pietrykowski, Bruce. (2001). "Information Technology and Commercialization of Knowledge: Corporate Universities and Class Dynamics in an Era of Technological Restructuring." *Journal of Economic Issues* 35, no. 2: 299–306.

Pitney, John J. Jr. (1997). "President Clinton's 1993 Inaugural Address." *Presidential Studies Quarterly* 27, no. 1: 91–103.

Plasticsurgery.org. (2007). "Indications for Men." http://plasticsurgery.org.

Plato. (1972). *The Laws.* Trans. Trevor J. Saunders. Harmondsworth: Penguin.

Plutarch. (1976). *The Rise and Fall of Athens: Nine Greek Lives by Plutarch.* Trans. Ian Scott-Kilvert. Harmondsworth: Penguin.

Poblete, Johanna Paola D. (2007, February 28). "The Filipino Adonis Comes of Age." *Business World:* S3.

Polanyi, Karl. (2001). *The Great Transformation: The Political and Economic Origins of Our Time.* Boston: Beacon Press.

"Poll Suggests World Hostile to US." (2003, June 16). http://news.bbc.co.uk.

Pollard, Jason. (2003). "Common Entrance Exams." *Index on Censorship* 32, no. 2: 70–81.

Pollard, Jason and Andrew Smith. (2003). "Migration by Numbers." *Index on Censorship* 32, no. 2: 40–41.

Pope, Harrison G. Jr., Katharine A. Phillips, and Roberto Olivardia. (2000). *The Adonis Complex: The Secret Crisis of Male Body Obsession.* New York: Free Press.

Porter, Roy. (1991). "History of the Body." *New Perspectives on Historical Writing.* Ed. Peter Burke. Cambridge: Polity Press. 206–32.

———. (2002). *Madness: A Brief History.* Oxford: Oxford University Press.

Portes, Alejandro. (2001). "Introduction: The Debates and Significance of Immigrant Transnationalism." *Global Networks* 1, no. 3: 181–93.

Portes, Alejandro and Rubén G. Rumbaut With Patricia Fernández-Kelly and William Haller. (2006). *Immigrant America: A Portrait.* 3rd ed. Berkeley: University of California Press.

Post, N. M. (2002, December 30). "Ground Zero Plan Expected Soon." *Engineering News-Record.*

Postrel, Virginia. (1999, August 2). "The Pleasures of Persuasion." *Wall Street Journal*.

———. (2003). *The Substance of Style: How the Rise of Aesthetic Value Is Remaking Commerce, Culture, and Consciousness*. New York: HarperCollins.

———. (2004, February 22). "A Prettier Jobs Picture?" *New York Times*.

Poulin, Christiane. (2001). "Medical and Nonmedical Stimulant Use Among Adolescents: From Sanctioned to Unsanctioned Use." *Canadian Medical Association Journal/Journal de l'association médical canadienne* 165, no. 8: 1039–44.

Power, Michael. (2004). *The Risk Management of Everything: Rethinking the Politics of Uncertainty*. London: Demos.

Powers, C. A. (2000). "The Pharmacology of Drugs Used for the Treatment of Attention Deficit Hyperactivity Disorder." *Attention Deficits and Hyperactivity in Children and Adults: Diagnosis, Treatment, Management*. 2nd ed. Ed. P. J. Accardo, T. A. Blondis, B. Y. Whitman, and M. A. Stein. New York: Marcel Dekker. 477–511.

President's Council on Bioethics. (2002a April). *Staff Working Paper 7: Distinguishing Therapy and Enhancement*.

———. (2002b, December 12). "Session 3: Prescription Stimulant Use in American Children: Ethical Issues."

———. (2003). *Beyond Therapy: Biotechnology and the Pursuit of Happiness: A Report by the President's Council on Bioethics*. Washington, DC.

President's New Freedom Commission on Mental Health. (2003). *Achieving the Promise: Transforming Mental Health Care in America*. Rockville.

Program on International Policy Attitudes and Knowledge Networks. (2003). *Misperceptions, the Media and the Iraq War*.

———. (2004a). *Americans on Climate Change*.

———. (2004b). *Americans on Globalization, Trade, and Farm Subsidies*.

———. (2004c). *Americans and Iraq on the Eve of the Presidential Election*.

———. (2004d). *US Public Beliefs on Iraq and the Presidential Elections*.

Project for Excellence in Journalism and Committee of Concerned Journalists. (2000). *A Question of Character: How the Media Have Handled the Issue and How the Public Has Reacted*. Pew Charitable Trusts.

Project for Excellence in Journalism. (2002). *The War on Terrorism: The Not-So-New Television News Landscape*.

Public Health Protection Act. http://www.commercialalert.org/phpa.pdf.

"Public Inquiry Call Over Drug." (2001, July 2). http://news.bbc.co.uk.

Pufendorf, Samuel. (2000). *On the Duty of Man and Citizen According to Natural Law*. Trans. Michael Silverthorne. Ed. James Tully. Cambridge: Cambridge University Press.

Pullen, Christopher. (2007). *Documenting Gay Men: Identity and Performance in Reality Television and Documentary Film*. Jefferson: McFarland.

"Pupil Power." (2000, November 18). *The Economist*: 40.

Purcell, Mark. (2003). "Citizenship and the Right to the Global City: Reimagining the Capitalist World Order." *International Journal of Urban and Regional Research* 27, no. 3: 564–90.

Putnam, Robert D. (2000). *Bowling Alone: The Collapse and Revival of American Community*. New York: Simon & Schuster.

Putnam, Robert. (2001, October 19). "A Better Society in a Time of War." *New York Times*.

Quaccia, Jon. (2004, August 12). "Big Business and Labor Working Hand in Hand." *Alter-*

native Press Review.

Quinn, P. O. and K. G. Nadeau. (2000). "Gender Issues and Attention Deficit Disorder." *Attention Deficits and Hyperactivity in Children and Adults: Diagnosis, Treatment, Management.* 2nd ed. Ed. P. J. Accardo, T. A. Blondis, B. Y. Whitman, and M. A. Stein. New York: Marcel Dekker. 215–27.

Rafavolich, Adam. (2001). "Disciplining Domesticity: Framing the ADHD Parent and Child." *Sociological Quarterly* 42, no. 3: 373–93.

Ragusa, Angela T. (2005). "Social Change and the Corporate Construction of Gay Markets in the *New York Times*' Advertising Business News." *Media, Culture & Society* 27, no. 5.

Rasmussen, Claire E. (2006). "We're No *Metro*sexuals: Identity, Place and Sexuality in the Struggle Over Gay Marriage." *Social & Cultural Geography* 7, no. 5: 807–25.

Rasmussen, Nicolas. (2004). "The Moral Economy of the Drug Company–Medical Scientist Collaboration in Interwar America." *Social Studies of Science* 34, no. 2: 161–85.

Raunig, Gerald. (2004). "La inseguridad vencerá: Activismo contra la precariedad y MayDay Parades." Trans. Marcelo Expósito. *Republicart.net* 6. http://republicart.net.

Rawlings, S. (1993, February 12). "Luring the Big Boys." *B and T*: 18–19.

Rawls, John. (1971). *A Theory of Justice.* Cambridge: The Belknap Press of Harvard University Press.

"Really Desperate Housewives." (2006, December 9). *The Economist:* 64.

"Real Men Get Waxed." (2003, July 3). *The Economist.*

Redden, Guy. (2002). "The New Agents: Personal Transfiguration and Radical Privatization in New Age Self-Help." *Journal of Consumer Culture* 2, no. 1: 33–52.

———. (2007). "Makeover Morality and Consumer Culture." *Makeover Television: Realities Remodelled.* Ed. Dana Heller. London: I. B. Tauris. 150–64.

Reeves, Jimmie L. and Richard Campbell. (1994). *Cracked Coverage: Television News, the Anti-Cocaine Crusade, and the Reagan Legacy.* Durham: Duke University Press.

Reinhardt, Mark. (2000). "Constitutional Sentimentality." *Theory & Event* 4, no. 1.

Reitman, Valerie. (2003, February 10). "Attention Deficit Disorder for Adults." *Los Angeles Times.*

Rendall, Steve and Tara Broughel. (2003 May/June). "Amplifying Officials, Squelching Dissent." *EXTRA!Update.*

Rendon, Jim. (2004, April 8). "Marketing Beyond the Metrosexual." *Business and Finance.*

Revkin, Andrew C. (2003, February 26). "Experts Fault Bush's Proposal to Examine Climate Change." *New York Times.*

Reygadas, Luis. (2002). *Ensamblando Culturas: Diversidad y conflicto en la globalización de la industria.* Barcelona: Editorial Gedisa.

Reznek, Lawrie. (1998). "On the Epistemology of Mental Illness." *History and Philosophy of the Life Sciences* 20, no. 2: 215–32.

Rich, Andrew and R. Kent Weaver. (2000). "Think Tanks in the U.S. Media." *Harvard Journal of Press/Politics* 5, no. 4: 81–103.

Rich, Frank. (1998, December 23). "Larry and Lucy." *New York Times:* A27.

———. (1999, August 14). "What Tony Soprano Could Teach Bill Clinton." *New York Times:* A13.

———. (2003, May 11). "The Jerry Bruckheimer White House." *New York Times.*

———. (2004, May 30). "It Was the Porn That Made Them Do It." *New York Times.*

———. (2005, February 20). "The White House Stages Its 'Daily Show.'" *New York Times.*

Rich, Ronda. (2006, October 15). "Dating a Metrosexual Man." *Sun-Herald*.

Rich, Vera. (2003). "The Price of Return." *Index on Censorship* 32, no. 3: 82–86.

"Riddlin' Kids." (2002). http://www.sony.com/index.php.

Rieder, Jonathan. (2003). "Getting a Fix on Fragmentation: *"Breakdown" as Estimation Error, Rhetorical Strategy, and Organizational Accomplishment.*" *The Fractious Nation? Unity and Division in American Life*. Ed. Jonathan Rieder. Assoc. Ed. Stephen Steinlight. Berkeley: University of California Press. 13–54.

Riesman, David With Nathan Glazer and Reuel Denney. (1953). *The Lonely Crowd: A Study of the Changing American Character*. Garden City: Doubleday Anchor.

Rifkin, Jeremy. (2002, May 17). "The World's Problems on a Plate." *Guardian*.

Rigakos, George S. and Richard W. Hadden. (2001). "Crime, Capitalism and the 'Risk Society.'" *Theoretical Criminology* 5, no. 1: 61–84.

Risol, Lara. (2003, July 22). "Bring on the Culture War." http://alternet.org.

"Ritalin Cures Next Picasso." (1999, August 4). *The Onion*: 27.

"Ritalin Prescriptions Up Again." (2001, June 19). *New Zealand Press Association*.

Ritter, Gretchen. (2000). "Gender and Citizenship After the Nineteenth Amendment." *Polity* 32, no. 3: 345–68.

Roberts, Donald F., Ulla G. Foehr, and Victoria Rideout. (2005). *Generation M: Media in the Lives of 8–18 Year-Olds*. Kaiser Family Foundation.

Robertson, Craig. (2003). *"Passport Please": The U.S. Passport and the Documentation of Individual Identity, 1845–1930*. PhD, University of Illinois.

Robinson, James. (2005, April 24). "The Loutish Lad Is Dead. Enter the Caring Lad in Cashmere." *Observer*.

Rocchio, Christopher and Steve Rogers. (2007, January 12). "Bravo Announces 'Queer Eye' to End, Final Episodes to Air This Summer." http://realitytvworld.com.

Roche, Walter F. Jr. (2006, October 22). "Bush's Family Profits From 'No Child' Act." *Los Angeles Times*: A1, A20.

Rodriguez, Roberto and Patrisia Gonzales. (1995, May 15). "Cultural Idea for Citizenship Is Catching On." *Fresno Bee*: B5.

Rogers, Patrick. (2001, July 23). "Drawing the Line." *People*: 50.

Rogers, Steve. (2003, November 20). "New 'Queer Eye' Episode Kicks Off New Episodes Run With Strong Ratings." http://realitytvworld.com.

Rojek, Chris. (2002). "The Post-Auratic President." *American Behavioral Scientist* 46, no. 4: 487–500.

"The Role of Intellectual Processes in the *DSM-V* Diagnosis of ADHD." (2006). *Journal of Attention Disorders* 10, no. 1: 3–8.

Romano, Allison. (2004, September 6). "Wants a Bigger Slice." *Broadcasting & Cable*: 10–12.

Romer, Daniel and Patrick Jamieson. (2003). "Introduction." *American Behavioral Scientist* 46, no. 9: 1131–36.

Rondinelli, Dennis A. (2002). "Transnational Corporations: International Citizens or New Sovereigns?" *Business and Society Review* 107, no. 4: 391–413.

Roosevelt, Franklin Delano. (1937, January 20). "Second Inaugural Address."

Rose, Nikolas. (1999). *Powers of Freedom: Reframing Political Thought*. Cambridge: Cambridge University Press.

———. (2003). "Neurochemical Selves." *Society* 41, no. 1: 46–59.

———. (2007). *The Politics of Life Itself: Biomedicine, Power, and Subjectivity in the Twenty-*

First Century. Princeton: Princeton University Press.

Rose, Nikolas and Peter Miller. (1992). "Political Power Beyond the State: Problematics of Government." *British Journal of Sociology* 43, no. 2: 173–205.

Rose, Steven. (2006). *The 21st-Century Brain: Explaining, Mending and Manipulating the Mind.* London: Vintage.

Rosen, Christine. (2004). "The Democratization of Beauty." *New Atlantis* 5: 19–35.

Rosen, Jeffrey. (2003, September 7). "How to Reignite the Culture Wars." *New York Times Magazine:* 48–49.

Rosenthal, Meredith B., Ernst R. Berndt, Julie M. Donohue, Arnold M. Epstein, and Richard G. Frank. (2003). *Demand Effects of Recent Changes in Prescription Drug Promotion.* Kaiser Family Foundation.

Ross, Ellen. (1980). "'The Love Crisis': Couples Advice Books of the Late 1970s." *Signs* 6, no. 1: 109–22.

Rotzer, Florian. (2003, January 7). "The World Is What the Media Reports." *Telepolis.*

Rousseau, Jean-Jacques. (1975). *The Social Contract and Discourses.* Trans. G. D. H. Cole. London: J. M. Dent.

Rowe, David. (1997). "Big Defence: Sport and Hegemonic Masculinity." *Gender, Sport and Leisure: Continuities and Challenges.* Ed. Alan Tomlinson. Aachen: Meyer and Meyer Verlag. 123–33.

Rowe, Jonathan. (2006, August 21). "Drug Ads Sell a Problem, Not a Solution." *Christian Science Monitor:* 9.

Rubin, Lawrence C. (2004). "Merchandising Madness: Pills, Promises, and Better Living Through Chemistry." *Journal of Popular Culture* 38, no. 2: 369–83.

Rubinstein, R. A., S. C. Scrimshaw, and S. E. Morrissey. (2000). "Classification and Process in Sociomedical Understanding: Towards a Multilevel View of Sociomedical Methodology." *The Handbook of Social Studies in Health & Medicine.* Ed. G. L. Albrecht, R. Fitzpatrick, and S. C. Scrimshaw. London: Sage. 36–49.

Ruddick, Sue. (2003). "The Politics of Aging: Globalization and the Restructuring of Youth and Childhood." *Antipode* 35, no. 2: 334–62.

Ruddick, Susan M. (1996). *Young and Homeless in Hollywood: Mapping Social Identities.* New York: Routledge.

Ruff, Michael E. (2005). "Attention Deficit Disorder and Stimulant Use: An Epidemic of Modernity." *Clinical Pediatrics* 44: 557–63.

Rundle, G. (1999). "Ten Years of Vitamin P." *Arena Journal* 13: 25–30.

Rush, Benjamin. (1812). *Medical Inquiries and Observations Upon the Diseases of the Mind.* Philadelphia: Kimber and Richardson.

Russell, J. (1997, December 1). "The Pill That Teachers Push." *Good Housekeeping:* 110–17.

Russell, James A. and Kaori Sato. (1995). "Comparing Emotion Words Between Languages." *Journal of Cross-Cultural Psychology* 26, no. 4: 384–91.

Saad, Lydia. (2003, March 13). "Americans Foresee Energy Shortage Within 5 Years." *Gallup News Service.*

"Salons Are Catering to Men Who Want More." (2006, January 4). *Los Angeles Times:* C3.

Salzman, Marian, Ira Matathia, and Ann O'Reilly. (2005). *The Future of Men.* New York: Palgrave Macmillan.

Sandberg, S. and J. Barton. (1996). "Historical Development." *Hyperactivity Disorders of Childhood.* Ed. S. Sandberg. Cambridge: Cambridge University Press. 1–25.

Sandberg, S. and M. E. Garralda. (1996). "Psychosocial Contributions." *Hyperactivity Dis-*

orders of Childhood. Ed. S. Sandberg. Cambridge: Cambridge University Press. 280–328.

Santer, Vanessa. (2007, February 28). "Pole Stars." *Sydney MX*: 23.

Santostefano, S. (1999). "A Psychodynamic Approach to Treating Attention Deficit/Hyperactivity Disorder: Recent Developments in Theory and Technique." *Understanding, Diagnosing, and Treating AD/HD in Children and Adolescents: An Integrative Approach. Reiss-Davis Child Study, Volume Three*. Ed. A. Incorvaia, B. S. Mark-Goldstein, and D. Tessmer. Northvale: Jason Aronson. 319–67.

Sarat, Austin. (2001). *When the State Kills: Capital Punishment and the American Condition*. Princeton: Princeton University Press.

Sardar, Ziauddin and Merryl Wyn Davies. (2002). *Why Do People Hate America?* Cambridge: Icon Books.

Sawhill, Isabel and John E. Morton. *Economic Mobility: Is the American Dream Alive and Well?* Economic Mobility Project of The Pew Charitable Trusts.

Sawyer, Terry. (2003, July 22). "Blind Leading the Bland." http://popmatters.com.

Sax, L. (2000). "Ritalin: Better Living Through Chemistry?" *The World and I* 15: 286.

"Scandal! They Haven't Tested Ritalin on the Children It's Not Prescribed for! Scandal! They're Going to Test Ritalin on the Children It's Prescribed for." (2001, January 2). *Washington Post*.

Scardino, Albert. (2005, March 9). "Sun Sets on US Broadcast Golden Age." *Guardian*.

Schachar, R., R. Tannock, and C. Cunningham. (1996). "Treatment." *Hyperactivity Disorders of Childhood*. Ed. S. Sandberg. Cambridge: Cambridge University Press. 433–76.

Scheffler, Richard M., Stephen P. Hinshaw, Sepideh Modrek, and Peter Levine. (2007). "The Global Market for ADHD Medications." *Health Affairs* 26, no. 2.

Scheid, T. L. (2000 August). "Commodification and Contradiction: The Rationalization of Mental Health Care." Paper presented to the American Sociological Association, Washington, DC.

Schell, Jonathan. (2003, July 7). "The New American Order." *The Nation*: 7.

———. (2005, April 25). "Faking Civil Society." *The Nation*: 6.

Scherer, Glenn. (2004, October 27). "The Goldy Must Be Crazy." http://grist.org.

Scherer, Michael. (2005 May/June). "The Side Effects of Truth." *Mother Jones*: 71–75.

Schiller, Dan. (1996). *Theorizing Communication: A History*. New York: Oxford University Press.

———. (2007). *How to Think About Information*. Champaign: University of Illinois Press.

Schiller, Herbert I. (2000). *Living in the Number One Country: Reflections From a Critic of American Empire*. New York: Seven Stories Press.

"Schizophrenia May Be Expanded." (2000, July 26). *Wall Street Journal*: B1, B4.

Schmidt, Ronald Sr. (2000). *Language Policy and Identity Politics in the United States*. Philadelphia: Temple University Press.

Schmitt, Eric. (2005, January 16). "New U.S. Commander Sees Shift in Military Role in Iraq." *New York Times*: 10.

Schmitz, Mark F., Prema Filippone, and Elaine M. Edelman. (2003). "Social Representations of Attention Deficit/Hyperactivity Disorder, 1988–1997." *Culture & Psychology* 9, no. 4: 383–406.

Schonfeld, Reese. (2002, July 22). "Artful Dodging: TV Accounting Methods." *Electronic Media*: 10.

Schubert, Sarah, Susan Hansen, and Mark Rapley. (2005). "'There *Is* No Pathological Test':

More on ADHD as Rhetoric." *Journal of Critical Psychology, Counselling, and Psychotherapy* 5, no. 3: 151–60.

Schudson, Michael and Susan E. Tifft. (2005). "American Journalism in Historical Perspective." *The Press.* Ed. Geneva Overholser and Kathleen Hall Jamieson. Oxford: Oxford University Press.

Schumpeter, Joseph A. (1975). *Capitalism, Socialism and Democracy.* New York: Harper-Perennial.

Schweder, Richard A., Martha Minow, and Hazel Rose Markus. (2002). "Introduction: Engaging Cultural Differences." *Engaging Cultural Differences: The Multicultural Challenge in Liberal Democracies.* Ed. Richard A. Schweder, Martha Minow, and Hazel Rose Markus. New York: Russell Sage Foundation. 1–13.

"Selling to the Developing World." (2003, December 13). *The Economist:* 8.

Senate Committee on Commerce, Science and Transportation Hearings. (2005, February 2).

Sender, Katherine. (2005). *Business, Not Politics: The Making of the Gay Market.* New York: Columbia University Press.

———. (2006). "Queens for a Day: *Queer Eye for the Straight Guy* and the Neoliberal Project." *Critical Studies in Media Communication* 23, no. 2: 131–51.

Sered, Susan Starr and Rushika Fernandopulle. (2007). *Uninsured in America: Life & Death in the Land of Opportunity.* 2nd ed. Berkeley: University of California Press.

Shafer, Jack. (2003, March 24). "POW TV." http://www.slate.com.

———. (2005, August 9). "The Meth-Mouth Myth." http://www.slate.com.

Shafir, Gershon. (1998). "Introduction: The Evolving Traditions of Citizenship." *The Citizenship Debates: A Reader.* Ed. Gershon Shafir. Minneapolis: University of Minnesota Press. 1–28.

Shannon, Brent. (2004). "ReFashioning Men: Fashion, Masculinity, and the Cultivation of the Male Consumer in Britain, 1860–1914." *Victorian Studies* 46, no. 4: 597–630.

Shapiro, Michael J. (2001). *For Moral Ambiguity: National Culture and the Politics of the Family.* Minneapolis: University of Minnesota Press.

Shaps, S. (1994, November 5). "When Moral Panic Is the Real Villain of the Piece." *Independent.*

Sharp, Lesley A. (2006). *Strange Harvest: Organ Transplants, Denatured Bodies, and the Transformed Self.* Berkeley: University of California Press.

Shattuc, Jane M. (1997). *The Talking Cure: TV Talk Shows and Women.* New York: Routledge.

Shaw, Randy. (1999). *Reclaiming America: Nike, Clean Air, and the New National Activism.* Berkeley: University of California Press.

Shea, Christopher. (2003, July 27). "The Last Prejudice?" *Boston Globe:* E1.

Sherman, Paul and Bill Vann. (2002, August 3). "The Pennsylvania Mine Rescue and the Human Cost of Coal." World Socialist Web site, www.wsw.org/articles/2002/aug2002/mine-a03_prn.shtml.

"Shire Buys Noven Attention-Deficit Patch." (2003, February 27). *Reuters.*

Shorter, Edward. (1997). *A History of Psychiatry: From the Era of the Asylum to the Age of Prozac.* New York: John Wiley.

Shreve, Jenn. (1997, July 15). "Gen Rx." http://www.salon.com.

Shulman, George. (2000). "Narrating Clinton's Impeachment: Race, the Right, and Allegories of the Sixties." *Theory & Event* 4, no. 1.

Shuman, Michael H. and Merrian Fuller. (2005, January 24). "Profits for Justice." *The Nation:* 13–22.

Sieg, K. G. (2000). "Neuroimaging and Attention Deficit Hyperactivity Disorder." *Attention Deficits and Hyperactivity in Children and Adults: Diagnosis, Treatment, Management.* 2nd ed. Ed. P. J. Accardo, T. A. Blondis, B. Y. Whitman, and M. A. Stein. New York: Marcel Dekker. 73–118.

"Sign the Call!" (2006). http://maydaysur.org/.

Simmel, Georg. (1976). "The Metropolis and Mental Life." *Sociological Perspectives: Selected Readings.* Trans. Kurt H. Wolff. Ed. Kenneth Thompson and Jeremy Tunstall. Harmondsworth: Penguin. 82–93.

Simpson, Mark. (1998). *It's a Queer World: Deviant Adventures in Pop Culture.* London: Harrington Park.

———. (2002, July 22). "Meet the Metrosexual." http://www.salon.com.

———. (2003, June 22). "Metrosexual? That Rings a Bell . . ." *Independent.*

———. (2004a, January 5). "MetroDaddy Speaks!" http://www.salon.com.

———. (2004b, June 27). "Forget New Man." *Observer.*

———. (2005). "Metrodaddy v. Ubermummy." *3amMagazine.*

———. (2006a). http://marksimpson.com/blog.

———. (2006b, April 7). "This Trend's Not Dead—Just Common." *The Times.*

———. (2006c, October 10). "Who Are You Calling Hummersexual?" *Guardian.*

Singer, Dorothy G. and Jerome L. Singer. (2001). "Introduction: Why a Handbook on Children and the Media?" *Handbook of Children and the Media.* Ed. Dorothy G. Singer and Jerome L. Singer. Thousand Oaks: Sage Publications. xi–xvii.

Singer, Natasha. (2006, November 30). "More Doctors Turning to the Business of Beauty." *New York Times.*

Singh, Ilina. (2002). "Bad Boys, Good Mothers, and the 'Miracle' of Ritalin." *Science in Context* 15: 577–603.

"Sins of the Secular Missionaries." (2000, January 29). *The Economist:* 25–27.

Skinner, David. (2003, August 14). "Queer Like Us." *Weekly Standard.*

Skocpol, Theda. (2003). "Social Provision and Civic Community: Beyond Fragmentation." *The Fractious Nation? Unity and Division in American Life.* Ed. Jonathan Rieder. Assoc. Ed. Stephen Steinlight. Berkeley: University of California Press. 187–205.

———. (2004 June). "The Narrowing of Civic Life." *American Prospect:* A5–A7.

Sloan, Ted, Stephanie Austin, and Daniel Noam Warner. (2006). "Critical Psychology in the Belly of the Beast—Notes from North America." *Annual Review of Critical Psychology* 5.

Smith, Clarissa. (2002). "Shiny Chests and Heaving G-Strings: A Night Out With the Chippendales." *Sexualities* 5, no. 1: 67–89.

Smith, Ken. (1999). *Mental Hygiene: Classroom Films 1945–1970.* New York: Blast Books.

Smith, Tom W. and Seokho Kim. (2004). *The Vanishing Protestant Majority.* National Opinion Research Center General Social Survey Report 49.

TheSmokingGun.com. http://www.thesmokinggun.com.

Smutniak, John. (2004, January 24). "Living Dangerously." *The Economist:* 3–4, Survey of Risk.

Snyder, Kirk. (2006, September 9). "Bringing the Outsiders In." *Guardian:* 3.

Sollisch, Jim. (2000, October 7). "Profits Before Ethics in Drug Company Ads." *Philadelphia Inquirer.*

Solon. (1994). "I Made the Crooked Straight." *Citizenship*. Ed. Paul Barry Clarke. London: Pluto Press. 38–39.

Sommerville, C. John. (1982). *The Rise and Fall of Childhood*. Beverly Hills: Sage Publications.

Soros, George. (1997 February). "The Capitalist Threat." *Atlantic Monthly*.

Souccar, M. K. (2002, November 11). "Groups Urge Link of Arts, NY Economy." *Crain's New York Business*.

Sparatos, Carla. (2001, September 4). "The People's Prozac." *Village Voice*.

Spiegel, Alix. (2005, January 3). "The Dictionary of Disorder." *The New Yorker*: 56–63.

Splendor in the Grass. (1961). Dir. Elia Kazan. NBI Productions.

Sproat, D. Kapura. (1998). "The Backlash Against PASH: Legislative Attempts to Restrict Native Hawaiian Rights." *University of Hawaii Law Review* 20: 321–73.

Squires, Peter. (2006). "New Labour and the Politics of Antisocial Behavior." *Critical Social Policy* 26, no. 1: 144–68.

Srinivas, Katta. (2002). "A Question of Citizenship." http://indiainfo.com.

St. John, Warren. (2003, June 25). "Un nuevo modelo de hombre, bien masculino pero sensible, invade los capitales del primer mundo." Trans. Claudia Martínez. *Clarín*.

Staiger, Janet. (2005). *Media Reception Studies*. New York: New York University Press.

Stearns, Peter N. (1994). *American Cool: Constructing a Twentieth-Century Emotional Style*. New York: New York University Press.

———. (2006). *American Fear: The Causes and Consequences of High Anxiety*. New York: Routledge.

Steele, Margaret, Peter S. Jensen, and Declan M. P. Quinn. (2006). "Remission Versus Response as the Goal of Therapy in ADHD: A New Standard for the Field?" *Clinical Therapeutics* 28, no. 11: 1892–1908.

Stein, Joel. (1999, July 19). "Only His Hairdresser Knows for Sure." *Time*: 78.

Steinberg, Jacques. (2003, March 25). "Weblogs: Facts Are In, Spin Is Out." *New York Times*.

Steinberg, L. (1999). "ADD or AD/HD Medication Treatment." *Understanding, Diagnosing, and Treating AD/HD in Children and Adolescents: An Integrative Approach. Reiss-Davis Child Study, Volume Three*. Ed. J. A. Incorvaia, B. S. Mark-Glodstein, and D. Tessmer. Northvale: Jason Aronson. 223–34.

Steinberg, Paul. (2006, March 7). "Attention Surplus? Re-Examining a Disorder." *New York Times*.

Steinberg, S. R. and J. L. Kincheloe. (1997). "Introduction: No More Secrets—Kinderculture, Information Saturation, and the Postmodern Childhood." *Kinderculture: The Corporate Construction of Childhood*. Ed. S. R. Steinberg and J. L. Kincheloe. Boulder: Westview Press. 1–30.

Steiner, Hans and Niranjan S. Karnik. (2006, September 1). "New Approaches to Juvenile Delinquency: Psychopathology, Development, and Neuroscience." *Psychiatric Times*: 15.

Stephens, Sharon. (1995). "Children and the Politics of Culture in 'Late Capitalism.'" *Children and the Politics of Culture*. Ed. Sharon Stephens. Princeton: Princeton University Press. 3–48.

Stevens, Jacqueline. (1999). *Reproducing the State*. Princeton: Princeton University Press.

Stewart, James B. (1999, July 4). "Consider the Sources." *New York Times Book Review*: 8.

Stiglitz, Joseph. (2002). "The Roaring Nineties." *Atlantic Monthly* 290, no. 3: 75–89.

Still, George F. (1902, April 12). "The Goulstonian Lectures on Some Abnormal Psychical Conditions in Children: The Goulstonian Lectures." *Lancet* 1: 1008–12.

Strange, Susan. (2000). *The Retreat of the State: The Diffusion of Power in the World Economy.* Cambridge: Cambridge University Press.

Streeter, Thomas. (1996). *Selling the Air: A Critique of the Policy of Commercial Broadcasting in the United States.* Chicago: University of Chicago Press.

"Stressed Out and Traumatised." (2005, March 5). *The Economist:* 30–31.

"Subsidising Virtue." (2005, March 12). *The Economist:* 57.

Stratton, Allegra. (2007, November 12). "Ritalin of No Long-Term Benefit, Study Finds." *Guardian.*

Striffler, Steve. (2002). "Inside a Poultry Processing Plant: An Ethnographic Portrait." *Labor History* 43, no. 3: 305–13.

"Study Reveals: Portrait of Gay America." (2006, April 24). OpusComm Group.

"Supercharging the Brain." (2004, September 18). *The Economist:* 27–29.

Superstar. (1999). Dir. Bruce McCulloch. SNL Studios.

Surowiecki, James. (2004, November 15). "The Risk Society." *The New Yorker:* 40.

Susman, Warren I. (1984). *Culture as History: The Transformation of American Society in the Twentieth Century.* New York: Pantheon.

Sutcliffe, Bob. (2003). *A More or Less Unequal World? World Income Distribution in the 20th Century.* Amherst: Political Economy Research Institute Working Paper Series 54.

Swatos, William H. Jr. (2007). "Televangelism." *Blackwell Encyclopedia of Sociology.* Ed. George Ritzer. Malden: Blackwell. 4963–65.

Szalavitz, Maia. (2005, April 26). "'Generation Rx' Label Dazzles Media." http://alternet.org.

Tafoya, Sonya. (2004 December). *Shades of Belonging.* Washington, DC: Pew Hispanic Center.

Taibo, Carlos. (2003). "Hegemonía con Quiebras." *Washington Contra el Mundo: Una Recopilación de Rebelión.org.* Ed. Pascual Serrano. Madrid: Foca. 23–32.

Tait, Gordon. (2001). "Pathologising Difference, Governing Personality." *Asia-Pacific Journal of Teacher Education* 29, no. 1: 93–102.

———. (2005). "The ADHD Debate and the Philosophy of Truth." *International Journal of Inclusive Education* 9, no. 1: 17–38.

Tan, Michael L. (2001, March 27). "Moral Panic." *Philippine Daily Inquirer:* 8.

Tavernise, Sabrina. (2004, May 10). "Authors, Get Out There and Break a Leg." *New York Times:* E1, E5.

"Tell Your Local NBC Affiliate You Want to See *Queer Eye for the Straight Guy.*" (2003, August 7). http://glaad.org.

Tepper, S. J. (2002). "Creative Assets and the Changing Economy." *Journal of Arts Management, Law & Society* 32, no. 2: 159–68.

Terry, J. (1995). "Anxious Slippages Between Us and Them." *Deviant Bodies.* Ed. J. Terry and J. Urla. Bloomington: Indiana University Press. 129–69.

Teter, C. J., S. E. McCabe, K. LaGrange, J. A. Cranford, and C. J. Boyd. (2006). "Illicit Use of Specific Prescription Stimulants Among College Students: Prevalence, Motives, and Routes of Administration." *Pharmacotherapy* 26, no. 10: 1501–10.

Thelen, David. (2000). "How Natural Are National and Transnational Citizenship? A Historical Perspective." *Indiana Journal of Global Legal Studies* 7: 549–65.

"Therapy of the Masses." (2004, September 18). *The Economist:* 12–16.

"There's a Word for That." (2004, November 6). *The Economist:* 14.

Thomaselli, Rich. (2007, March 19). "Gold's Hasta La Vista, Musclemen." *Advertising Age.*

Thompson, Kenneth. (1998). *Moral Panics.* London: Routledge.

Thumma, Scott, Dave Travis, and Warren Bird. (2006). *Megachurches Today 2005: Summary of Research Findings.* Hartford: Hartford Institute for Religion Research and Leadership Network.

Tien, Ellen. (1999, June 20). "The More Hairless Ape." *New York Times:* 3.

Tienda, Marta. (2002). "Demography and the Social Contract." *Demography* 39, no. 4: 587–616.

"Time to Act on Inequality." (2007, April 23). *The Nation:* 3.

"Time for a Makeover." (2006, August 12). *The Economist:* 11.

Timimi, Sami. (2002). *Pathological Child Psychiatry and the Medicalization of Childhood.* Hove: Brunner-Routledge.

Timimi, Sami and Eric Taylor. (2004). "ADHD Is Best Understood as a Cultural Construct." *British Journal of Psychiatry* 184: 8–9.

Timimi, Sami and 33 Coendorsers. (2004). "A Critique of the International Consensus Statement on ADHD." *Clinical Child and Family Psychology Review* 7, no. 1: 59–63.

Tiryakian, Edward A. (2003). "Assessing Multiculturalism Theoretically: *E Pluribus Unum, Sic et Non.*" *International Journal on Multicultural Societies* 5, no. 1: 20–39.

Titanic. (1997). Dir. James Cameron. Twentieth Century-Fox.

Titus, Jordan J. (2004). "Boy Trouble: Rhetorical Framing of Boys' Underachievement." *Discourse* 25, no. 2: 145–69.

Tomasky, Michael. (2003, March 3). "Spooky Story." *American Prospect.*

"To Those That Have, Shall be Given." (2007, December 22). *The Economist:* 53–54.

Toy Story. (1995). Dir. John Lasseter. Walt Disney Pictures.

Toy Story 2. (1999). Dir. John Lasseter and Ash Brannon. Pixar Animation Studios.

"Trade Trouble Ahead." (2005, January 15). *The Economist:* 59.

Trapani, C. (2000). "Psychoeducational Assessment of Children and Adolescents With Attention Deficit Hyperactivity Disorder." *Attention Deficits and Hyperactivity in Children and Adults: Diagnosis, Treatment, Management.* 2nd ed. Ed. P. J. Accardo, T. A. Blondis, B. Y. Whitman, and M. A. Stein. New York: Marcel Dekker. 197–214.

Trebay, Guy. (2004, August 1). "When Did Skivvies Get Rated NC-17?" *New York Times.*

Treichler, Paula. (1999). *How to Have Theory in an Epidemic: Cultural Chronicles of AIDS.* Durham: Duke University Press.

Trepp, Anne-Charlott. (1994). "The Private Lives of Men in Eighteenth-Century Central Europe: The Emotional Side of Men in Late Eighteenth-Century Germany (Theory and Example)." Trans. Ursula Marcum. *Central European History* 27, no. 2: 127–52.

Trew, Jonathan. (2002, July 24). "I Love Me so Much." *Scotsman.*

"Trials and Tribulations." (2004, June 19). *The Economist:* 62–63.

Tripathi, Salil. (2003). "Powers of Transformation." *Index on Censorship* 32, no. 3: 125–31.

Tryhorn, Chris. (2003, March 25). "When Are Facts Facts? Not in a War." *Guardian.*

Tuchman, Gaye, Arlene Kaplan Daniels, and James Benet, eds. (1978). *Hearth and Home: Images of Women in the Mass Media.* New York: Oxford University Press.

Tugend, Alina. (2003 May). "Pundits for Hire." *American Journalism Review.*

Tully, Shawn. (2007, April 1). "A Profit Gusher of Epic Proportions." *Fortune.*

Turkel, Studs. (2003, October 30). "In Bed With Bush." *In These Times.*

Turner, Christopher. (2006, April 22). "Boys Behaving Badly Score Their Own Literary Genre." *Guardian.*

———. (2007, January 7). "Oracle Worker." *Daily Telegraph*.

Twain, Mark and Charles Dudley Warner. (1874). *The Gilded Age: A Tale of To-Day*. Hartford: American Publishing.

Tyler, Deborah. (1993). "Making Better Children." *Child and Citizen: Genealogies of Schooling and Subjectivity*. Ed. Denise Meredyth and Deborah Tyler. Brisbane: Institute for Cultural Policy Studies. 35–59.

Ungar, Sheldon. 2001. "Moral Panic Versus the Risk Society: The Implications of the Changing Sites of Social Anxiety." *British Journal of Sociology* 52, no. 2: 271–91.

———. (2002). "Moral Panic versus the Risk Society: The Implications of the Changing Sites of Social Anxiety." *British Journal of Sociology* 52, no. 2: 271–91.

UNICEF. (2007). *Child Poverty in Perspective: An Overview of Child Well-Being in Rich Countries*. UNICEF Innocenti Research Centre Report Card 7. Florence: UNICEF.

United Nations Development Programme. (2004). *Human Development Report 2004: Cultural Liberty in Today's Diverse World*.

Urban, Robert. (2006, March 28). "Gay Men Survive—and Thrive—on Reality Television." http://www.afterelton.com.

US Census Bureau News. (2007, May 17). "Minority Population Tops 100 Million."

"U.S. Children Still Traumatized One Year After Seeing Partially Exposed Breast on TV." (2005, January 26). *The Onion*.

"Us versus Us." (2003, November 8). *The Economist*: 8–12.

van Ham, Peter. (2001). "The Rise of the Brand State: The Postmodern Politics of Image and Reputation." *Foreign Affairs* 80, no. 5: 2–6.

Vannini, Phillip and Aaron M. McCright. (2004). "To Die For: The Semiotic Seductive Power of the Tanned Body." *Symbolic Interaction* 27, no. 3: 309–32.

van Zoonen, Liesbet. (2005). *Entertaining the Citizen: When Politics and Popular Culture Converge*. Lanham: Rowman & Littlefield.

Vastag, Brian. (2001). "Pay Attention: Ritalin Acts Much Like Cocaine." *Journal of the American Medical Association* 286, no. 8: 905–6.

Vico, Giambattista. (1970). *The New Science*. 3rd ed. Trans. Thomas Goddard Bergin and Max Harold Fisch. Ithaca: Cornell University Press.

Vonnegut, Kurt. (2004, August 6). "I Love You, Madame Librarian." *In These Times*.

"Vote in the *Ad Age* Weekly Online Poll." (2005, January 20). *Advertising Age*.

"The Vote Next Time." (2005, March 5). *The Economist*: 39.

Wade, Robert Hunter. (2003, March 13). "The Invisible Hand of the American Empire." http://www.opendemocracy.net.

Wagner, D. (1997). *The New Temperance: The American Obsession With Sin and Vice*. New York: Westview Press.

Wallas, Graham. (1967). *The Great Society: A Psychological Analysis*. Lincoln: University of Nebraska Press.

Wallechinsky, David. (2006, April 23). "Is the American Dream Still Possible?" *Parade*.

Wallerstein, Immanuel. (1989). "Culture as the Ideological Battleground of the Modern World-System." *Hitotsubashi Journal of Social Studies* 21, no. 1: 5–22.

———. (2003). *The Decline of American Power: The U.S. in a Chaotic World*. New York: New Press.

Wallis, Claudia. (2006, February 10). "Getting Hyper About Ritalin." *Time*.

"Wall Street's Crisis." (2008, March 22). *The Economist*: 11–12.

Wartella, Ellen. (1996). "The History Reconsidered." *American Communication Research—*

The Remembered History. Ed. Everette E. Dennis and Ellen Wartella. Mahwah: Lawrence Erlbaum. 169–80.

Washko, Rita M. (2005). "The Ghostwriting Controversy: Time for a Proper Burial?" *Science Editor* 28, no. 6: 187.

Wasko, Janet. (2005). "Introduction." *A Companion to Television.* Ed. Janet Wasko. Malden: Blackwell.

Watanabe, Teresa. (2007, May 17). "California Is Leading Nation in Diversity." *Los Angeles Times:* B2.

Waters, Mary C. (2003). "Once Again, Strangers on our Shores." *The Fractious Nation? Unity and Division in American Life.* Ed. Jonathan Rieder. Assoc. Ed. Stephen Steinlight. Berkeley: University of California Press. 117–30.

Waters, R. (2000, May 2). "Generation Rx." *Family Therapy Newsletter.*

Waters, Rob. (2004 November/December). "Prosecuting for Pharma." *Mother Jones:* 22–24.

Watson, Alison M. (2004). "Seen But Not Heard: The Role of the Child in International Political Economy." *New Political Economy* 9, no. 1: 3–21.

Watson, Rod. (1973). "The Public Announcement of Fatality." *Working Papers in Cultural Studies* 4: 5–20.

Watts, Michael J. (2000). "The Great Tablecloth: Bread and Butter Politics, and the Political Economy of Food and Poverty." *The Oxford Handbook of Economic Geography.* Ed. Gordon L. Clark, Maryann P. Feldman, and Meric S. Gertler with the assistance of Kate Williams. Oxford: Oxford University Press. 195–212.

Webster, Bruce H. Jr. and Alemayehu Bishaw. (2006). *Income, Earnings, and Poverty Data from the 2005 American Community Survey.* U.S. Census Bureau, American Community Survey Reports, ACS-02.

Weiss, David. (2005). "Constructing the Queer 'I': Performativity, Citationality, and Desire in *Queer Eye for the Straight Guy.*" *Popular Communication* 3, no. 2: 73–95.

Weiss, Michael. (2002 October). "Chasing Youth." *American Demographics.*

Welch, H. Gilbert, Lisa Schwartz, and Steven Woloshin. (2007, January 2). "What's Making Us Sick Is an Epidemic of Diagnoses." *New York Times.*

Wells, M. (1994, October 10). "Slimmer Dooner Revs Up McCann." *Advertising Age:* 50.

Westcott, Kathryn. (2005, February 14). "Pressure Builds for US Climate Action." *BBC News.*

Westerfelhaus, Robert and Celeste Lacroix. (2006). "Seeing 'Straight' Through *Queer Eye:* Exposing the Strategic Rhetoric of Heteronormativity in a Mediated Ritual of Gay Rebellion." *Critical Studies in Media Communication* 23, no. 5: 426–44.

Westheimer, Joel. (2004). "Introduction." *PS: Political Science & Politics* 37, no. 2: 231–34.

Westheimer, Joel and Joseph Kahne. (2004a). "Educating the "Good" Citizen: Political Choices and Pedagogical Goals." *PS: Political Science & Politics* 37, no. 2: 241–48.

———. (2004b). "What Kind of Citizen? The Politics of Educating for Democracy." *American Educational Research Journal* 41, no. 2: 237–69.

Whewell, William. (1840). *Philosophy of the Inductive Sciences.* London: Longman.

Whitaker, Brian. (2002, August 19). "US Thinktanks Give Lessons in Foreign Policy." *Guardian.*

White House, The. (2002, September 17). *The National Security Strategy of the United States of America.*

"Who Are 'We'?" (2004 February). *EXTRA!Update:* 2.

Wichtel, Diana. (2002, December 14). "Music That Makes for Moral Panic." *New Zealand Herald*.

Wilce, H. (2000, August 3). "Is There Life After Ritalin?" *Independent*.

Wilgoren, Jodi. (2002, April 20). "Scholar's Pedophilia Essay Stirs Outrage and Revenge." *New York Times*: A18.

Wilke, Michael. (2003, February 18). "Super Bowl Delivers Gay Ad Themes, Companies Remain Mum." *Commercial Closet*. http://www2.commercialcloset.org.

Williams, Andrew. (2005, September 15). "Mark Simpson." *Metro Café*.

Williams, Patricia J. (2002, June 3). "Racial Prescriptions." *The Nation*: 9.

Williams, Raymond. (1983). *Keywords: A Vocabulary of Culture and Society*. Rev. ed. New York: Oxford University Press.

Williams, Zoe. (2006, September 27). "Metrosexual Mendacity." *Guardian*: 31.

Willis, Cecil L. and Stephen J. McNamee. (1990). "Social Networks of Science and Patterns of Publication in Leading Sociology Journals." *Knowledge: Creation, Diffusion, Utilization* 11: 363–81.

Wilson, Robert. (2004). *The Vanished Hands*. New York: Harcourt.

Winthrop, Robert. (2002). "Exploring Cultural Rights." *Cultural Dynamics* 14, no. 2: 115–20.

Wittgenstein, Ludwig. (2007). *Lectures and Conversations on Aesthetics, Psychology, and Religious Belief*. Comp. Yorick Smythies, Rush Rhees, and James Taylor. Ed. Cyril Barrett. Berkeley: University of California Press.

Wolfe, Alan. (2006, August 23). "This Panic Won't Create Air Safety." *Boston Globe*.

Woodworth, Terrance. (2000, May 16). *Ritalin—The Fourth R in Schools: Discussing the Use of Psychotropic Drugs for Youth: DEA Congressional Testimony Before the Committee on Education and the Workforce: Subcommittee on Early Childhood, Youth, and Families*. United States Drug Enforcement Administration.

World Economic Forum. (2004). *Global Governance Initiative Annual Report 2004*.

"A World of Exiles." (2003, January 4). *The Economist*: 41–43.

"The World Through Their Eyes." (2005, February 26). *The Economist*: 23–25.

World Trade Organization. (2003). *World Trade Developments in 2001 and Prospects for 2002*. Geneva.

Wright, Richard and Richard Rosenfeld. (2003, January 26). "We're Racing Toward Moral Panic." *St. Louis Post-Dispatch*: B3.

Wucker, Michele. (2005). "The Perpetual Migration Machine and Political Power." *World Policy Journal* 21, no. 3: 41–50.

Yarborough, Marti. (2004, February 23). "The Metrosexual Male: What Sisters Really Think of Them." *Jet*: 34.

Yates, Michael D. (2005). "A Statistical Portrait of the U.S. Working Class." *Monthly Review* 56, no. 11: 12–31.

"The Year of the Retrosexual." (2006, December 31). *Scotsman*.

Younge, Gary. (2007, September 3). "In the US, Class War Still Means Just One Thing: The Rich Attacking the Poor." *Guardian*.

Youngers, Coletta. (2003 June). "The U.S. and Latin America after 9-11 and Iraq." *Foreign Policy in Focus Policy Report*.

Youniss, James, Jeffrey A. McLellan, and Miranda Yates. (1997). "What We Know About Engendering Civic Identity." *American Behavioral Scientist* 40, no. 5: 620–31.

Yúdice, George. 1990. "For a Practical Aesthetics." *Social Text* 25–26: 129–45.

"Yu to Propose 5 Fresh Policy Goals Today." (2004, September 17). *Taiwan News.*

Zarembo, Alan. (2005, April 26). "Drug Ads Often Lead to Unnecessary Prescriptions." *Los Angeles Times.*

Zernike, Kate and Melody Petersen. (2001, August 19). "Schools' Backing of Behavior Drugs Comes Under Fire." *New York Times:* 1.

Zinn, Howard. (2004). "An Occupied Country." *The Long Term View* 6, no. 2: 88–91.

Zito, J., D. J. Safer, S. dos Reis, J. Gardner, M. Boles, and F. Lynch. (2000). "Trends in the Prescribing of Psychotropic Medications to Preschoolers." *Journal of the American Medical Association* 283, no. 8: 1025–30.

Žižek, Slavoj. (2005, February 19). "The Empty Wheelbarrow." *Guardian:* 23.

Zorach, Rebecca. (2003, March 9). "Insurance Nation." *Boston Globe:* D2.

Zyvatkauskas, Caz. (2007, February 3). "Theatre Critic." *The Economist:* 18.

INDEX